BATTLING THE BOARD

Emerging Frontiers in the Global Economy

EDITOR J. P. Singh

SERIES TITLES

Financial Inclusion: How An Idea Became a Global Agenda
Tyler Girard, 2026

Shadow Negotiators: How UN Organizations Shape the Rules of World Trade for Food Security
Matias E. Margulis, 2023

Poverty as Subsistence: The World Bank and Pro-Poor Land Reform in Eurasia
Mihai Varga, 2023

Jobless Growth in the Dominican Republic: Disorganization, Precarity, and Livelihoods
Christian Krohn-Hansen, 2022

Precarious Asia: Global Capitalism and Work in Japan, South Korea, and Indonesia
Arne L. Kalleberg, Kevin Hewison, and Kwang-Yeong Shin, 2022

Unwitting Architect: German Primacy and the Origins of Neoliberalism
Julian Germann, 2021

Revolutionizing World Trade: How Disruptive Technologies Open Opportunities for All
Kati Suominen, 2019

Globalization under and after Socialism: The Evolution of Transnational Capital in Central and Eastern Europe
Besnik Pula, 2018

Discreet Power: How the World Economic Forum Shapes Market Agendas
Christina Garsten and Adrienne Sörbom, 2018

Making Money: How Taiwanese Industrialists Embraced the Global Economy
Gary G. Hamilton and Cheng-shu Kao, 2017

Sweet Talk: Paternalism and Collective Action in North-South Trade Relations
J.P. Singh, 2016

For a complete listing of titles in this series, visit the Stanford University Press website, www.sup.org.

Battling the Board

SHAREHOLDER ACTIVISM, SUSTAINABILITY, AND SOCIAL MOVEMENTS IN AUSTRALIA

Ainsley Elbra

STANFORD UNIVERSITY PRESS
Stanford, California

Stanford University Press
Stanford, California

Library of Congress Cataloging-in-Publication Data
Names: Elbra, Ainsley, author
Title: Battling the board : shareholder activism, sustainability, and social movements in Australia / Ainsley Elbra.
Other titles: Emerging frontiers in the global economy
Description: Stanford, California : Stanford University Press, 2026. | Series: Emerging frontiers in the global economy | Includes bibliographical references and index
Identifiers: LCCN 2025044433 (print) | LCCN 2025044434 (ebook) | ISBN 9781503646162 cloth | ISBN 9781503647145 ebook
Subjects: LCSH: Social responsibility of business—Australia | Stockholders—Political activity—Australia | Corporations—Investor relations—Australia | Corporate governance—Australia | Social movements—Australia
Classification: LCC HD60.5.A8 E43 2026 (print) | LCC HD60.5.A8 (ebook) | DDC 658.4/08—dc23/eng/20250923
LC record available at https://lccn.loc.gov/2025044433
LC ebook record available at https://lccn.loc.gov/2025044434

Cover design: Susan Zucker
Cover photograph: Shutterstock / Michael Parfitt
Typeset by Newgen in ITC Galliard Pro, 10/14

The authorized representative in the EU for product safety and compliance is: Mare Nostrum Group B.V. | Doelen 72 | 4831 GR Breda | The Netherlands | Email address: gpsr@mare-nostrum.co.uk | KVK chamber of commerce number: 96249943

Printed and bound by CPI Group (UK) Ltd, Croydon, CR0 4YY

For Josh and Sam

Contents

Acknowledgments

I BEGAN THIS RESEARCH in late 2020, six months after the devastating Black Summer Bushfires and as Rio Tinto's board faced its shareholders over the destruction of the 46,000-year-old caves at Juukan Gorge. A career lifetime ago, I had worked on a campaign run by employees of one of Australia's largest banks, urging our employer not to fund a pulp mill project that would have led to the destruction of a section of Tasmanian wilderness. It felt like a full circle moment, one that encouraged me to turn my attention to understanding how activists could challenge companies to address these issues through the discourse and forums that executives and directors understood best.

The result is a book that highlights attempts to address two of the most pressing issues facing Australian society today. Firstly, Aboriginal and Torres Strait Islander peoples' long-running battle to protect country. First Nations Australians are often pitted against well-resourced corporate interests in attempts to preserve traditions and sacred sites, on land that was never ceded. I am grateful to the Darkinjung people, on whose lands this book was written, and all First Nations Australians, who bear much of the cost of the country's fixation on mining.

The politics of climate change in Australia are vitriolic and increasingly used to divide (particularly rural) communities. Yet, the politics belies the facts. The Black Summer Bushfires were unprecedented in terms of the loss of lives, livelihoods, and property. Australia's ecosystem will also never recover from the harm sustained that summer. The events of 2019 and 2020 remain permanently etched in many Australians' memories. My aim in this work is to reveal an often-overlooked pathway for addressing these challenges.

In the course of researching this book I was fortunate to speak to many environmental, social, and governance (ESG) activists, who deserve credit for directing their energy, time, and resources to these causes. In particular, I owe a debt of gratitude to the Australasian Centre for Corporate Responsibility (ACCR) for doing the groundbreaking work in documenting these resolutions, establishing their shareholder filings database, and being willing to share their institutional knowledge of older filings. None of the findings in this book are intended to detract from the hard work of activists, whose efforts have made real and visible impact.

I have been most fortunate in being supported by the editorial team at Stanford University Press's Emerging Frontiers in the Global Economy series. I could not have asked for more understanding and encouraging editors in Dan LoPreto and J. P. Singh, whose advocacy and enthusiasm for the project have made working on this book such a joy.

Aspects of this work have been presented at the European Consortium for Political Research General Conference, Australian International Political Economy Network annual workshop, Australian Political Studies Association Annual Conference, the Centre for Governance and Public Policy at Griffith University, and a number of classes at the University of Sydney. The research was funded by the Faculty of Arts and Social Sciences at the University of Sydney through various internal grants and a period of sabbatical.

No book is the work of one person alone, and my colleagues have been a constant source of intellectual stimulation. Over the course of this and related research, I have been fortunate enough to benefit from discussions with and mentoring from John Mikler, Hannah Murphy, Erin O'Brien, Martijn Boersma, Justine Coneybeer, Susan Park, Sarah Phillips, and Laura Shepherd, as well as my AIPEN colleagues. The book also greatly benefited from the work of my research assistant, Georgia Peters, and the two anonymous readers.

Lastly, thanks go to my friends and family. I am lucky enough to be surrounded by brilliant women who encourage and inspire. Thanks to Tim for the support you gave me during this project, especially as we navigated the challenges of homeschooling during long lockdowns. My greatest thanks are to Sam and Josh—you make me so proud. I hope this book is an insight into why I remind you to aim high and to pursue what matters.

BATTLING THE BOARD

INTRODUCTION

CORPORATIONS AROUND THE WORLD are under growing pressure from investors, regulators, and consumers to address urgent environmental and social challenges. The use of corporate governance mechanisms is emerging as a key strategy for investors to influence companies to align with sustainability and ethical business practices. Investors are increasingly recognizing that strong corporate governance can help ensure that companies not only deliver financial returns but also address environmental, social, and governance (ESG) issues effectively. This book explores the use of corporate governance mechanisms, namely shareholder resolutions, to pressure large, listed, Australian firms to respond to some of the country's most pressing issues, where governments have failed to adequately respond. In doing so, it provides new insights into the effectiveness of market-based activism and the impact of regulator attempts to legislate against investor voice.

In 2024, Australia's largest oil and gas company, Woodside Energy Group Limited, held an annual general meeting (AGM) dominated by intense debate over the company's approach to emissions reduction. Two years earlier, the company had yielded to activist demands to allow shareholders a biannual "say on climate" vote. Woodside's say on climate vote was an invitation to investors to vote on the company's strategy to reduce its carbon emissions, including those of downstream customers, which had increased 78 percent over the prior two years (Conservation Council of WA 2024). By 2024, the board, and in particular high-profile Chair Richard Goyder, were under immense pressure to demonstrate they were responding to calls to reduce the company's emissions. The company's shareholders questioned the adequacy of Woodside's climate strategy, and the unresponsiveness of its leadership, which had until then largely escaped serious scrutiny over the scale of the company's emissions. In an unfortunate piece of timing, Goyder was also facing a shareholder vote on re-election as Woodside's Chair in the same year that he had been forced out of the leadership of the country's national air carrier (Knight 2024).

As the AGM approached, proxy advisors, CGI Glass Lewis, issued a recommendation that investors vote against both the climate plan and Goyder's re-election (Macdonald-Smith 2024). Institutional investors also weighed in. The pension fund, HESTA, supported Goyder's re-election but rejected the emissions reduction plan, emphasizing the need for substantial climate action (HESTA 2024). Allianz Global Investors announced their intention to vote against both the climate plan and Goyder's re-election, highlighting growing investor impatience with Woodside's climate strategy (Allianz Global Investors 2024). At the AGM, 58 percent of shareholders voted down the company's climate transition plan (Woodside Energy Group Limited 2024). Goyder survived as Chair but not without a punishing protest vote, which reflected shareholders' dissatisfaction with the company's ability to present a strategic plan for emissions reduction.

Woodside's 2024 AGM experience represented the culmination of seven years of sustained shareholder activism aimed at reforming Australian corporations' approaches to ESG challenges. This wave of activism has seen shareholder activist groups work with wealthy investors, institutional investors, and fund managers to engage directly with management and boards to reform corporate behavior. Much of this activism took place through the filing of ESG shareholder resolutions at companies' AGMs. Corporate AGMs include a series of resolutions, put forward by the company and its board, voted on by shareholders. These usually pertain to board re-election and executive remuneration. Shareholders may also file resolutions if they wish to express a view on management. Shareholder resolutions have traditionally focused on improving the financial metrics of a firm (through refusing to endorse remuneration packages, forcing board or executives out, etc.); however, this mechanism is increasingly being used by activist shareholders to signal issues of ESG concern to the company.

While ESG shareholder activism has a long history in comparable liberal market economies, Australia's experience with this form of activism is relatively short. Ad hoc ESG shareholder resolutions were raised throughout the early 2000s, however these amounted to no more than a dozen attempts at lobbying firms through corporate governance mechanisms. Australia's restrictive corporations law and its interpretation by the Federal Court places significant hurdles in the way of this form of activism. Despite this, a small group of committed investors developed pathways around regulatory barriers, and from 2017 onwards ESG shareholder resolutions have been a fixture of large Australian corporate AGMs. There were no ESG resolutions raised at 2016 company AGMs, yet between 2017 and 2022, 174 resolutions were filed by activists. Australia's economy is dominated by firms whose business activities heavily impact the environment and the country's First Nations peoples, two areas at which ESG shareholder activism has traditionally been directed. This book explores the emergence of a concentrated pair of activist organizations in Australia, focused heavily on the politics of climate change, with the resources to target the country's largest listed companies via their shareholdings. The concentration of activists leads to a narrower range of target companies and issues over which engagement is sought. As such, the archetypical example of ESG shareholder activism in Australia is that which targets a large mining, oil, or gas firm over their climate credentials. As is explored in this book, while other issues and industries are on the radar of activists, it remains that climate change is the overriding focus of investor activists.

The analysis suggests that the emergence of shareholder activism in Australia is a result of a governance gap driven by societal expectations of corporate behavior, and the rules that govern firms. This is particularly evident in the issue areas of climate action and First Nations' land rights. This is demonstrated through analyses of corporations' responses to climate change, and mining companies' impacts on First Nations' communities. The book also argues that while Australia's *Corporations Act 2001* (Cth) ("Corporations Act") poses unique barriers to this form of participation, it has not prevented a rise in shareholder activism. Instead, it has created space for a narrow duopoly of activist shareholders supported by institutional investors, pension funds, and, occasionally, wealthy investors to lobby corporate management. The legal barriers in place mean that Australia lags behind other liberal democracies in the emergence of ESG shareholder activism. Nonetheless, the gap between societal expectations, corporate behavior, and government inaction has led to the model environment for such activism to emerge. A noticeable outcome of these legal impediments is activists' heavy focus on climate change, with far less attention paid to social issues. This anomaly, when compared to other similar jurisdictions, suggests Australia represents a unique and important case study for the potential effectiveness of anti-corporate activism in a hostile legal environment. The case also sheds light on the impacts of anti-ESG lawmaking, in an era of heightened rhetoric globally.

The contributions of this book include intervention in debates around the effectiveness of anti-corporate social movements, and the impact of pro-business regulators in limiting calls for greater business sustainability. It is shown that anti-corporate activism is most successful when it targets a single issue that resonates universally among activists, their financial backers, and the wider shareholder population. In Australia, coalescence around climate change provided the conditions for the emergence of such activism, and its success is evidenced by the forced early closure of coal-fired power stations. However, these necessary conditions did not materialize over other pressing societal issues. Activists' prioritization of climate change has shielded corporations from scrutiny over social issues including Indigenous land rights, human rights, modern slavery, and non-climate-related environmental concerns.

Much of the research on investor voice and ESG shareholder activism has focused on the United States, European Union, and the United Kingdom (Allen et al. 2012). There is far less written about the intersection of sustainable business practices and investors in other liberal market economies including Australia. Yet, as explored in this book, overlapping issues are at stake globally, and activists have worked within these jurisdictions, as well as transnationally, to advance their causes. There is much to be learned from the experiences of ESG shareholder activism in these previously overlooked jurisdictions, acknowledging the variation in geographical and regulatory environments in which activists, investors, and companies operate. Furthermore, many key ESG actors operate at a global or transnational level, and thus the scholarship can benefit by understanding how practices and norms are disseminated into new markets. This book sets out to explore the unique characteristics of ESG shareholder activism in a jurisdiction where legal impediments are high. In doing so, it asks: What are the drivers of the sudden emergence of ESG shareholder activism in Australia? Is there any evidence that this form of activism has forced change at the corporate, industry, or regulatory level? And finally, is lobbying firms through corporate governance mechanisms effective in addressing some of society's most pressing challenges? In order to respond to these questions, the introductory chapter explores some of the key debates and concepts driving the emergence of ESG shareholder activism globally and in Australia, including sustainability, ESG, the role of the corporation, and the corporate governance mechanisms used to lobby firms.

Sustainability and ESG Investing

The term "sustainability" first emerged in the 1970s to refer to an economic, social, and environmental ideal that recognized the finitude of resources that humans were depleting in their quest for economic growth (Caradonna 2022). Sustainability can broadly be defined as "a moral way of acting, and ideally habitual, in which the person or group intends to avoid deleterious effects on the environmental, social, and economic domains, and which is consistent with a harmonious relationship with those domains that is conducive to a flourishing life" (Bañon Gomis et al. 2011, 176; Sheehy 2022). This approach has been applied to business in an effort to define attempts to meet the long-term goals of organizations, whereby companies respond to short-term incentives without compromising their (or others') ability to meet their long-term needs (Brundtland 1987; Bansal and DesJardine 2014). In a business sense, sustainability can be defined as value creation that "ensures the long-term stability and resilience of the ecosystems that support human life" and that "facilitates the achievement of human rights and other basic social rights" (Sjåfjell and Bruner 2019, 11). The three pillars of ESG (environmental, social, and governance) are all central to the concept of sustainable business practice. The embrace of sustainable business practices places corporations under increasing pressure to meet management and shareholders' desires for short-term returns, whilst simultaneously considering the long-term sustainability of their business models (Porter and Derry 2012).

While activists have engaged corporations on non-financial matters through the market since the nineteenth century, the term "ESG" only came into use in 2004 after it appeared in a United Nations report titled *Who Cares Wins* (Bowley and Hill 2024a). The report advocated for embedding ESG principles in capital markets, whilst simultaneously striving for good business outcomes such as growth in profitability and higher shareholder returns (United Nations Global Compact 2005). *Who Cares Wins* was a response to calls from the then UN Secretary General Kofi Annan for established guidelines on how to integrate ESG concerns into investment decisions under the UN Global Compact. The result was the UN Principles for Responsible Investment (UNPRI), which promotes a set of values designed by world's largest institutional investors, as advised by a panel of investors, intergovernmental organizations, and civil society (United Nations Principles for Responsible Investment 2023). Transnational actors, such as the UNPRI, work collectively to improve the accountability of businesses, but also to promote a shift in business–society relationships, which see investors working with civil society to "shape new norms of corporate behavior by redefining investor and fiduciary responsibilities" (MacLeod 2010, 47).

Since its inception, ESG has grown rapidly as a concept of interest to scholars, a codified approach to achieving sustainability through business practices, and most notably as a key driver of investment decisions (Macey 2022). Investors are playing an increasingly important role by foregrounding ESG stewardship—that is, using their influence, through their ownership stake, to prompt their corporations to address the ESG challenges facing society (Bowley and Hill 2024a). Since specific ESG-focused funds have emerged as an asset classification, funds under management have grown exponentially. Globally, ESG assets under management reached US$30 trillion in 2022 and are expected to grow to US$40 trillion by 2030 (Bloomberg Intelligence 2024). Half of all investors globally currently direct some of their capital to ethical or ESG funds (Macey 2022). Over 2023 and 2024, markets observed a decline in ESG funds under management. A range of reasons have been put forward including the tightening of Securities and Exchange Commission (SEC) rules around ESG funds, the growing backlash due to the politicization of the concept, and a general market softening. Yet, despite this market correction, ESG funds under management remain a significant portion of investment flows.

This rapid growth in funds under management reflects the fact investors are increasingly being drawn to "impact investing" (Scholtens 2006), or socially responsible investment (SRI) funds, where they are able to both generate returns and create societal value (Nilsson 2008). Simultaneously, many investors perceive ethical funds as a pathway to higher returns, where the risks of a socially or environmentally irresponsible company are seen as a potential drain on earnings. It is possible to envisage ESG investors existing on a spectrum: at one end are those who consider socio-ecological risks only in terms of their impact on returns on investment, and at the other, those who place ESG considerations at the forefront of their capital allocation decisions for ethical reasons alone (Bowley and Hill 2024a). Studies show that the majority of investors sit closer to the focus on returns on investment end of this scale, considering these risks as a factor in portfolio decision-making where the aim remains the maximization of financial returns (V. H. Ho 2015; Pollman 2021). For example, an investor may consider a mining company's poor engagement with local communities as a potential risk to operations and may express this through divestment or portfolio composition choice. Here, the driver of this investment decision is a risk to returns, rather than a moral commitment to improved engagement with mining communities. Nonetheless, while investors remain motivated by a mix of financial and non-financial metrics, it is clear that companies' ESG credentials are an essential part of guiding investment decisions.

Given the rise in ESG-focused funds under management, we might expect not only for companies to be under increasing pressure to respond to ESG claim-making, but also higher valuations for those that proactively comply. There is considerable debate in the financial literature over the impact of ESG shareholder activism on corporate value, as measured through share valuation and associated market capitalization (Barko et al. 2022). Some quantitative studies have shown little significant impact, in the long run, on a company's share price following ESG activism against the firm (English II et al. 2004; Nelson 2006; Gillan and Starks 2007; Greenwood and Schor 2009), whereas other authors have been able to demonstrate improved financial returns for investors where a company is the target of ESG activists (Brav et al. 2008; Bebchuk et al. 2015). This was shown in one of the first studies on the effects of ESG shareholder activism on US public sector pension funds, which found that such attention generated growth in shareholder wealth (M. P. Smith 1996). These divergent results suggest that there is no clear demonstrable gain from corporations' engagement on ESG issues from a valuation point of view. It remains, however, that companies may wish to head off ESG risks by proactively assessing and addressing potential financial and reputational impacts.

The Role of the Corporation

Debates over the role of companies in addressing ESG challenges lead to questions about the role of the firm in society. There remains considerable tension between advocates of responsible investing, or ESG, and those who focus narrowly on the fiduciary duties of the firm, and its board and management. Put simply, contestation exists over whether or not the corporate purpose extends beyond profit maximization and if it does, how the interests of actors other than shareholders are represented in board decision-making (I. MacNeil and Esser 2022). This question, of course, assumes that profit maximization and societal interests do not overlap. The analysis in this book resists this approach and argues that they do, however in general much of the debate has been focused on theorizing the role of firms in going *beyond* the goal of profit maximization to achieve ESG goals, as though these are two clearly delineated objectives.

This debate is reflected in the evolution of the approach taken by the Business Roundtable, a non-profit lobbying association made up of over two hundred US CEOs. In its 1997 statement on the purpose of business, the group stated that the primary goal of business was to generate returns for shareholders and owners, and if broader stakeholder concerns were addressed, these should only be taken into account so far as they were linked to shareholders' interests (Business Roundtable 1997). At the time, this statement reflected the prevailing norm of shareholder primacy, which dominated the understanding of the role of the corporation. According to this approach, the role of management was to enhance corporate value and, in the process, explicitly subordinate the interests of non-shareholders (Sjåfjell and Taylor 2019). This approach also laid out clear expectations of company boards, with directors mandated to prioritize returns over societal concerns (Shariati 2024).

In more recent times this de facto position has been challenged, most notably in 2018, when BlackRock CEO Larry Fink highlighted in his influential annual letter to CEOs that society now expected business to fulfill a social purpose (Fink 2018; Rock 2020). Then in 2019, the Business Roundtable updated its approach to the role of corporations through its statement titled *The Purpose of a Corporation,* where it outlined that there was a growing expectation that business would "support the communities where they operate and adopt sustainable practices" (Business Roundtable 2019). These high-profile statements supported the reframing of the purpose of business to include a wider cohort of stakeholders including employees and those impacted by business operations. Recent case law decisions in the US have reflected an embedding of this shift through the recognition of the rights of non-shareholders (I. MacNeil and Esser 2022). The impact of large corporates on the environment, climate, and communities near which they operate is reflected in the rising instance and acceptance of ESG shareholder resolutions as a legitimate form of investor expression. The power of financial actors (including shareholders) has grown, providing a counterforce to management authority and the prioritization of financial returns alone (Peetz and Murray 2013; Clapp 2014; Baines and Hager 2021). The evolution of views on the rights of investors to express voice is not, however, uniform. Those that refer to themselves as anti-woke capitalists have called for ESG issues to be banished altogether from "serious AGM business." At the opposite end of the ideological spectrum, critical scholars have suggested ethical investing is simply a vehicle for factoring the risk of ESG issues into expected portfolio returns (Parfitt 2024).

As these divergent views on ESG investing demonstrate, the practice is not without its critics. A large segment of this criticism has been directed at investment managers and proxy advisors. While the emergence of the UNPRI and the sheer growth in ESG investing outlined above suggest a shift in soft law and investment trends toward including ESG considerations in investment decisions, hard law has not followed suit. Instead, many legal rulings in the US have interpreted fund managers' and proxy advisors' fiduciary duty as the prioritization of returns on investment over social and environmental considerations (Schanzenbach and Sitkoff 2020; I. MacNeil and Esser 2022). The UNPRI and other similar initiatives seek to hold business accountable for factors beyond financial materiality, yet critics argue that the focus of corporations and investors should be limited to financial metrics, driven solely by the profit motive. Corporate lobbyists and pro-business regulators have also placed anti-ESG pressure on intermediaries, including everything from proposals to tighten regulations governing the role of proxy advisors through to more explicit outright bans on funds engaging in ESG activism. The implications of these anti-ESG regulatory efforts are outlined in the following chapter, and in chapter 5, which explores attempts by US regulators to limit shareholder political expression.

The contestation outlined above suggests the focus on the corporation as a vehicle for achieving public goods is not without its challenges. The shareholder corporation lacks social embeddedness and places a small financial elite at the center of corporate responses to challenges of climate change, human rights, and other social ills (Sheehy 2017). Yet, there are a number of public policy issues, including those related to sustainability, that cannot be solved without targeting corporate actors (Greenfield 2019). At the same time, there is considerable evidence that increased inequality in society can be partly blamed on growing corporate power, business lobbying, and the capture of political agendas (Kanbur 2019). The legal corporation, as Benedict Sheehy (2022, 275) notes, sits "at the intersection of public interests in conservation and private wealth through exploitation. It is the legal actor making decisions, buying and selling in markets and responding to various regulatory landscapes. It is the critical actor in the contest for ecological and social sustainability." This research moves forward on this basis, motivated by the claim that the corporation is responsible for and therefore centrally placed to address many of society's greatest challenges; and, that markets are not solely guided by exogenous forces but are reflective of the web of social relations between actors that can be leveraged in order to generate long-lasting change.

A Brief History of Shareholder Activism

Shareholder activism is defined as "the use of ownership position to actively influence company policy and practice" (Sjöström 2008). While this exercise of influence includes divestment campaigns and other forms of protest, the literature on shareholder activism focuses predominantly on the filing of shareholder resolutions at company AGMs (Marquardt and Wiedman 2016). Since the mid-twentieth century, shareholder resolutions have been used in liberal market economies, such as the US and UK, to impose financial discipline on companies (Gillan and Starks 2000). They have traditionally been filed by investors in response to poor financial performance, targeting levers such as executive pay, composition of board members, or the overhaul of management teams.

Historically, the use of shareholder resolutions to address ESG issues has been far less common: between 1998 and 2008, ESG shareholder resolutions made up just 3 percent of total shareholder resolutions filed in the UK (Filatotchev and Dotsenko 2015). However, more recently the use of shareholder resolutions to draw corporate leadership's attention to ESG issues has grown (Sjöström 2008). One of the most notable global campaigns occurred in 2015, when activists pressured British Petroleum and Royal Dutch Shell (hereafter 'Shell') to commit to stronger action on climate change. UK activist group ShareAction filed ESG shareholder resolutions calling for both companies to test whether their business models were compatible with the global pledge to limit warming to 2 degrees, and to link corporate bonuses to climate action (Carrington 2015). The pressure from investors, society, and the media was so great that both company boards ultimately supported this resolution, drawing 98 percent support from both companies' shareholders—meaning the resolutions were binding under UK law (ShareAction 2017). The campaign against British Petroleum and Shell built on ShareAction's 2010 "Counting the Cost" campaign, which drew attention to the future financial risks facing these firms, and their shareholders, of continued mining of tar sands in Alberta, Canada (Ivanova 2016). The success of these campaigns led to the realization that corporate governance mechanisms could potentially be used as a tool for addressing urgent ESG concerns, such as climate change.

Although highly successful campaigns, such as that waged against British Petroleum and Shell, can elicit majority shareholder support, even without this backing ESG shareholder resolutions are a method by which activists and shareholders can signal the importance of an issue to the company's board and management using existing institutional channels. Filing ESG shareholder resolutions has been shown to improve the performance of companies on ESG issues, even with only a moderate level of support at the AGM (Grewal et al. 2016). Often, resolutions are introduced at repeated AGMs, and there is evidence that these repeated proposals garner incrementally more support each time they are introduced—whilst also signaling the embedded salience of an issue to boards and management (Gillan and Starks 2000; Freeburn and Ramsay 2021a).

While the filing of an ESG shareholder resolution is visible and observable activism, it is often not the start or end point of this form of engagement. Usually, a company has been in dialogue with activists and investors over the ESG issue of concern. As a result of these discussions, resolutions are occasionally rescinded prior to the AGM, and other times, they are not filed at all (Freeburn and Ramsay 2021a). The concept of ESG shareholder activism incorporates the negotiations and discussions that take place around the AGM, as this firm-level dialogue has the potential to shift corporate behavior without resorting to filing shareholder resolutions (Neville et al. 2019). Scholars of anti-corporate activism have noted a shift from subversive action, which takes a company by surprise, to much more mainstream activity whereby firms are part of the negotiation process around the content of resolutions, and whether they need to be raised at the AGM or if aims can be achieved prior through dialogue between activists and management (Rehbein et al. 2013). In the interviews undertaken as part of this research, examples of negotiation ahead of and after AGMs were common. Activists recounted stories of large mining companies approaching activists, proxy advisors, and institutional investors following the public outcry over mining company Rio Tinto's destruction of First Nations' cultural heritage to assure investors and activists that their company's internal governance systems would not allow something so controversial to occur within their operations. There are also many instances of resolutions that are withdrawn ahead of the AGM, or after they have appeared in the AGM notice but prior to the actual meeting. An example of this occurred in 2020, when BHP was targeted over its cultural heritage policy. Activists filed and then rescinded a resolution before it could go to the AGM as the company and activist organization the Australasian Centre for Corporate Responsibility (ACCR) reached an agreement on the required change to corporate practices. Regular, ongoing, or pre- and post-AGM dialogue has the potential to shift corporate behavior without resorting to shareholder resolutions (Neville et al. 2019).

Shareholder resolutions, once filed, appear in the company's notice of AGM. They are accompanied by commentary from both the filer and the board, each presenting their views on the issue and their plans to address it. The board offers an opinion on how shareholders should vote, usually against activist claim-making. Investors are commonly split into two groups. The first, retail investors, sometimes referred to as "Mom and Pop shareholders," own a small parcel of shares either as an investment or as part of their pension fund. Retail shareholders may or may not possess the information to assess the resolution at hand and decide whether or not to support it. However, if they do, they are less likely to impact the overall support of a resolution due to their minimal shareholding. Instead, it is the votes of the second group of investors, institutional shareholders who control large percentages of a company's shareholding, that are most likely to sway sufficient votes to send a message to the company on a particular issue. As such, institutional investors tend to be the target of activists.

Adding another layer of complexity to this process is the role played by proxy advisory firms (hereafter proxy advisors). Proxy advisors are engaged by large institutional investors to provide reporting and recommendation services. In this role, they regularly report on a company's performance as well as key issues facing the firm and its industry, while also recommending how institutional investors should vote on AGM and EGM (extraordinary general meeting) resolutions (Sheehy et al. 2021). While proxy advisors operate behind the scenes through private engagement, they have the capacity to influence the success or failure of very public activist campaigns. Proxy advisors' recommendations, as we saw in the Woodside case, can be highly influential in determining the vote of institutional investors over contentious AGM resolutions. Furthermore, prior to the AGM a proxy vote is taken from those shareholders who are not physically attending the meeting via a proxy voting form provided to investors ahead of the meeting. This form allows shareholders to "hand over" their vote to another individual or company, including the company chair or proxy advisors. The delegation of voting rights to proxy advisors is a common approach taken by investors, cumulatively providing a significant voting share to these intermediaries. The crucial aspect to note about this process is that proxy votes are tallied ahead of the AGM, which means that an indication of support for ESG (and other) resolutions is available to the company prior to the AGM. Under Australian corporations' law, companies may share this information before or after the meeting; nonetheless, this vote indicates to management the salience of the issue amongst non-activist investors and, depending on their willingness to engage, may prompt more discussions between activist groups and company management.

For an ESG issue to resonate with the board and non-activist investors, it must also represent a material financial threat. In other words, the issue must have the potential to impact the company's profitability and shareholder returns. It is insufficient and ineffective for ESG activists to appeal only to the moral or ethical concerns of market actors such as institutional investors or company boards in order to effect change. In the case of climate change, activists have repeatedly highlighted the risk of stranded assets, such as superseded coal-fired power stations, to motivate investors and their companies to bring forward an end to emissions-intensive energy production. In this sense, ESG shareholder activism channels an increasing concern with the chasm between profit and the burden of production (Clapp 2002; Neville et al. 2019). However, in the case of social issues, it is less likely that activists can leverage tangible assets in their claim-making. Instead, activists need to highlight the possibility of reputational damage, litigation, and financial penalties, including those that may be applied to directors themselves where a dereliction of duty can be shown. Such individualized financial disincentives may come in the form of lost bonuses, reduced severance payments, or even litigation aimed at board members who have been shown to fail in their fiduciary duties.

One key area in which activists have leveraged such incentives is at the intersection of Traditional Owners' interests and those of mining firms. Protection of cultural heritage is a global challenge for First Nations' communities, and this is growing in relevance and urgency as a result of the race to renewable energy. Studies have shown that, globally, 54 percent of the minerals required for the transition to green energy are located on, or near to, Indigenous peoples' lands (Owen et al. 2023). In response, companies usually seek a social license to operate, that is, an informal contract which demonstrates "ongoing acceptance and approval of a [project] by local community members and other stakeholders that can affect its profitability" (Moffat and Zhang 2014, 61). Such a license requires continuing and dynamic engagement with communities, as attitudes and impacts evolve over time. Companies' acquisition of a social license to operate does not guarantee permanent and enduring positive relations with local communities, and it can be withdrawn at any time (Bice et al. 2017). In the cases where these relations break down, companies and their investors risk financial costs. It is the potential for such economic losses that activists can use to draw investor, board, and management's attention to the importance of free, prior, and informed consent (FPIC) and a social license to operate. As John Ruggie, the architect of the United Nations Guiding Principles on Business and Human Rights, noted, even fifteen years ago, "for a world class mining operation there's a cost somewhere between $20 million and $30 million a week for operational disruption by [dissatisfied] communities" (Ruggie 2011). This quantification of the risk of poor engagement with First Nations' communities, which would be considerably greater today, shows the value that ESG shareholder activists can provide companies, boards, and non-activist shareholders in pushing to improve social engagement by firms. The material financial risk posed by poor social engagement is a strategic focal point for activists (Cerrato and Ferrando 2020).

Shareholder Activism in Australia

The Australian economy is dominated by financial services, mining, oil, and gas firms. This is reflected in the composition of the leading share market index, the ASX 200, which is comprised of 30 percent banking and financial services firms and 20 percent materials or mining firms (S&P Dow Jones Indices 2022). Natural resource extraction and the companies that fund mining projects sit at the heart of debates around corporations' role in addressing salient issues such as climate change and Indigenous peoples' land rights. As such, they have been the target of almost all ESG shareholder resolutions filed in Australia. This includes an early campaign against the country's largest four banks, who together control the financial sector, over lending to emissions-intensive industries and projects. The mining, oil, and gas sectors have been key targets of activists over their contribution to global warming as well as their ongoing relations with Australia's First Nations people.

Australian public companies are required, under the *Corporations Act,* to hold an AGM each year. They may also hold extraordinary general meetings under special circumstances. At these meetings, the Chair and CEO present a summary of the past year and future plans to shareholders. They are joined by the board in these presentations. Following this, shareholders vote on a series of resolutions. Normally, these resolutions call for investors to vote on mundane matters of corporate governance including the election or re-election of board members and approval for remuneration packages for executives and board members. They usually receive very high "yes" votes on the basis of board, management, and proxy advisor support, aside from occasions where shareholders have chosen to "punish" a company for perceived poor performance by refusing to re-elect board members or by voting down pay proposals. If a company's remuneration resolution is the subject of a "no" vote greater than 25 percent, the board is said to have experienced a "first strike." A second strike the following year requires the entire board to go up for election (*Corporations Act 2001*). The re-election of entire boards is commonplace globally but not in Australia, where board members have overlapping terms.

Shareholders may also file their own resolutions at AGMs, calling on other investors to support claim-making against the company. While this process is common in most liberal market economies, there are particular rules governing shareholder resolutions that vary between corporate governance regimes. For example, each jurisdiction has a minimum ownership threshold for shareholders to meet before they can file a resolution. In the UK and Australia this is a number of shareholdings or a percentage share in a company; in the US this pertains to the length of time shareholders have held their investments as well as a minimum shareholding requirement. These regulations exist in order to eliminate what some may perceive as "nuisance" resolutions. Depending on the jurisdiction, resolutions may also be binding or non-binding. Binding resolutions require management to act on an issue if a threshold "yes" vote is achieved. The likelihood of a binding ESG resolution reaching threshold is normally very low, and as such, many activists see non-binding resolutions as the preferred way to garner wider support for a message that they would like management to take seriously. In this sense, "advisory resolutions" (or non-binding resolutions) provide shareholders with a lower risk approach of engaging with management and the board, "without risking the interference in management" (Sheehy et al. 2023, 19).

In the period since 2017, the number of ESG shareholder resolutions filed at large listed Australian corporate AGMs has increased dramatically. This rapid rise is somewhat surprising, as the country's legal system presents significant barriers to filing such resolutions. As a result, in the Australian context, shareholder resolutions have traditionally been seen as a blunt tool of governance. They have been leveraged less frequently than in other liberal market economies (Sheehy et al. 2023). The Australian *Corporations Act* and its subsequent interpretation by the Federal Court of Australia in a 2015 test case severely curtailed advisory resolutions by shareholders. The ruling is explored in full in the next chapter, however, the intention was to curb investor voice through the implementation of legal barriers to shareholder resolutions. Instead, in the years following this ruling, two key activist organizations in Australia devised a method of bypassing the strict requirements around filing non-binding, advisory resolutions. In doing so, they opened up a path for this duopoly of dedicated activist groups to file ESG shareholder resolutions on a handful of large, listed corporations (Elbra 2023). As a result of these impediments and the emergent duopoly of activists, not only were ESG shareholder resolutions used as a tool of anti-corporate politics much later than in other jurisdictions, but they have also been filed over far fewer issue areas and at far fewer company AGMs.

Shareholder activism in Australia has predominately focused on environmental concerns, specifically addressing a rapidly warming climate. This focus is a result of a number of contributing factors. Firstly, as explored in this chapter, the legal regime in Australia is highly hostile to shareholder expression of political views. This in turn has resulted in just two organizations possessing the resources required to file advisory resolutions against Australian companies. The two organizations with the ability to file shareholder resolutions, ACCR and Market Forces, have an overwhelming focus on climate change. In fact, Market Forces is mandated only to lobby corporations over climate change, while ACCR has a broader mandate but remains heavily focused on this issue. As a result, anti-corporate politics in Australia is characterized by a heavy bias toward environmental issues, particularly climate change. This is due to the structure of the activist organizations, their funding sources, and the priorities and representativeness of activists and non-activist shareholders. While there are historical and contemporary examples of activists targeting companies over non-climate environmental, social, and governance concerns, these are far less frequent than resolutions calling for companies to decrease emissions. The reasons for this are explored in detail in chapter 4 of this book, which explores a lack of claim-making over social issues in Australia, but can be attributed to the funding, composition, and remit of the narrow range of actors in this space.

Historically, conflicts over the corporate governance of firms, including debates around the rights of shareholders or owners, managers, and workers, have varied between local corporate cultures (Gourevitch and Shinn 2005; Callaghan 2018). These debates have focused on the strategic direction, allocation of resources, and distribution of profits within firms. Frameworks that analyze the tension between these actors and combinations thereof illustrate how national corporate governance systems produce particular distributional outcomes (Gourevitch and Shinn 2005). For example, US corporate governance is considered to be a battle of interest groups, contrasted with a European focus on shareholder blocks, and historical cooperation between government and business in some East Asian states. These characterizations reflect varying regulations governing shareholder voice, the rights of workers, and the responsibilities of management. They also reflect the political institutions and distribution of power that have led to regulatory systems of corporate governance. This book intervenes in debates around frameworks of corporate governance through analysis of the Australian case, where regulation of investor voice is stringent, yet we see active debate emerge between owners and managers over companies' ESG responsibilities. Debates between workers and management are notably absent from contemporary shareholder activism in Australia, despite this specific combination of contestation being central to the earliest iterations of Australian anti-corporate political movements.

The rise of ESG shareholder activism in Australia can be linked to growing tension between societal expectations, regulation, and the behavior of firms, particularly around the country's approach to reducing carbon emissions. Frustration at government inaction is redirected to lobbying corporations, who are seen as being capable of, and potentially responsive to, reducing carbon emissions. Adding a layer of urgency to this action is the fact Australia faces a looming climate catastrophe, the effects of which are already being seen through the unprecedented duration and intensity of bushfire seasons, regular record floods, and prolonged drought. Australia's 2019 "megafires" represent the country's costliest natural disaster to date (P. Read and Denniss 2020).

According to the country's 2023 *Intergenerational Report*, climate change could cost Australia A$423 billion over the next forty years, while Australians are five times more likely than Europeans to be displaced by a climate-fueled disaster[1] (Steffen and Bradshaw 2021; Commonwealth of Australia 2023). Yet, Australia lags behind other Organization for Economic Co-operation and Development (OECD) states in its government-led response to climate change (Taylor 2014). Robert MacNeil (2021, 1) argues "on most metrics, Australia has, for the past quarter century, been the worst performing industrialized state in the world when it comes to climate policy." The country has no price on carbon and continues to subsidize fossil fuel industries to the value of A$12 billion per annum[2] (Australian Productivity Commission 2020). There are limited market signals encouraging producers or consumers to move away from carbon-intensive energy production to clean energy. Such government inaction has meant that corporate Australia has been the target of activists pushing for a transition to clean energy and the end to coal mining and other high-emission energy production.

Growing shareholder activism focused on climate change is evidence that Australian government inaction on this issue has transformed corporate governance into a site of contestation over emissions reduction. Michael MacLeod and Jacob Park (2011, 55–56) argue that investor activism serves as "an emerging form of private environmental governance that redirects the growing relevance of socially responsible investing in the business community with investors acting as a powerful force articulating a clear business case for why climate change is, and will remain, a critical sustainable business issue in the global economy." ESG activists have been successful in leveraging this governance deficit by pushing corporations to make public commitments to addressing climate change and extracting greater commitments from those who already have.

In addition to ACCR and Market Forces, there is an increasing push globally for pension funds (known in Australia as superannuation funds) to divest from emissions-intensive sectors (Hirsch 2021). While such commitments had previously been the sole focus of ethical investment funds, mainstream pension funds and investors are coming under greater pressure to manage their portfolio ESG risk. In April 2021, the Australian Council of Superannuation Investors (ACSI) published an updated climate policy, which called for greater disclosure of climate risks and the alignment of corporate strategy to the Paris Agreement objective of net zero emissions by 2050 (Australian Council of Superannuation Investors 2021). The policy notes that where these alignments are not occurring,

ACSI may recommend its members vote against directors of ASX-listed companies, laying the responsibility for improvement in ESG behavior at the feet of individual directors.

A second area in which a significant gap has also emerged between societal expectations and corporate behavior is approaches to Australia's First Nations peoples' culturally significant sites. In May 2020, mining multinational Rio Tinto destroyed the Juukan Gorge caves, a site of significant importance to the local Indigenous population and First Nations peoples more broadly. The sacred site in the Western Australian Pilbara region demonstrated 46,000 years of continual civilization and provided a 4,000-year-old genetic link to present-day occupants (Wahlquist 2020). The destruction of the caves, which enabled Rio Tinto to access A$135 million worth of iron ore at the site, shocked much of Australian society (Young and Toscano 2020). Rio Tinto had sought permission to mine the caves under section 18 of the Western Australian Aboriginal Heritage Act in December 2013, which meant the company could not be prosecuted for "excavating, destroying, damaging, concealing or in any way altering any Aboriginal site." Nonetheless, these actions were widely condemned as unethical. The Juukan Gorge caves demonstrate the wide schism between what is permitted under Western Australian law and what society expects of corporations. Rio Tinto has since faced a parliamentary inquiry, and its Chair, CEO, and three senior executives were forced to resign. The incident has also led to a rise in the number of ESG shareholder resolutions directed at mining firms demanding that destruction of culturally significant sites be preemptively ruled out. In 2020, Origin Energy and BHP both faced shareholder resolutions demanding the companies commit to respecting First Nations' lands beyond what is required by law, and that mining companies operating in areas that are known to contain culturally significant sites strengthen their governance structures to move beyond legal requirements, to be in line with societal expectations around the rights of Australia's First Nations peoples (ACCR 2025). BHP responded preemptively to this resolution and agreed to cease acting on section 18 approvals, which allow for mining on culturally significant land, and, as noted prior, the resolution was withdrawn ahead of the AGM (BHP 2020a).

There are signals that ESG shareholder activism is gaining traction amongst non-activist, or mainstream, investors in Australia. The first resolution to receive more than 50 percent shareholder support in defiance of the board's support was filed at Woodside Petroleum's 2020 AGM (Freeburn and Ramsay 2021a). The resolution, which garnered 50.16 percent shareholder support, called for Woodside to commit to emissions targets in line with the Paris Agreement, both within the company and further down its supply chain. This resolution is often touted as a breakthrough moment in ESG shareholder activism in Australia, and evidence suggests that it was the precursor to more well-supported climate change resolutions directed at Australian companies (Freeburn and Ramsay 2021a). Resolutions focused on climate change, rather than other environmental issues or social concerns, have the highest support among shareholders, even when these are not supported by management (ACCR 2025). In 2021, the first instance of an ASX-listed company board encouraging shareholders to support an ESG shareholder resolution occurred. Rio Tinto supported two ESG shareholder resolutions related to climate change, one filed by ACCR and one by Market Forces (ACCR 2025). Support from the Rio Tinto board followed the trend of climate change resolutions attracting relatively stronger support than resolutions on governance or societal issues. The resolutions were also supported by the new CEO, who was keen to improve Rio Tinto's public image in light of the company's destruction of the Juukan Caves. Support from the CEO and board, as well as the focus on climate change, saw these resolutions both receive 99 percent shareholder backing. Activists remain cautious, suggesting the board's support stemmed from the ongoing reputational pressures facing Rio Tinto and that supporting these shareholder resolutions was more of a symbolic move by the board than a genuine response to calls for emissions reduction (Market Forces 2021). Nonetheless, this suggests there is potential for activists to pressure large corporations to change, where societal expectations have shifted.

Finally, AGMs are a historical feature of the joint stock corporation. They were introduced when physical gatherings of shareholders were the only options for investors to discuss issues of importance to companies including board elections and remuneration. Communication methods have since changed, and well before the Covid-19 pandemic the Australian government had raised the potential for greater flexibility through hybrid and online attendance at AGMs (Corporate and Markets Advisory Committee 2012). The motivation for flexible, hybrid, or virtual

AGMs was to encourage wider participation and allow a more diverse range of shareholders to attend, including those with limited accessibility and people located outside Australia's largest cities. As pandemic-induced lockdowns were introduced, in March 2020, the Australian Securities and Investments Commission (ASIC) agreed to a "no action" rule, whereby it would not penalize companies that held their AGMs online, given the inability for shareholders to meet physically (Freeburn and Ramsay 2021b). This has since been formalized in legislation. ASIC guidelines suggest that shareholders present at a virtual AGM should be provided the same opportunity to participate in the meeting as if they were attending in person (ASIC 2021). However, there are serious concerns that online platforms can be used to exclude shareholders from asking pertinent questions (and follow-ups), mask voting irregularities, and generally dissuade participation—and ultimately allow board members to evade accountability (Freeburn and Ramsay 2021b). It has been noted that "while virtual annual meetings work reasonably well for most plain vanilla, uncontested situations they are not designed for corporate battles involving activist investors or dissident shareholders who want to see and hear an accountable management and board. A proposal presented remotely is far less impactful than one presented 'from the floor'" (Goldfarb 2020).

Shareholder activist groups, primarily ACCR and Market Forces, are effectively directing public concerns regarding the insufficient action on climate change and the deliberate destruction of culturally significant sites to corporations, using systems of corporate governance previously reserved for conventional issues related to financial performance. Activists are targeting large corporations as a result of the disconnect between public expectations and corporate behavior. Moreover, they are doing so due to the governance gap that has emerged from regulatory inaction. Australia remains a climate laggard, despite the direct impacts of global warming being felt across the country through warmer weather, reduced rainfall, and increased frequency and intensity of natural disasters. Furthermore, various sub-national legal systems allow the destruction of First Nations peoples' sites of cultural significance, in exchange for the extraction of minerals and metals that further exacerbates climate change. This governance gap is being addressed in a way that bypasses traditional forms of government and instead relies on corporate governance. In this sense, activists and large corporations are leading governments on the reform of some of the most salient societal issues. Shareholder support for climate change resolutions continues to rise. These observations suggest that traditional understandings of power and governance need to consider the role of non-state actors, such as social movements and firms.

This book sets out to explore the implications of ESG shareholder activism in the unique case study of Australia. The research employs qualitative research methods including thematic content analysis, interviews with key actors, and participant observation at corporate AGMs, in addition to the collation and analysis of a database of ESG shareholder resolutions. It examines how and why activists chose to target large corporations in a country beset by environmental, climate, and Indigenous relations challenges, and where companies appear to be operating with impunity in relation to these issues. It assesses the implications of a legal regime designed to stymy investor activism and limit shareholders' rights to lobby their companies' boards and management, a question that remains pertinent as investors, companies, and regulators navigate the rapid growth in ESG funds and investments globally. The book demonstrates that anti-ESG regulation does not necessarily eliminate investor voice, but it can severely limit the issues over which shareholders express political views and the targets of anti-corporate politics. The research reveals the ability of this form of activism to pressure firms and successfully hasten industries' response to pressing societal issues. However, it also warns that this level of change is yet to produce regulatory reform, embedding the very governance gaps that drive anti-corporate activism in the first place. The analysis of how corporate governance mechanisms have been leveraged in Australia offers insights into larger questions about how and why civil society views corporations as potential drivers of societal change and why this approach is likely to be sustained despite the shifting global political landscape. It offers generalizable lessons for addressing governance gaps in analogous political and economic settings. These lessons include the potential for activist-investors to supersede traditional ethical market actors, and, where specific political economic conditions arise, opportunities for an increased role for previously marginalized groups such as First Nations communities to steer responses to ESG issues, including climate change, through corporate governance processes. Countering this, however, is the finding that governments remain capable of reversing many of these gains through weak regulation that fails to respond to societal imperatives.

The book is organized as follows: Chapter 1 traces the global history of ethical investing and the local ecosystem in Australia, including the emergence of this form of lobbying, the key players, and the issues being addressed. It argues that legal impediments to investor voice have served to produce a duopoly of investor-activists rather than activist-investors, as is the case elsewhere globally. Chapter 2 explores the theoretical basis of the book, synthesizing the social movement scholarship with the literature on private governance to develop a framework that allows us to understand how and why activists target certain firms and the role these companies play in leading change in their industries. Here, the research methods are also introduced. Next, chapter 3 applies this novel framework to the politics of climate change, demonstrating the power of effective social movements in forcing change within large companies and their industries, as well as the limitations faced by activists in forcing legislative change. Chapter 4 moves to the trickier question of the *S* in ESG, arguing that legal limitations on investor voice produce a duopoly of actors with a narrow focus on climate change; and that, while the field of play remains small, the funders, activists, and the non-activist investors they target are unlikely to prioritize social issues such as First Nations' land rights, modern slavery, or workers' rights. Chapter 5 explores the lessons that can be learned from Australia's experience with shareholder activism in liberal market economies elsewhere. Beginning with an examination of transnational investor activism and its implications for markets globally, the chapter moves on to highlight specific implications arising from attempts to legislate against investor voice and market-based attempts to meet the challenges faced by First Nations peoples in settler-colonial societies. The book concludes with an explanation of the successes and failures of ESG activists in Australia, an examination of the implications of the legal regime, and a discussion of the potential impact of the rise of ESG activism and investing on the major issues facing society.

CHAPTER 1
ESG Shareholder Activism

AUSTRALIA'S RESPONSE TO CLIMATE change has been bound by political inaction on both sides of the political aisle since the 1990s (Christoff 2005; Bailey et al. 2012). As noted in the introduction to this book, there remains no price on carbon, or any other market signal to disincentivize ongoing investment in emissions-intensive activities. By the 2000s, attempts to introduce a market for carbon had become the subject of vitriolic political discourse, despite Labor Prime Minister Kevin Rudd labeling climate change "the greatest moral, economic and social challenge of our time" (Bailey et al. 2012). The politicization of this scientific issue led to Rudd failing at two attempts to introduce a price on carbon and, ultimately, the loss of his prime ministership. Rudd's successor and Australia's first female prime minister, Julia Gillard, introduced a price on carbon at the behest of climate-friendly cross benchers, a decision which later led to her downfall as prime minister. Yet, the country remains harmfully exposed to more frequent and intense natural disasters including floods, fires, and extreme heat. Australia's 2019 megafires burnt through seven million hectares of land, in the most extreme fire event since European invasion (Collins et al. 2021). Just two years later Northern NSW experienced flooding so severe that it took the lives of twelve people and decimated large parts of the region in Australia's costliest natural disaster in history (M. Read 2023). Australia's lack of climate action also impacts its nearest neighbors, low-lying Pacific Island states (Enari and Viliamu Jameson 2021). Sea levels in the Western Pacific are rising at three to four times the global average, affecting already vulnerable populations (Perkins and Krause 2018). In many aspects, Australia's lack of climate policy sits not only uncomfortably with persistent natural disasters but continues a pattern of relations seemingly blind to a history of colonial displacement at home and in the Pacific. Many of the companies at the heart of this research not only contribute to carbon emissions but also to the deep concern over the protection of Australia's First Nations peoples' cultural heritage.

Australian corporations play a key role in addressing some of the most pressing issues facing the country, including increasing emissions output and reconciling Australian society with its history of dispossession. Frustration with the behavior of under-regulated firms has encouraged activists to engage in an increasing variety of ways. One of these is through market-based solutions, that is using tools of corporate governance, boycotts, divestment campaigns, and naming and shaming to pressure firms to reform their behavior (O'Brien et al. 2022). Of particular interest here is the recent emergence of ESG shareholder activism in Australia. This chapter maps the emergence of a unique form of shareholder activism in Australia, placing it in its global historical context. In doing so, it identifies the key players in this arena including those who pioneered this style of activism in Australia and the two key organizations that dominate the contemporary space. The chapter sketches the ecosystem of ESG shareholder activism by outlining the issue areas over which this contestation is taking place, principally and historically, climate change, but also First Nations' land rights, the protection of culturally sacred sites, modern slavery, and non-climate environmental concerns. This reveals the relations between groups and their potential for impacting corporate behavior and legislative change.

Since 2017, Australia has experienced a marked increase in the instances of ESG shareholder activism (Grewal et al. 2016). As shown in Figure 1, in 2016 there were no ESG shareholder resolutions. However, a total of 174 ESG resolutions were filed over the following six years. In 2021 alone, 38 ESG resolutions were filed at the AGMs of Australian listed companies. As Figure 1 shows, activists are pressuring firms to respond to

FIGURE 1. ESG shareholder resolutions per year, 2002–2022. Source: Author's database.

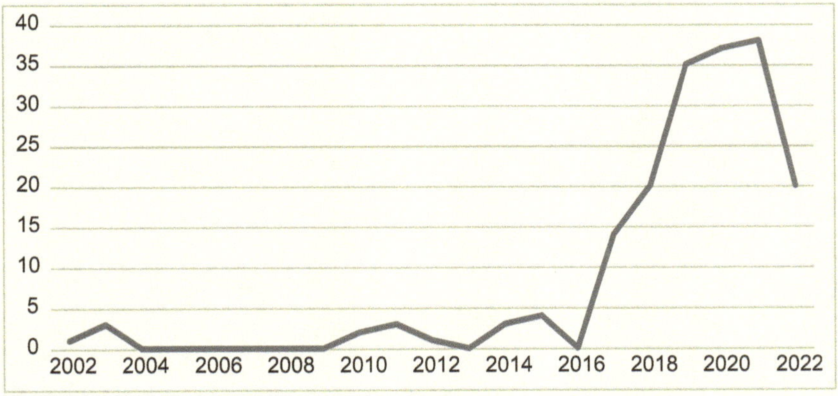

the challenges of climate change, Indigenous land rights, human rights, and corporate governance. This unprecedented action seeks to engender a new wave of corporate accountability and political participation.

Not all sectors of the economy have been targeted equally. Mining, oil and gas, and financial services (including banking, pension and funds management) firms were the targets of 92 percent of all resolutions filed between 2017 and 2022. Table 1 shows that almost all these resolutions related to firms' approach to climate change, while the remainder focused on cultural heritage (including FPIC) and human rights (including workers' rights and modern slavery). Furthermore, the number of filers is also highly concentrated, with 91 percent of the resolutions raised between 2017 and 2022 emerging from one of two groups, ACCR and Market Forces, both of whom are at the forefront of this trend. Unlike their international counterparts such as the US Interfaith Center for Corporate Responsibility (ICCR) and the UK's ShareAction, these organizations are usually *not* joined by wealthy investors, trade unions, and ethical institutional investors to file resolutions at Australian firms' AGMs. In the majority of cases, either ACCR or Market Forces is the only filer. On occasion, they have been joined by civil society actors from overseas, such as ethical or religious investors who have decided to target an Australian corporation and rely on the activists' shareholdings to file the resolutions. The lack of coalition-building is the key difference between Australian investor activism and its international counterparts, and can be attributed

TABLE 1. ESG Shareholder Resolutions Filed Between 2017 and 2022, Categorized by Industry and Issue. Source: Author's database.

	Climate	Cultural Heritage	Human Rights	TOTAL
Oil and Gas	41	8	1	50
Finance	25			25
Mining	22	2		24
Property/Retail			4	4
Aviation			2	2
Other	3			3

to the legal barriers dissuading activists from using shareholdings to lobby companies. In jurisdictions such as the US and UK a range of actors leverage their professional identity to move between activism and finance in order to drive change (Seabrooke and Wigan 2018). Instead, in the Australian case, ACCR and Market Forces file alone, but rely on a strategy of appealing to institutional shareholders to "vote up" their resolutions, given their significant shareholdings.

While the Australian experience varies from that of other jurisdictions, largely due to the concentrated nature of activist groups that have emerged as a result of high legal barriers to investor activism, there are similarities in the drivers and approach of ESG shareholder activists globally. The next section explores the global history of ESG activism, beginning with early modern forms of investment screening.

A History of Ethical Investment

In the eighteenth and nineteenth centuries, Quaker and Methodist immigrants introduced what is now known as ethical investing to the United States. The approach taken by these religiously motivated investors prohibited believers from investing in stocks or businesses that traded in war or slavery (Schueth 2003). For Methodist founder John Wesley, the use of money was one of the most important lessons of biblical teachings (Schueth 2003). The decision not to invest in stocks that ran against these Christian beliefs was the beginning of "social screening" in the modern world. By the twentieth century this had transformed to practices of wider negative screening, principally banning investment in "sin stocks" including companies profiting from gambling, alcohol, and tobacco (Guay et al. 2004). This form of investment differs from the standard approach to trading, which is based solely on judgments about financial materiality. The definition of financial materiality has evolved over time, but the description posited by the United States Supreme Court, and used by the Securities and Exchange Commission (SEC), is: "a fact is material if there is a substantial likelihood that the disclosure of the omitted fact would have been viewed by the reasonable investor as having significantly altered the 'total mix' of information made available" (US Supreme Court 1976). European regulators have moved beyond this narrow definition to one that more explicitly incorporates ESG concerns, acknowledging that ESG challenges represent the dynamic or double materiality concerns facing investors and their corporations (D. A. Katz et al. 2021). The discrepancy between the two definitions is reflected in contemporary debates about the role of corporations in addressing ESG concerns in the face of governance deficits, the central focus of this book.

Religion may have motivated the original ethical investors, yet it was the heated political climate of the United States in the 1960s that drove the rapid emergence of what is now known as Socially Responsible Investment. The rapid growth in political movements and their supporters, including those opposing the Vietnam War, supporting the US civil rights movement, and pushing for women's liberation, drove much of the professionalization of SRI (Schueth 2003). SRI moves beyond narrow definitions of materiality and instead focuses on an "investment approach that uses both financial and non-financial criteria to determine which assets to purchase, but whose distinguishing characteristic is the latter" (Guay et al. 2004, 126). Investors motivated by SRI principles examine three "social" factors: the firm's internal practices and policies, external practices and policies, and their industry—thus a firm with equal opportunity hiring practices and a strong environmental record in a non-harmful industry may be a candidate for SRI (Guay et al. 2004). The first contemporary SRI fund was established in the US in 1971, Pax World Funds. This was followed by a number of other SRI funds including Calvert Social Investment Fund (1982) and Friends Provident Stewardship Fund in the UK in 1984 (Guay et al. 2004). SRI accelerated in the 1970s largely due to the formation of the ICCR in 1973, which built on previous campaigns to establish an interfaith group of activist investors with an interest in directing capital for social good. A pioneering advocacy coalition, the ICCR represents more than three hundred global institutional investors and holds more than US$4 trillion in managed assets (Interfaith Center on Corporate Responsibility 2023a). The ICCR outlines its investment objectives as to "to improve corporate practices on vital environmental, social, and governance concerns and, in doing so, build more sustainable, and financially resilient companies" (Interfaith Center on Corporate Responsibility 2023b). In this sense, the organization promotes the three components of ESG in its approach to investing.

The emergence of ICCR and other SRI funds and campaigns legitimized the idea that investing in a company meant implicitly supporting the company's actions. Furthermore, investors also began to see their shareholdings as a mechanism through which they could signal to boards and management dissatisfaction with corporate behavior. As such, shareholders pursued strategies of lobbying in cases where "management is not acting in the best interests of shareholders, and threaten[ing] to do something about it" (Guay et al. 2004). The threatened "something" may vary from private discussions with management to public petitions, boycotts, filing shareholder resolutions, bringing media and other activists on board, or visible protests. Often, the lobbying tactic chosen reflects the particulars of corporate law in that country, as we will see in the case of Australian shareholder activism (Jefferies 2019). An approach which allowed for investor voice took hold from the late 1970s onwards, with protests over management and labor issues, as well as the anti-nuclear movement (Schueth 2003). Drawing on these experiences, what followed in the decade after was the most widespread and encompassing investor campaign yet, where US citizens, churches, universities, and city and state pension funds pushed for companies to exit and funds to divest from Apartheid South Africa (Soule 1997; Schueth 2003; Guay et al. 2004). Although anti-Apartheid campaigns had existed in various forms from the 1950s, media coverage of the state-sanctioned violence against Black South Africans, which increased from the 1960s onwards, meant this movement acquired much greater support in the US (Sethi and Williams 2000). Activists urged US firms operating in South Africa to support the Sullivan Principles. These six (and later, seven) principles were designed by General Motors board member Reverend Leon Sullivan and demanded the equal treatment of employees, regardless of race, both inside and outside of the workplace. The Sullivan Principles conflicted directly with the policy of segregation pursued by the Apartheid South African regime. When companies refused to abide by these principles they were pressured to withdraw from their South African operations with activists pushing for boycotts and divestments from companies that continued to operate in the country (Sethi and Williams 2000). Apartheid South Africa dominated the investor activist space until the dismantling of the regime and the transition to majority rule in the early 1990s (Graves et al. 2001). Since this time, shareholder activism has been used in a more diverse range of issues, and as a tool in almost every social movement campaign including civil rights, feminism, LGBTQI rights, and environmentalism (L. King and Gish 2015). Often, these issues are highlighted by religious, ethical or public sector investment funds, which research, and engage with companies. Where a solution cannot be reached, ethical institutional investors may file resolutions at AGMs (Sheehy et al. 2021).

While the strategies outlined above have proven successful in achieving a certain level of environmental and social reform, the type of active shareholder activism studied in this book moves beyond the establishment of SRI or ethical funds, and divestment and boycott. It instead focuses on more contentious strategies for forcing corporate change, specifically the use of corporate governance mechanisms such as shareholder resolutions to lobby firms to reform corporate behavior. ESG shareholder activism first emerged in the United States in the postwar era, when a series of stockholders, often referred to as "gadflies," sought entry to stockholders' meetings to press companies on social issues. These interlopers included Wilma Soss, who confronted the management of US Steel about the possibility of appointing a woman to the Board, and James Peck and Bayard Ruskin, who purchased a single share each in Greyhound in order to raise integrated bus seating in the US South at the stockholders' meeting (Marens 2002). These activists had minimal budgets, and would often borrow or purchase small parcels of shares in order to permit them to file shareholder resolutions (L. King and Gish 2015). These early attempts at leveraging existing shareholdings or purchasing shares for the express purpose of pursuing such social goals are often overlooked in the literature. Instead, most accounts of ESG shareholder activism place the origins of this practice in the 1960s and 1970s United States (L. King and Gish 2015). Throughout the 1960s and into 1970 three early campaigns shaped the ESG shareholder activist movement in the US. The first was Saul Alinsky's pathbreaking campaign against Kodak on civil rights; the second, the campaign against Dow Chemical's sale of Agent Orange (which was being used against civilians in the Vietnam War); and finally, the campaign against General Motors on the basis of civil rights and other progressive causes (Guay et al. 2004; L. King and Gish 2015). In the cases of Dow Chemicals and General Motors, the US SEC was forced to make a ruling regarding the legitimacy of using shareholder resolutions for social purposes. The resulting decision in favor of allowing activist shareholders to file such resolutions opened the door for this practice in the US, and eventually other jurisdictions. It also signaled a legitimate place for ESG concerns in the boardrooms of major corporations.

The emergence of shareholder activism in the mid-twentieth century represents a move away from a strategy of divestment, also known as the "Wall Street rule," whereby shareholders unhappy with their company's actions would simply divest, by selling their shareholdings (Drucker 1996). By the early 1980s the Wall Street rule, or a strategy of exit, had been replaced with one of voice, that is a belief that shareholders should use their stake in companies to improve their ESG performance. This was particularly the case for institutional investors who hold significant parcels of shares in corporations, and were increasingly acting as "patient capitalists," or shareholders with a long-term investment horizon, unafraid of challenging management by upending understandings of investor–management relations (Barnard 1990, 1152; Fligstein 2001; Davis 2009; Lee and Lounsbury 2011). More recently, this has evolved into what is commonly referred to as "universal ownership," whereby it is understood that institutional investors hold a broad portfolio of shares in most companies listed on a respective exchange (Lydenberg 2007). There is therefore no gain for these investors if one company generates negative externalities at the expense of others or if one manipulates the political system to its sole advantage (Sheehy et al. 2021). The recognition of the importance of ESG concerns by investors suggests a natural affinity between concerned shareholders, activists, and ethical investors, who may together push for more sustainable business practices (Lydenberg 2007). The universal ownership approach is assumed to inform ethical investors' approach to AGMs, board engagement, and ESG issues. It is also encapsulated in the UNPRI, a set of guidelines for signatory institutional investors with funds under management of US$121 trillion (United Nations Principles for Responsible Investment 2023). Investors who are signatories to UNPRI are often sought out by activists to support claims against companies due to their commitment to "incorporate ESG issues into our ownership policies and practices" (United Nations Principles for Responsible Investment 2023).

Universal ownership, or universal stewardship, is clearly demonstrated through the tactics and approach of three US asset managers: BlackRock, Vanguard, and State Street. Referred to as the "Big Three," these investors control 80 to 90 percent of assets under management in US passive equity funds—that is, funds that replicate established stock indexes such as the Dow Jones Index, or FTSE 100, and where investors do not actively buy and sell, but instead allow their portfolio to follow the market (Fichtner et al. 2017).[1] The implications of this concentration are explored in chapter 5 of this book, however it is important here to acknowledge the power these investors have over the direction of companies, and entire sectors, within the US and internationally. All three can be considered permanent universal owners, in that they do not buy and sell based on investment strategies, but instead hold stocks based on when companies fall in and out of various indices (Fichtner and Heemskerk 2020). Given their ownership stakes in companies, they hold the power to vote on behalf of investors, with a commitment to do so in "investors' best interests" (Griffin 2019). Thus, their position on ESG issues, expressed through their power to lobby companies in which they hold large shareholdings and through their votes on ESG resolutions, carries significant weight in determining businesses' approaches to environmental and social issues. The Big Three's ESG stance has evolved over time, however all three asset managers have in recent years explicitly noted their commitment to ESG issues, and have voted accordingly.

In the UK, as in Australia, the term "ethical investment" is used in place of SRI when referring to market-based activism. The UK legal regime, set out in the Companies Act (2006), allows shareholders to file both directive (or advisory) and conditional resolutions. Directive resolutions are non-binding and signify to the company's board an issue of importance to shareholders, whereas conditional resolutions require a company to act on the claim-making, where a threshold of 75 percent support is reached. As in Australia, there is a legal requirement that before a resolution can be filed it must have the support of 100 shareholders, or

5 percent of the total voting shares. Thus, there are far fewer ESG shareholder resolutions filed in the UK compared to the US (Sheehy et al. 2021). This is not to suggest, however, that UK shareholders are less engaged on ESG matters; it may be that legal barriers have forced a greater deal of private engagement with companies.

Peter Newell (2001) refers to shareholder activism as leveraging the "hassle factor" by disrupting otherwise uneventful corporate governance procedures. This characterization aligns with arguments that this form of activism is most effective where it forces the company to devote a disproportionate amount of resources at a fraction of their operations through disruptive efforts such as ESG shareholder resolutions (Rodman 1998; Luders 2006; Lee and Lounsbury 2011). The unwanted attention to the company's operations also increases the cost of doing business while negative publicity can also prove costly (Clark et al. 2008; B. King 2008a; Logsdon and Van Buren 2008). Thus, dialogue between some firms and activists has increased, driven by management and boards that see value in addressing activist concerns before they reach shareholders and the media (Logsdon and Van Buren 2008). Newell (2001) explores the UK case of activist pressure on Shell to improve its environmental and human rights record in Nigeria, which was supported by civil society actors WWF and Amnesty International. Activists' grievances were given added legitimacy when it was revealed that former Shell director Geoffrey Chandler and the then Duke of Edinburgh were acting as Amnesty and WWF's legal representatives (Marinetto 1998). Shareholders holding 1 percent of the company's shares filed a resolution at the 1997 AGM calling for one Shell director to be assigned responsibility for improving the company's human rights and environmental accountability measures (W. Lewis 1997). Shell then attempted to preemptively ward off this action by publishing an improved Statement of General Business Principles, which included a greater focus on human rights and sustainable development (Caulkin 1997). In the end, the resolution was supported by eighteen public and private pension funds, five religious funds, and one academic fund—but was ultimately defeated (saving Shell much embarrassment) by the board's ability to lobby City of London investors to vote the resolution down (Marinetto 1998). While this attempt to embed ESG principles into the board's responsibilities and role was unsuccessful, this campaign is often referred to as the starting point for the modern ESG shareholder movement. From this point onwards, such campaigns increased in frequency, and individual board members found themselves the targets of campaigns for ethical investment.

As this form of activism has matured the field of investors has grown more sophisticated. Increasingly, for-profit investors are seeking to transform the behavior of companies, driven by reputational, moral, and profit imperatives. In these instances, the logic of social justice activism intersects with the logic of profit, and rather than competing, they are seen as complementary (L. King and Gish 2015). This process has been referred to as the monetization of activism, where for-profit socially responsible investing leads to higher expected returns on investment (L. King and Gish 2015; Michelon et al. 2020). This has also created a duality whereby resolutions are raised by activists driven by social and ethical considerations, and by investors driven by profit-seeking motives, where it is believed that increased monitoring of ESG issues is good for business (Michelon et al. 2020). In most liberal market economies ESG shareholder activism is dominated by diversified firms offering investments that achieve ESG and profit goals, simultaneously. Corporations and investors remain motivated by logics of profit, measured in shareholder value, however SRI practitioners, in the US in particular, have "influenced how financial risk is conceptualized and calculated among an ever growing set of investors" (L. King and Gish 2015, 726).

As the volume of ESG shareholder activism has increased globally in liberal market economies such as Australia, the UK, Canada, and particularly in the US, a greater number of investors and pension fund members have sought guidance that their investments meet ESG standards (Sheehy et al. 2023). At the same time, the public has gained a greater awareness of some of the issues ESG activists target, including human rights, climate change, environment more generally, and the rights of First Nations' peoples. Together, this has led to increasing pressure on company boards to treat ESG issues as part of the overall profitability equation. Firms face the potential for reputational harm where ESG issues are not addressed, as well as financial penalties for breaching legislation governing modern slavery, diversity and inclusion, and environmental harm.

The increasing pressure on boards and management to address ESG issues has drawn the ire of corporate lobby groups and led to government attempts in the United States and Australia to constrain shareholder voice.

Proxy advisory firms, who guide institutional investors in how to respond to ESG claims, have been key targets of this legislative response. In 2023, the American Securities Association President Chris Iacovella argued "the proxy advisory process must be reformed to prioritize the interests of working families, retirement savers, and small public companies—not activist investors with a political agenda" (American Securities Association 2023). Such statements emerged in parallel with attempts to introduce 165 pieces of "anti-ESG" legislation in US state legislatures. These bills were aimed at curbing the ESG activities of government pension funds and restricting investors' rights to lobby their companies on non-financial issues (Gibson and Sawyer 2023). This followed the tightening of regulations in 2018 when the US SEC withdrew a ruling that allowed investment advisors to rely on proxy advice in lieu of their own analysis. And in 2019, when the SEC also tightened regulation of proxy advisors by requiring them to disclose potential conflicts of interest and allowing firms to respond to voting recommendations prior to their release (Boone et al. 2020). Proxy advisors have also attracted the attention of regulators in other jurisdictions. In 2021, the Australian government attempted to constrain the power of proxy advisors by proposing strict new regulations (Frydenberg 2019). This action was in spite of the regulator ASIC's recommendation that no changes were required. The proposal was described as "regulating against contrary views" (Radzyminski 2022) and seen as an attempt to undermine activists' efforts to harness the power of proxy advisors to influence companies on climate change, and other ESG issues. Similar criticisms have been levelled at the SEC's regulatory changes, including accusations of overreach (Boone et al. 2020).

Despite the surge in ESG shareholder activism, and the corresponding attempts by some jurisdictions to limit this tool of corporate governance being used for social issues, there remains conflicting evidence as to the efficacy of this approach. While significant difficulties lie in isolating the drivers of investor voting patterns, corporate change, or financial metrics such as share price, it has been suggested that this practice is ineffective largely due to the low levels of support for these resolutions (Rehbein et al. 2013; M. Pepper et al. 2021). While it is rare for ESG shareholder resolutions to achieve a significant in-favor vote from the broader shareholder population, others have argued that it is the very disruptiveness of ESG shareholder resolutions that drive potential outcomes (Elbra 2023).

There are anecdotal examples of successful campaigns around issues outlined earlier in the chapter such as forcing companies to withdraw from Apartheid South Africa (Meznar et al. 1994), banning the use of harmful packaging (O'Rourke 2003), improved pollution management (Lee and Lounsbury 2011), forcing companies to disclose their GHG footprint (Reid and Toffel 2009), and, as explored in this book, campaigns to bring forward the closure of coal-fired power stations. The success of these campaigns, despite low levels of shareholder support, may lie in the wider community response to the campaigns, media attention, and Newell's (2001) earlier argument, that regardless of the likely voting outcome, ESG shareholder resolutions force firms to devote significant resources to one particular issue.

One way that corporations can limit the costs of this attention, particularly if the practice being targeted by activists is considered peripheral to core business operations, is to address activist concerns directly. It is not necessarily the ultimate goal for activist investors to see their resolutions voted on at the AGM. Jeanne Logsdon and Harry Van Buren (2009) dispute the David and Goliath narrative that depicts a small group of committed activists publicly taking on large corporations, and instead note that a significant amount of social change takes place in private dialogue that cannot be seen by outsiders. Studies on UK and Canadian funds' behind-the-scenes engagement with activists has demonstrated effectiveness in increasing shareholder value (Becht et al. 2009; Doidge et al. 2015). While a shareholder vote at an AGM sits at the end of the activism spectrum, there are substantive gains to be made from the prior stages of negotiation, including through dialogue with the target firm, negotiations, and threats to file a resolution, and even filing and rescinding a resolution on the basis of a mutually agreed outcome. Shareholder resolutions are often withdrawn before AGMs, particularly in instances where education, dialogue, or commitments from the company have swayed activists to avoid a more confrontational path (Logsdon and Van Buren 2009).

Australian Shareholder Activism

Australia has a much shorter history of ESG shareholder activism, when compared to the global experience described in the previous section. One reason for this is that according to a strict Federal Court interpretation of the *Corporations Act* shareholders are not permitted to file advisory resolutions at AGMs, as is the case in the US, the UK, and Canada. Prior to this ruling, the earliest ESG shareholder activism was undertaken by environmental groups in the 1960s and 1970s, and then trade unions and environmental groups, in a sporadic fashion, throughout the 1990s and early 2000s (Anderson et al. 2007). In the early 2000s, trade unions, frustrated at management's attempts to stymy or ignore their workplace concerns, began leveraging shareholder activism to further their causes (Anderson and Ramsay 2006). These cases represent examples of the early worker versus owner and manager battles referred to previously. One example was that of the Transport Workers Union claim-making at the 2003 Boral AGM, where the union made the case for considering workplace health and safety as a corporate governance issue. This claim was supported by an independent report provided by wealth manager BT Financial, which noted that workplace health and safety was a material financial risk to companies in terms of reputation, remediation, and potential fines, thus reiterating to the Boral management and directors that ESG issues should be considered at the board level (Rawling 2006). Three years earlier, the Construction, Forestry, Mining and Energy Union (CFMEU) had filed resolutions at Rio Tinto's AGM calling for independent board members to be appointed, and a right to collective bargaining under the International Labour Convention. In 2004, the Finance Sector Union put a resolution to the Commonwealth Bank of Australia AGM calling for the appointment of an independent expert to examine the legality of proposed job losses (Anderson et al. 2007). And in the same year, the Australian Workers Union filed five shareholder resolutions over executive remuneration, appointment, and tenure at Bluescope Steel (Rawling 2006; Anderson et al. 2007). These trade union coordinated efforts reflect the lack of employee voice in corporate governance processes. John Maitland, the then national secretary of the CFMEU, announced that unions would not confine their bargaining to the workplace; instead they would utilize shareholder activism as an alternative, because unions' rights to bargain collectively were being curtailed (Anderson et al. 2007). This campaign occurred at a time where there was a historical trend downward in workers' rights at the expense of management control. The majority of this activism took place in heavily unionized sectors of the economy, reflecting the ability of workers to coordinate and engage in claim-making against employers over workers' rights.

Several years passed before ESG resolutions were again raised at Australian company AGMs. Three resolutions were filed by investors and activists Ethinvest, GetUp!, and The Wilderness Society in 2010 and 2011 on issues including climate disclosure (ANZ), ending investment in the Narrabri Gas Project (Santos), and acting to limit the harm from gaming machines (supermarket giant Woolworths). While these resolutions were disparate and not part of a coordinated campaign, they signaled that ESG shareholder activism was emerging as a tactic of Australian activist groups.

Australian corporations law follows in the tradition of UK legal rights, although there has been divergence between the two. Shareholder resolutions are bound by the same requirements as in the UK, whereby one hundred individual shareholders or those who own 5 percent of the company must band together to file the resolution. The one-hundred-shareholder rule is not met through an activist organization holding one hundred shares in a company, but instead obtaining the support of one hundred shareholders as signatories to the resolution. However, several constraints have been placed on ESG shareholder activism in recent times in Australia through the setting of precedents circumscribing their use. Firstly, law reform that removed the right of one hundred shareholders to call an *extraordinary* general meeting severely limits the opportunities for activists to file resolutions at any time, restricting these exclusively to *annual* general meetings (Riddell 2016). Secondly, in a move that signaled a shift away from US-style engagement whereby shareholders have a path to voice concerns about management strategy, advisory resolutions were ruled unlawful by the Federal Court in a 2015 test case brought on by activist group ACCR. The case revolved around the decision by the Commonwealth Bank of Australia to refuse to include two of three resolutions filed by ACCR on behalf of one hundred shareholders in their 2014 Notice of AGM (North 2020). ACCR brought the case to court where it argued that shareholders have a right to propose non-binding resolutions over issues that are under the control of management and boards. ACCR lost this case, with the Full Court of the Federal Court of Australia denying the resolutions; declaring them to be "an incursion by shareholders into the exclusive management domain of directors," the court ruled that "shareholders have no right to express an opinion about how directors are exercising their power" (Sheehy et al. 2023, 18). This ruling was originally interpreted by many as the end of the limited ESG shareholder activism that had taken place. The decision can be seen as an attempt to prevent even "pious or precatory resolutions that have no binding force or legal effect," but that signal shareholder concerns to management (Riddell 2016, 172). This judicial attempt to shut down advisory resolutions was described as overreach. Moreover, as noted by Stephen Bottomley (2019, 106), "an advisory resolution is not binding on the directors: it does not attempt to do the work of the directors or remove, curtail, or bind the exercise of their managerial power," thus it is not clear why they should be restricted in this globally unique manner.

Despite the legal rulings that appeared to end the path to advisory resolutions, one of two main activist groups involved in ESG shareholder activism today developed a strategy to work around the *Corporations Act* and the ACCR vs. CBA precedent. From late 2015 onwards, given the difficulties in filing an advisory resolution, ACCR introduced an approach whereby it would file a binding, or non-advisory, resolution seeking to amend the company's constitution or call for the removal of directors *and* a second substantive resolution, the advisory resolution itself. The requirement that shareholders first propose to dissolve the board, or amend the company's constitution, in order to express concerns about an unrelated matter is now a feature of market-based activism in Australia. However, it is not the intention of shareholders to either remove the board or amend the constitution; instead this must be proposed for the non-binding resolution to be filed. The first of these resolutions consistently achieves a low "yes" vote, and as a result, the second resolution is not voted on at the AGM. However, given that the majority of shareholders vote on resolutions via proxy, and the outcome of the first vote is not known ahead of the AGM, proxy votes on the advisory resolution are tallied and published in the results of the AGM. Therefore, those observing this vote, including boards and management, receive a clear insight into shareholders' and proxy advisors' position on the proposition. This "double-barreled" approach thus became the "standard approach to shareholder advisory resolutions in Australia" from 2017 onwards (Sheehy et al. 2021, 171).

The legal barriers explored above explain why the Australian shareholder activism movement has a short history relative to other liberal market economies. By extension, we should be unsurprised to discover that it has been leveraged over far fewer social issues than elsewhere, and, given the ownership requirements, that claim-making has been filed at comparably fewer company AGMs. However, while ESG shareholder activism emerged relatively late as a tool of anti-corporate politics, there was a rapid rise in this form of activism from 2017 onwards. This was dominated by two key players that employed methods to circumvent legal restrictions on this form of protest, ACCR and Market Forces. These two organizations' histories and approaches have come to determine the shape and volume of shareholder activism in Australia. Domination of the landscape by these two actors has led to a strong focus on mining, oil and gas, finance and insurances sectors, and "blue-chip" ASX-listed firms, as well as a tendency (although not solely) to focus on climate change as a key issue area.

Australia has a unique history of ESG shareholder activism, which stands in contrast with the international experience, where hedge funds, pension funds, and ethical investors have traditionally formed coalitions with activist groups to channel the trillions of dollars under funds management away from socially irresponsible firms. At the core of these coalitions are pension or hedge funds, often joined by civil society organizations whose role it is to direct investor activism activities (MacLeod and Park 2011). In contrast, the Australian experience has not typically been led by pension funds, and only very rarely involves funds as co-filers, this is despite the pension market's ranking as the world's third largest. Instead, two activist organizations have operated by acquiring the minimum parcel of shares and leveraging this stake to file ESG resolutions at company AGMs. While much of the literature on lobbying treats actors as either possessing insider or outside status, Erin O'Brien et al. (2023, 7) refer to the actors undertaking this tactic as *unnatural insiders*, that is "those who have intentionally sought to change their status from outsiders to insiders for the purposes of lobbying." It is through the use of this strategy that from 2017 onwards, the two key organizations behind Australia's shareholder resolutions took on a more professional turn. These groups organized registers of shareholders that could be called on to "donate" their vote to a shareholder resolution and employed a growing number of professional activists whose job it was to liaise with companies and push for more ethical company policies, particularly around climate change. This section sets out the historical emergence of the key players, supporting actors, and the key issue areas that Australian shareholder activism has focused on.

Actors

The ecosystem of actors partaking in ESG shareholder activism in Australia is relatively small. Although, the size of the country's pension system leads to an outsized amount of power bestowed on these actors. We can conceptualize this ecosystem by categorizing actors the following way: activists, shareholder representatives, institutional investors, and proxy advisors. These groups and their composite actors are shown in Figure 2 and explored in this section.

Activists

Australian Ethical Investments (AEI)

Prior to ESG shareholder activism's late takeoff in Australia, AEI was one of the earliest proponents of market-based activism globally, and Australia's first ethical pension investment fund. The organization was formed in 1986 by Caroline Le Couteur, Howard Pender, and James Thier. Three years later, in 1989, AEI launched the first public trust offering SRI in Australia. AEI pioneered Australian shareholder activism as one of the many tools for ethical investment used by the company, seeking for the first time to replicate the US experience in corporate lobbying through investor holdings. AEI filed shareholder resolutions against Aquila and Paladin at their AGMs as part of the company's Climate Advocacy Fund in 2010 and 2011 (Pender 2011; Sheehy et al. 2021). Pender then filed a shareholder resolution at Woodside Petroleum's 2011 AGM, which asked the company to detail its capital expenditure plans on the basis of carbon emissions, a carbon price and demand for oil (Pender 2011). The resolution gained the support of 5.7 percent of Woodside's shareholders. However, by 2012 all three founders had departed the organization, moving on to

FIGURE 2. Australian ESG Shareholder Activism Ecosystem.

other sustainable investment projects, including ACCR, where Howard Pender remains on the board of directors (West 2012). It can be argued that these original AEI shareholder resolutions represented the first systematic approach to anti-corporate activism in Australia. Their filings also took place prior to the Federal Court ruling that limited the ability of shareholders to file an advisory resolution. AEI was the first organization to file shareholder resolutions over ESG issues, outside of individual trade union campaigns of the early 2000s and earlier sporadic environmental resolutions.

Australasian Centre for Corporate Responsibility

ACCR was founded by Howard Pender and Robert Howell in 2013, the year after Pender departed AEI (West 2012). As one interviewee for this research noted, ACCR was founded on the premise that there was significant opportunity to more widely implement the model of shareholder activism that had been imported from the US and used earlier by AEI. The founders of ACCR observed the lack of organizations like the ICCR in Australia and began importing these tactics, which increased in frequency when Executive Director Brynn O'Brien was recruited in 2017 (ACCR 2023). ACCR is a small organization, with twenty-two staff members, and is funded through donations from Pender, the Sunrise Project (an Australian-based social justice advocacy group), and a range of private family trusts, without support from listed companies or institutional investors.

In 2014 and 2015, Caroline Le Couteur (then Executive Director of ACCR) led a short-lived campaign against two of Australia's largest banks, Australia and New Zealand Banking Group (ANZ) and the Commonwealth Bank of Australia (CBA) (author's own database). The Australian financial services sector is dominated by what is known as the Big Four banks, which together control 73 percent of the deposit and home loan markets, compared to the US, where the largest four institutions hold 45 percent of deposits (Muroi 2023). ACCR held discussions with all four banks around their financing of emissions-intensive energy projects, however two, ANZ and CBA, remained unwilling to meet ACCR's demands. Of the four, ANZ's balance sheet was the most exposed to emissions-heavy projects. ACCR's resolutions called on the banks to disclose the extent of emissions financed by their loans, or what is now referred to as scope 3 emissions. While ACCR faced a legal challenge from

CBA that prevented resolutions from being heard at the 2015 AGM, the bank nonetheless implemented many of the requests of the activists due to the amount of media attention generated by the legal battle (Hey 2015). It also set a precedent whereby shareholder activists utilized a loophole allowing them to raise non-binding resolutions at company AGMs, that is through first raising a binding, constitutional amendment resolution. This was accompanied by resolutions filed at the 2015 AGMs of Origin Energy and AGL over a lack of planning for emissions reduction and commitments to pathways to limit global warming (author's own database). Both companies would become repeat targets of activist groups due to their unwillingness to depart from a business model that was heavily reliant on the continued production of coal-fired power and extraction of gas, including prospecting for new gas reserves.

Over 2015 and 2016, ACCR focused its efforts on securing the requisite share parcels to file resolutions against Australia's biggest emitters, and from 2017 onwards rapidly increased the number of resolutions it filed to the level seen in Figure 1. ACCR attempts to engage companies in this form of activism by speaking in a language familiar to boards and investors. While the group holds only a fraction of a percentage of shares in these companies, resolutions are expressed in the voice of investor ownership, that is what is good for "our company," in order to sway non-activist investors. In addition to filing ESG shareholder resolutions, ACCR continues to engage companies privately over ESG risks as well as liaise with media on proposed or actual resolutions.

Market Forces

Market Forces, an affiliate project of Friends of the Earth Australia, was formed in 2013. The organization has a single-issue focus on climate change, leading it to solely target companies that produce significant carbon emissions. Julien Vincent is the founder and Executive Director of Market Forces, and previously worked for Oxfam and Greenpeace and was awarded the Goldman Environmental Prize in 2022 (The Goldman Environmental Prize 2023). Market Forces has twenty-four members of staff and receives funding from philanthropic institutions and individual donors.

Market Forces began filing ESG shareholder resolutions in 2017. As with ACCR, Market Forces acquired control of at least one hundred shares of a range of large, listed companies whose emissions profile classifies them as a target for climate activists, and has since filed multiple claims on these companies each year. Unlike ACCR, Market Forces' resolutions are solely climate related, with a focus on the mining, oil, gas, financial, and insurance sectors. Market Forces has been heavily focused on preventing new coal projects in Australia, doing so by targeting miners as well as their financial backers, banks, and insurance companies. One key feature of its campaigns has been to draw investors and management's attention to the fact that coal projects will likely become stranded assets in the near future. Market Forces combines these anti-corporate tactics with grassroots campaigns that encourage employees and customers to agitate against banks and insurers over these commitments. In 2019, leading insurance companies QBE Insurance and Suncorp Insurance both agreed not to insure any new coal projects, and to exit their existing projects by 2030, meaning there are no longer any Australian insurers willing to underwrite new coal projects. And, as a result of ACCR and Market Forces' campaigns, between 2019 and 2021, all four major Australian banks agreed to cease lending to new coal projects.

Wilderness Australia (previously the Colong Wilderness Foundation)

Originally known as the Colong Committee, this grassroots organization organized Australia's first shareholder campaign, a predecessor to contemporary ESG shareholder activism. As part of the group's opposition to the mining of a proposed limestone cave in the Blue Mountains, a world heritage site west of Sydney, the Colong Committee purchased a parcel of shares in the Associated Portland Cement Manufacturers and distributed these amongst members who attended AGMs in the late 1960s and early 1970s in protest (Wilderness Australia 2023). The campaign was successful in protecting the cave and represents an early practice of utilizing tools of corporate governance to force change in company behavior. The group has since been involved in a series of protection measures for Australian wilderness areas.

In 2021, the Colong Wilderness Foundation filed shareholder resolutions against two insurance companies, QBE and IAG. These Australian insurance companies were publicly backing the proposed raising of the Warragamba Dam wall. The Warragamba Dam is located on the fringes of South Western Sydney, and calls to raise the dam wall have been heard regularly following serious flooding events that have impacted the Sydney basin. Wilderness Australia is committed to campaigning against the raising of the wall, citing the damaging impact this will have on nearby ecosystems. The organization opposes the "developer-driven proposal that will destroy 65 kilometers of wilderness rivers and inundate 4,700 hectares of the world heritage listed Blue Mountains National Park" (Wilderness Australia 2023). Wilderness Australia varies from other activist groups in its direct focus on the protection of world heritage sites. This stands in stark contrast to organizations focused on global environmental issues, such as climate change.

Wilderness Australia employs a wide variety of activist tools to lobby governments to protect world heritage areas. In 2021, the group worked with ACCR and Market Forces to co-file shareholder resolutions to target insurance companies over ceasing support for the dam wall raising and in favor of developing clear world heritage protection policies. The group has been successful in bringing the peak insurance body, the Insurance Council of Australia (ICA), on board and isolating those pushing for the raising of the dam wall. Yet, to date no large insurer has delivered on Wilderness Australia's request that insurers develop a comprehensive world heritage policy.

GetUp!

GetUp! is a citizens rights group, formed in 2005. The organization is a leader in online, multi-issue campaigning (Marks 2010). The group has a large membership base with more than one million members. Its founders, Jeremy Heimans and David Madden, had worked in the Democratic-Party-aligned MoveOn in the United States. Their importation of this model is part of the "MoveOn effect," which saw the emergence of progressive organizations such as GetUp!, characterized by a small core of paid staff organizing a large distributed network of supporters through close data monitoring and micro-donations (Karpf 2012). The organization has campaigned on a wide variety of issues including electoral enrolment reform, reproductive rights, mental health policy, and same sex marriage rights—in what Ariadne Vromen (2015) refers to as post-material issues related to quality of life, environmental protection, and freedom of expression.

GetUp! is not formally aligned with any political party in Australia, however it does have strong links to progressive politics. It was founded through a A$50,000 donation from Unions NSW in 2005, and in the 2010 national election campaign received the largest historical donation not to go to a political party, from the CFMEU (Vromen 2017). The board of GetUp! has also included declared Greens Party members. GetUp! has participated in ESG shareholder activism in Australia since 2012, when the organization and its then Campaigns Director Paul Oosting filed a demand for Woolworths to hold an extraordinary general meeting, at which the company's board would respond to calls to limit the harm caused by its gaming machines, a case which is explored further in chapter 4. GetUp! was not directly involved in ESG shareholder activism again until 2021, when the organization's ownership stake in Origin allowed it to lobby against proposed fracking in the Beetaloo Basin.

Shareholder Representative Organizations

Australian shareholders are represented by two key bodies: retail investors through the Australian Shareholders Association (ASA), and institutional investors through the Australian Council of Superannuation Investors (ACSI). ACSI also serves as a quasi-proxy advisor given its role in providing research and advisory services to institutional clients. Both organizations clearly state that they are not ethical investors but are instead primarily concerned with material financial risks impacting their shareholders' investments. In their role, ASA and ACSI recommend to their members how they should vote on shareholder resolutions, as well as engage with companies on ESG concerns. Given the relative size of institutional shareholders' ownership stakes, ACSI's powers of recommendation can significantly influence the "yes" vote on ESG resolutions, although the organization is more heavily focused on board member re-elections and remuneration resolutions. While there is some overlap in what activists are seeking from companies and how ASA and ACSI perceive risk, often the claim-making from activists is seen as too strong a demand, and not financially prudent. Interviews with both organizations revealed that while shareholders might support, for example, the decarbonization of a company over the long term, activists' "asks" for radical responses such as the near-term divestment of emissions-intensive parts of the business are too extreme and risk the financial viability of their companies. As such, they are unlikely to be supported by shareholder representative organizations.

Ethical and Institutional Investors

Unlike similar liberal market jurisdictions, Australia does not have a strong history of religious or ethical institutional investors or pension funds. This is despite the fact the country has a relatively large pension system, predicted to become the world's largest by 2031. Compulsory and universal employer contributions, which are mandatorily preserved until a predetermined age, have led to the accumulation of US$4 trillion in pension assets under management (Super Members Council 2025). Yet, Australian funds have been largely reluctant to engage in market-based activism. Unlike their peers in the US, and particularly in the EU, there is little evidence of sustained activism by pension funds on behalf of members. Where pension funds have exercised investor voice, this has generally been as a result of activist campaigns, which have encouraged funds to divest members' retirement savings from contentious projects such as Australia's offshore detention operations and the Adani Carmichael coal mine (O'Brien et al. 2022).

Given the reluctance of Australian pension funds to engage directly in market-based activism or to use their shareholdings to lobby companies, their power is limited to the number of shareholder votes they control at AGMs. Like ASA and ACSI, these funds will ordinarily not support ESG resolutions on purely ethical grounds, but will consider the financial risks including reputational, stranded assets, maintenance capital, and the risk of litigation. There are examples of overseas investors filing resolutions against Australian listed companies, but these are in the minority and very much overshadowed by the role of Market Forces and ACCR. Groups such as St. Columban's Mission Society, Mercy Investment Services, and the Church of England are connected through their membership in the ICCR, as well as denomination of specific groups such as Laudato Si', which was Pope Francis's second encyclical emphasizing care for the natural environment. These groups also cite a commitment to the United Nations' Sustainable Development Goals as a guide to investment activities including disinvestment, SRI, and shareholder activism. In 2019, St. Columban's Mission Society co-filed a resolution against Coles supermarket group, alongside the Labor Union Cooperative Retirement Fund and Mercy Investment Services—although the lead filer in this instance was ACCR. This resolution was focused on modern slavery and the disclosure of risks along Coles' supply chain.

Proxy Advisors

The final set of actors explored in this section has an overlooked central role in the efficacy of campaigns for ethical investment, often described as neutral, technical experts (Elbra et al. 2025). The role of proxy advisors is to regularly report to companies and investors on issues of concern facing industries and sectors, provide platforms to cast and receive shareholder votes, and make voting recommendations at shareholder meetings (Malenko and Malenko 2019; Boone et al. 2020). The services sold by proxy advisors are often described as "report and recommend." That is, they firstly provide regular reporting on issues of financial salience to investors (including ESG issues). Secondly, they recommend how institutional investors should vote on resolutions filed at company AGMs. As is the case globally, the Australian proxy advice market is dominated by two firms, Institutional Shareholder Services (ISS) and CGI Glass Lewis (CGI). This duopoly dominates the global proxy advice market, with 97 percent market share in jurisdictions including the US, Australia, the UK, and Canada (Sharfman 2020; Spatt 2021; C. Shu 2022).

While proxy advisors are not directly involved in the voting process, they provide advice to institutional investors in making informed decisions. Most institutional investors rely on proxy advisors to deliver advice on how to vote on shareholder resolutions proposed at their companies' AGMs (Sheehy et al. 2021). Given the concentrated duopoly of advisors, their recommendations hold significant political influence, when the issues being voted on are of societal importance. In a functional sense, they serve to reduce the transaction costs of investors by providing a service (report and recommend) that would otherwise be done repeatedly by individual investors or institutional shareholders (Larcker et al. 2015). It is through this lens that they are seen to ostensibly maintain a politically neutral position. However, their capacity to heavily influence investors' decisions has political implications for the success or failure of activist groups' campaigns, as investors influence companies (Elbra et al. 2025).

Key Issues

The interests of shareholder activists are a product of their societal context, and as such, these shift over time (Graves et al. 2001). Furthermore, as both regulation and corporate practices evolve (potentially in response to this activism) shareholder activists may shift their attention to alternative issues, or may move on to other less responsive firms. In some instances, previously hot-button issues may altogether drop off the political agenda. An example of this is the high volume of shareholder resolutions filed against US companies in the 1980s over their investment and operations in Apartheid South Africa—at the point of transition to majority rule, these were no longer required and the issue fell away (Graves et al. 2001).[2]

Non-climate-change environmental issues were the impetus for ESG shareholder activism in Australia. The Colong Wilderness Foundation's campaigns of the 1960s and 1970s were followed in the early 2000s by resolutions filed against lenders and forestry company Gunns Limited, in an attempt to limit deforestation in Tasmanian old-growth forests. These resolutions were succeeded by a small number of loosely related resolutions filed by trade unions over labor rights and corporate governance. However, in the contemporary era of ESG shareholder activism, which is the focus of this book, climate change represents the overwhelming majority of ESG shareholder resolutions filed at large Australian corporations' AGMs. This began as early as 2010 with AEI's climate resolutions against Australian banks, supported by Howard Pender's report titled *Financed Emissions, Unburnable Carbon Risks and the Major Australian Banks* (Pender and ACCR 2014). As suggested by the title, this report called on the four major Australian banks to disclose the carbon emissions they were exposed to through their balance sheets. The banks, at this stage, had strong internal environmental policies that ACCR and others suggested concealed their real contribution, which was financed climate risks. Following the release of this report, a campaign against the big four banks' climate policies commenced, and banks began to provide much more detailed disclosure to investors about their exposure to fossil fuel financing (Sheehy et al. 2021).

In jurisdictions with a longer history of ESG shareholder activism, such as the US and UK, various environmental issues have entered and then fallen off the political agenda as they pique the interest of activists, and then attention drops away (Graves et al. 2001). In Australia, where this form of activism only commenced in any systemic fashion in the mid-2010s, there is far less variation in issue areas and an unsurprising focus on the most pressing issue facing contemporary society, climate change. While there have been resolutions filed in regards to non-climate environmental issues such as those seeking to protect world heritage sites, in the Australian case, and recently elsewhere globally, climate change is *the* issue for shareholder activists. It is unquestionably the focus of much of their work and where the most progress from lobbied companies can be seen.

More recently, ESG shareholder activists have leveraged their shareholdings in Australia's largest companies to push for change over social issues. This has principally come in the form of resolutions calling for greater attention to the rights of First Nations Traditional Owners, particularly from new and expanded mining projects. Analysis of Australia's settler-colonial history reveals maltreatment and disregard for Indigenous peoples' rights. For example, unlike in New Zealand and Canada no treaty-making has taken place with Australia's First Nations populations, whose land was historically referred to as *terra nullius*, meaning "nobody's land" in legal parlance. Aboriginal and Torres Strait Islander rights to Native title were only recognized in 1992, when the High Court of Australia affirmed this through the *Mabo (No2)* ruling, which led to passing of the Native Title Act 1993 (*Cth*). These strained and uneven relations were brought to the attention of many Australians in 2020, after Rio Tinto's destruction of the Juukan Caves. Following the public outcry to this destruction, other companies found themselves under greater pressure to consult more broadly with First Nations communities over protection of culturally significant sites, as well as quasi-environmental issues such as the protection of water sources and land from the impacts of mining more generally.

Australian companies have also found themselves targeted over a range of human rights concerns, namely the enforcement of labor rights and the detection and elimination of modern slavery in supply chains. Unlike the issue areas outlined above, which mainly impact mining, oil, and gas companies or their financiers, these resolutions are most frequently filed at the AGMs of supermarkets, airlines, and property groups, all companies with long, and sometimes opaque, supply chains. The filing of these resolutions coincides with the legislating of Australia's *Modern Slavery*

Act 2018, which required large companies, including those targeted by shareholder activists, to report on their efforts at the prevention and redress of modern slavery risks in their supply chains.

Missing from the Australian context are resolutions filed over governance issues, which are largely absent from any form of Australian ESG shareholder activism. As yet, no company has faced a shareholder resolution over diversity or any other corporate governance claim. The concentration of shareholder resolutions on climate at the expense of other pressing issues, including First Nations' land rights and modern slavery, is explored in chapter 5 of this book, which argues that the duopoly of actors, their limited resources, and priorities of their financiers most likely leave these issues untouched. Yet there may be scope in the future for resolutions to be filed over issues such as representation of minorities on company boards, something that proxy advisors have flagged as significant and that has been the subject of resolutions in other jurisdictions.

The history of market-based activism through shareholder resolutions locates this method of anti-corporate politics amongst other forms of political investorism, which has grown rapidly over recent years in Australia. It is clear that legal impediments to the expression of investor voice have impacted the opportunities for market-based activism in Australia. The emergence of two key actors equipped to overcome these regulatory hurdles has shaped the practices of ESG activists, including the target companies and issues. The result is a nascent duopoly of ESG shareholder activists focused predominantly on climate change, at the expense of other environmental and social issues. The implications of this are taken up in chapters 3 and 4 of this book. Prior to this, the following chapter outlines the theoretical approach taken in this analysis, that is the synthesis of social movement theory and private governance scholarship, which when taken together assist in explaining the tactics, successes, and failures of anti-corporate politics in Australia.

CHAPTER 2
Mobilizing ESG Shareholder Activism

THIS CHAPTER DEVELOPS THE core theoretical approach of the book by engaging with the literature on democratic participation, social movement theory, and the role of business in setting regulatory agendas. ESG activism, like other social movements, aims to reform the behavior of actors to better respond to societal concerns. In this sense, it is both a social movement and a political act (Davis and Thompson 1994). Social movements are defined as an "organized, sustained, and self-conscious challenge to authority," in this case the authority rests with the firm and its board of directors (Tarrow 1994, 4). Drawing on this definition, this chapter explores the specific form of activism aimed at business, known as anti-corporate activism. Anti-corporate activism represents a "unique form of social movement activism that seeks changes in corporate social behavior," often in regards to ESG issues (Lee and Lounsbury 2011, 159; see also Sadler 2004). This chapter develops a framework for understanding the power relations at play when financial market actors coalesce around social movements. It brings together contributions from international political economy and social movement scholarship to develop a novel framework for understanding ESG shareholder activism in Australia.

Much of the extant scholarship on ESG shareholder activism classifies this form of social movement engagement as anti-corporate politics. Anti-corporate politics has been situated in the social movement literature at the juncture of contentious politics (that is, social movement activity where government is the target or object) and private politics (where business is the target) (Baron 2003; McAdam et al. 2001). This chapter contests this definition, advocating for a third option, that activists are targeting government *through* corporations (Soule 2009, 34). Taking this approach, ESG shareholder activism can be considered a specific form of anti-corporate politics, where the goal of activists is to challenge companies to lead the way in addressing ESG challenges. While there remains significant variation in the drivers of this form of activism, the ultimate goal of activists is to enhance corporate value through ethical practices. This chapter develops this argument further. By synthesizing the social movement and private governance scholarships, it shows that activists are targeting powerful firms in order to cascade change throughout an industry, in place of government regulation, the absence of which is a key driver of activism. This is an extension of the scholarship on private governance, which highlights the authority of large corporations and their ability to set standards, lead industry change, and ultimately influence how sectors are regulated. This chapter demonstrates that this authority has been harnessed by activists in order to force a change in corporate behavior, and in turn address governance deficits. This book draws on the theoretical frameworks implemented by Sarah Soule (2009), Hilary Boudet (2011), and Kate Neville (2021; Neville et al. 2019), which have been developed using earlier work on social movements (McAdam et al. 2001; McAdam 2017). By synthesizing the literature on social movement theory and that on private authority, a new framework for understanding shareholder activism is developed, which sees ESG shareholder activism as a nascent form of governance, aimed at aligning the interests of previously assumed adversarial actors, business and civil society, in order to meet societal expectations until now ignored by governments. This framework is developed in response to Donatella Della Porta and Elias Steinhilper's (2021) call for international relations scholars to strengthen their analysis of counter-mobilizations and backlash by drawing on sociology and social movement scholarship and considering civil society contestation in their analysis. In particular, it acknowledges a need for international relations scholars to recognize the importance of opportunity structures in understanding change at the transnational level, particularly where such change is driven by social movement activism (N. Hall and Reiners 2025).

Given the recency in which ESG shareholder activism has emerged in the Australian context, this framework helps to explain what sparked mobilization at this particular historical moment. And, what drove activists to coalesce around the specific issues that have emerged as central in shareholder activism—that is, climate change and Indigenous land rights? The aim of this chapter is to take the theoretical insights from social movement theory and apply them to the corporate realm, in order to explain how the social movement organization tools can be directed at firms and, by extension, governments. ESG shareholder activism's emergence as a result of governance gaps has led to suggestions that this form of engagement represents an opportunity to widen political participation. To understand this potential, this chapter explores the extant literature on SMOs, including those specifically targeting private actors such as corporations. Augmenting this scholarship with that on private governance, the framework for analysis is presented, followed by an explanation of the research design and methodologies used to undertake the analysis.

Understanding the Potential of ESG Shareholder Activism

Governance Deficit

ESG shareholder activism can be viewed as part of a broader civil society attempt to address issues such as climate change, human rights breaches, and other failures of corporate governance. Peter Newell (2001) notes that these attempts by civil society are a direct response to the "governance deficit;" between the size and power of large corporations, and the unwillingness, or inability, of governments to regulate industry. In short, "people are turning to corporations for solutions to problems that are typically in the government's domain because government has failed" (Macey 2022, 258). As Soule (2009) notes, the era of deregulation heralded in by the Reagan and Thatcher administrations in the late 1970s in the US and UK, respectively, coincided with a decline in the power of organized labor, and the growth in mergers between large corporations. This led to a noticeable rise in corporate power and influence over government, and declining protections for workers and consumers. Together, these trends have driven much of the anti-corporate politics we have witnessed over the past five decades. Over this time, activists have increasingly looked to target the corporations seen as responsible for poor corporate practices, rather than (or alongside) governments with the power to regulate these firms and industries (Vogel 1978). Where governments have been seen to be slow to respond to issues, such as LGBTQI rights, activists have found more success directly lobbying companies (Raeburn 2004). Evidence of governance gaps abound, from the aforementioned LGBTQI rights movement to Apartheid South Africa, civil rights, First Nations' rights, and, in contemporary times, governments' inability or unwillingness to respond to climate change. Activists have consistently sought to influence private actors to respond to such issues, where they perceive that regulation has failed to keep pace with societal expectations.

It is on the basis of this governance deficit that civil society more broadly has sought to "engag[e] the corporate sector in the rapidly expanding web of corporate social responsibility initiatives" to "help narrow the governance gaps that now exist between global markets and state-based authority structures" (Ruggie 2007, 35). Civil society activists have stepped into this void, leveraging traditional methods and creating new mechanisms to govern corporate actors including market-based lobbying such as shareholder activism, boycotts, and divestment campaigns. There is considerable evidence that activists' strategies of leveraging firms' corporate governance models to compensate for the democratic deficit have yielded results (Scherer et al. 2013a). As such, civil society is increasingly turning to financial markets in order to undertake governance interventions. Firms have responded to these new modes of governance by altering their corporate practices and policies, particularly where they perceive high costs or risks for not doing so (Gallagher and Weinthal 2012). The potential costs for firms failing to respond to activist claims include reputational damage, litigation, and the risk of holding stranded assets, such as investments in blacklisted states or in coal-fired power plants as the shift to renewables takes place.

Corporations have engaged with these campaigns in a variety of ways, and some have been more responsive than others. Corporate reactions to these interventions are sometimes morally based, that is, safeguarding human rights because it is the right thing to do. This follows a logic of appropriateness, whereby corporations wish to be seen to be doing good. Others retain an element of a logic of consequences, where firms perceive potential penalties for noncompliance and as such adjust their behavior to minimize risks to the business (March and Olsen 1998). Institutional investors also respond to these twin logics, guided by the mandates of their funds and their risk appetite. These investors' decisions to invest in, or divest from, certain industries or companies in light of particular corporate practices are an exercise in power. However, investors also make decisions based on socially responsible metrics because these increasingly represent materially less risky investment options; in this case, they are obeying a logic of consequences. As investor-civil society coalition CERES (2002, 2) notes, "the bottom line is straightforward: climate change represents a potential multi-billion dollar risk to a wide variety of U.S. businesses and industries." As explored in the introduction to this book, the sheer growth of ESG investing suggests that environmental and social concerns are part of a suite of considerations made by investors. It can be argued that civil society is socializing investors to govern firms, by rewarding or punishing those that comply with changing norms and societal expectations (MacLeod 2010). If firms are driven by a combination of logics and socialization, then a possible explanation for greater firm buy-in of social concerns is that business norms and values have shifted to more closely represent those of society (Cutler et al. 1999; Dashwood 2012). For example, breaching community standards brings with it the risk of a financial cost in the form of boycotts or even fines if regulation catches up with societal expectations (Sjöström 2008). This book contributes to the literature on anti-corporate politics and the governance deficit by arguing that activist investors have demonstrated a degree of effectiveness in channeling their grievances through market-based mechanisms, and that there is evidence that this form of activism has led to changed behavior for large corporations, under sustained pressure, particularly over their contribution to carbon emissions (MacLeod and Park 2011).

Democratic Participation

The ability of individuals, through either private shareholdings or through the shareholdings of their pension funds, to support ESG shareholder resolutions is often argued to represent a growing and under-examined space for activism and political participation (Gillan and Starks 2000; Scherer et al. 2013a). As explored above, the changing governance role of listed corporations is a result of the "shift in focus from direct public regulation to market-based instruments" (Gómez-Baggethun and Naredo 2015, 385). This form of activism also continues the trend that sees non-state actors, such as civil society and firms, as capable of shaping political outcomes, thereby broadening the scope of actors with the power to influence how society is governed (Keohane 2009). The emergence of non-state actors as key players in the political process has been particularly visible in the area of environmental politics, where activists, NGOs, and the scientific community have engaged in this process (Bernstein and Cashore 2007; J. F. Green 2013).

The corporate governance scholarship has grappled with the efficacy of shareholder voting rights and their influence over boards and management (Andrei et al. 2023). These debates have explored the role of shareholders in determining board composition, executive remuneration, and responses to takeover bids and other merger and acquisition activity. On one side of the debate, scholars argue that from a strictly material perspective there is little chance that minority shareholders could command enough votes required to effect change in their organizations, labeling them "paper tigers" (Cai et al. 2013). Conversely, others suggest that minority shareholder voting rights are a fundamental part of investor expression, occasionally enabled by large block holder investors and family trusts to act as a bulwark against recalcitrant management (Bebchuk 2004; Villalonga et al. 2015). Beyond a strictly material view, even where minority shareholders remain powerless against management and boards, researchers focused on the behavioral impacts of shareholder expression suggest that voting rights do empower investors to influence corporate governance (Fiss and Zajac 2004; Westphal and Zajac 2013). The normative legitimacy of shareholder voting, acquired over time, allows minority shareholders to use their voice symbolically (Sauerwald et al. 2018). Alina Andrei et al. (2023, 1737) argue that by "decoupling the formal function of a proposal voted on at a shareholder meeting from its symbolic use" minority shareholders have been able to use their "expressive voting dissent" as a vote of no confidence in management. While these votes are not sufficient to sway the outcome of major decisions, they do serve as a signal to management, boards, and other investors. These signals are particularly important in ESG issues, where majority votes are exceedingly rare. However, as explored in this book, minority votes on environmental and social matters serve as an important vehicle for activists, minority shareholders, and sometimes institutional investors to communicate issues of importance to management. While such symbolic actions may not bring immediate change to the company's corporate governance, they provide a pathway to investor expression that boards and management may choose to respond to.

Much of the existing literature perceives shareholders as possessing the ability to "discipline" boards and management over underperformance (Grundfest 1993; Del Guercio et al. 2008). In this sense, shareholders are usually seen as decision-takers. Investors own voting rights attached to their shareholding and possess the right to exercise these in debates over their company's board composition, remuneration, and potential takeover bids. However, as listed companies are increasingly the target of anti-corporate politics, investors are frequently being asked to vote on ESG proposals. Moreover, shareholders themselves are taking the lead in filing shareholder resolutions that challenge management's existing approach to such issues. It is the expansion of investor voice beyond material financial concerns that has added weight to the suggestion that ESG shareholder activism represents a democratizing force, capable of widening political participation (Gillan and Starks 2000; Scherer et al. 2013b). This argument draws on the political participation literature, where authors have moved beyond a formal division between the "political" and the "non-political," and recognized that non-institutionalized forms of political participation (i.e., those that exist outside formal party structures) are growing in number and influence (Klingemann and Fuchs 1995). Market-based activism in various forms including boycotts, divestment campaigns, and shareholder activism all constitute forms of lobbying and decision-making that sit outside traditional arenas of politics.

Using the case of ESG shareholder activism in Australia, this book contests the argument that ESG shareholder activism represents a growing space for political participation. Instead, it demonstrates that claim-making on corporations is directed by a narrow constituency of actors, who are largely unrepresentative of wider society. This has implications for the issues that companies are targeted over, and those that they are not. Firstly, a common representation of shareholder voting rights often assumes that they are spread between a high number of shareholders, including retail investors, and a wide variety of institutional funds. However, in reality, this is rarely the case, even in countries where dispersed ownership of corporations is the norm, such as the UK and US (Bebchuk 2004). Instead, it is most often the case that institutional investors and fund managers hold large stakes in listed companies (Fichtner and Heemskerk 2020). These investors exercise the right to vote on behalf of their investors, with a commitment to do so in the best interests of the shareholders (Griffin 2019). It is difficult to theorize how the best interests of such a large group of passive investors could be defined. Even if this were possible, it is impossible that all investors would have matching preferences, a characteristic challenged by the fact fund managers vote identically for all the shares they own in a single company (Fichtner et al. 2017). In reality, a small number of fund managers vote uniformly on behalf of thousands of clients, a scenario that is incongruent with arguments advocating ESG shareholder activism as a mechanism for widening political participation.

If we consider the more dispersed "mom and pop" shareholders, or retail shareholders, it remains difficult to identify evidence that shareholder activism widens political participation. Retail shareholders are far less likely than institutional investors to exercise their right to vote at board meetings, with this prerogative usually handed over to a proxy who exercises the voting rights of passive investors (Kastiel and Nili 2016). Given the size of the ownership stakes of institutional investors, combined with the fact that many retail investors do not exercise their right to vote on proposals, the power of investor blocks over the corporate governance of large, listed companies cannot be understated (Griffin 2019). Moreover, not all interested parties are capable of engaging in shareholder activism, because corporate rights are provided in return for payment. These rights are most effectively exercised at significant volumes not available to the average person. This challenges the narrative of a dispersion of voting rights amongst a large number of retail investors, and fails to demonstrate direct pathways to influence for the average citizen, even if purchasing a share portfolio is within one's financial means. The distribution of these rights occurs in a commercial context, where "justice only comes to those with the resources to pursue it" (Sheehy 2017, 290).

The population of shareholders with the power to influence the vote on proposals raised at AGMs is quite narrow. Fund managers, proxy advisors, and retail investors with the means to purchase shares and the time and interest can engage in the corporate governance process. Yet, this group of individuals is not representative of modern society, and in this sense, it is difficult to convincingly argue that shareholder voting rights represent wider democratization. Even when we focus only on activist investors, or those pushing for change on corporate boards and to corporate governance, diversity remains difficult to identify. As explored in chapter 4 of this book, activist investors are likely to be as representative of the general population as fund managers, proxy advisors, and institutional investors. There is little evidence to suggest that they are reflective of a broader cross-section of society and therefore represent greater democratization. The most noticeable absence amongst investors (activist or non-activist) are those whose rights are being addressed as part of ESG campaigns. While this is not a universal conclusion, certainly in the areas of modern slavery and First Nations' land rights there is little evidence that those primarily affected by corporate actions in this space have obtained voting rights to effectively lobby companies to improve their ESG performance.

While there is little evidence of widening political participation through shareholder activism, shareholder voting rights do open space for political deliberation and contestation. The concentrated nature of block shareholding, and the reduced number of vote holders this creates, in many ways increases the opportunities and impact of ESG shareholder activism. Activists have transported the tactics and strategies of SMOs to the market, leveraging the shareholder model and associated corporate governance mechanisms to achieve their goals.

Theorizing Social Movement Organizations

Social movement organizations (SMOs) are defined as "collectivities acting with some degree of organization and continuity, partly outside institutional or organizational channels, for the purpose of challenging extant systems of authority" (Snow and Soule 2010, 6). Social movements represent one of the key forms of action through which collective groups can express grievances and concerns to an audience capable of responding in a meaningful way. SMOs reject politics through more official channels due to the fact they are often unable to access formal political institutions, or when they do, fail to be heard through such conventional measures. As a result, SMOs engage in claim-making through alternative modes of action. These actions can take many forms including protest, petition, boycott, and lobbying. While more formal and institutionalized avenues of expression exist for dissatisfied parties, particularly in liberal democracies, social movements have a long and rich history of providing an avenue for expressing political and social concerns (Snow et al. 2004).

Social movements typically exhibit three or more of the following characteristics: collective action, change-oriented goals, a degree of organization, a clear institutional target, and some measure of temporal continuity (Snow et al. 2004; Lee and Lounsbury 2011). They are defined by their attempts to bring about, or in some cases prevent, social change. Social movement activists can agitate in non-institutional settings or in more formalized arenas such as government, religious institutions, corporations, or any other realm where authority may be challenged (Snow et al. 2004; Soule 2009). According to these definitional parameters, ESG shareholder activism fits neatly into the definition of a social movement (Lee and Lounsbury 2011, 160). ESG shareholder activists are organized and work collectively, often co-filing resolutions with other groups in order to bring about social change. This activism is not an ad hoc event, but instead has a rich history in addressing a wide variety of social and political concerns. ESG activists target institutions, specifically corporations, to achieve non-market goals. And finally, this activism is change oriented in its attempts to reform corporate behavior. Ultimately, ESG shareholder activists "target companies in which they see opportunities and motivation to trigger or facilitate social change by executing their ownership influence" (Semenova and Hassel 2019, 146). It is in this sense that they can be seen as SMOs.

In order to theorize the emergence, effectiveness, and impact of ESG shareholder activism, we can look to social movement theory, which explains how grievances catalyze into political mobilization. Traditionally, social movement studies focused on explanations for the emergence of social movements, where collective interests were implied and instead the independent variable was access to resources that allowed movements to organize (Gamson 1975; Tilly 1977). As this field of study grew, researchers then began to question the assumption of a given or natural identity, seeking to better interrogate the social, cultural, and political networks and identities that led people to participate in mobilization (Polletta and Jasper 2001). Until the late 1990s much of the social movement scholarship was focused on explaining the emergence and fluctuations in social movements themselves, stopping short of examining their political implications (Soule 2009). However, a new scholarly agenda emerged in the late 1990s, calling researchers' attention to a wider set of considerations including the outcomes, impacts, and consequences of social movement mobilization (Giugni et al. 1999; Soule 1999). The scholarship that emerged was heavily focused on the ability of social movements to force policy change (Bosi et al. 2016). Embedded in this research was the assumption that most mobilization was directed at, and elicited a response from, the state. Studies on issues as broad as civil rights, women's rights, the environment, LGBTQI rights, and labor rights have all focused on the effectiveness of social movements in producing "state-related outcomes" (Amenta et al. 2010).

While traditional social movement studies concentrated on state-focused activism, an adjacent body of literature emerged that examined activism directed at non-state actors and organizations. The genesis of this scholarship measured the impact of social movements on organizational policy, for example on the lobbying of firms to widen hiring practices or to divest from the South African Apartheid regime (B. King and Soule 2007; B. King 2008b; Lee and Lounsbury 2011). While these works bring into focus the corporation as a target of activism and a driver of social change, they have primarily focused on the formation of company (or other non-state actors such as universities) *policy-making* in response to social movements. This characterizes target organizations as "rule-takers" on issues such as gender, the environment, climate change, LGBTQI rights, human trafficking, and child labor. Much of this work focuses on the role played by radical activists undertaking outsider protest and boycott, while less attention has been paid to "activism inside corporations . . . that facilitates the creation of legitimate agenda items in corporate decision-making processes" (Lee and Lounsbury 2011, 157). Such "insider tactics" are a reference to socially concerned actors using their financial stake in a business to call for increased transparency, better reporting, or policy changes within that business (Soule 2009; L. King and Gish 2015). While many social theory accounts treat activism as exogenous, or something which originates from outside to challenge business or the state, this book shares the approach taken by scholars such as Steffen Böhm and Annika Skoglund (2022), whereby the distinction between insiders and outsiders is not seen as binary but as an enmeshing of power and its challengers (O'Brien et al. 2023).

The lack of attention to lobbying from market-based actors or insiders comes despite this gap in anti-corporate politics being identified as early as forty-five years ago (Zald and Berger 1978). In order to identify how corporate behavior is reformed through activism, we must examine the internal and external drivers of success. The next section explores the strategies and tactics used by social movements actors in their attempts to drive change through anti-corporate activism.

Strategies of Anti-Corporate Activists

ESG shareholder activists utilize a range of tactics and strategies against multiple targets including corporations, industry associations, and legislators. Given the breadth of this social movement, we can draw on multiple conceptualizations of collective interactions explored in the literature. First amongst these is the concept of contentious politics, whereby social movements or other collective bodies target the state or some element thereof (McAdam et al. 2001). Actors engage in contentious politics in order to push for legislative change. This is the most common and well-rehearsed form of social movement activism. However, activists have moved beyond the state in efforts to enact reform, including through the targeting of non-state actors such as corporations, universities, and other organizations. This strategy has been conceptualized as "private politics" (Baron 2003), which draws parallels with Ulrich Beck's (2000) sub-politics. That is, it does not directly attempt to influence governments but instead relies on lobbying for change at the sub-state level. The scholarship on anti-corporate politics has engaged with issues such as labor standards (Fransen 2011), palm oil extraction (Berenschot et al. 2022), the impacts of pollution on city residents (E. Shu and Lewin 2024), and divesting from countries ruled by antidemocratic regimes (Soule et al. 2014).

The tactics and maneuvers used in contentious politics and private politics are important considerations when analyzing anti-corporate politics (Soule 2009). This is because while strategies may be considered part of either contentious or private politics, they can often be applied to both. And, as is argued here and elsewhere (see Soule 2009; Neville 2021), we are increasingly witnessing anti-corporate politics aimed predominantly at reforming corporate behavior but with secondary goals of forcing legislative change. Repertoires of contention, or the possible array of performances political actors can use to make political claims on another, are a fundamental part of contentious politics (Tilly and Tarrow 2015). Shareholder activists have extended these repertoires by harnessing mechanisms of corporate governance not previously utilized for this purpose: that is, the use of shareholder resolutions to make claims against non-state actors and draw the attention of governments. Claim-making relies on a combination of performances across time and space (Tilly and Tarrow 2015). For ESG shareholder activists, this often means repetitive claim-making at corporate AGMs over multiple years. Anti-corporate activists also rely on the use of shared scripts and tactics, something that scholars such as Charles Tilly and Sidney Tarrow (2015) suggest is common to contentious politics. In the case of ESG shareholder activism, activists have grown increasingly sophisticated in their claim-making, overcoming legal and institutional barriers to activism and targeting companies with more specific and demanding claims over time. In this sense, their activism has evolved, drawing ideas and inspiration from anti-corporate protests elsewhere globally. This modular approach to claim-making is outlined by Tilly and Tarrow (2015), who note that performances can be adapted and adopted to a wide range of sites of contention, learning from shared experiences and drawing on media reporting of activism in other jurisdictions or undertaken by other activists to localize claim-making.

Activists harness a range of strategies in targeting market-based actors such as corporations. Of all the tactical repertoires available to activists, the approach most commonly attributed to ESG shareholder activism is the action-reaction model, which relies on threatening and disrupting normal operating procedures in order to persuade elites and decision-makers of the importance of an issue (Piven and Cloward 1977; Gamson and Meyer 1996; Andrews 2001). In the initial stages, ESG activists use corporate governance mechanisms, including AGMs, to threaten political and corporate elites by filing resolutions that sit outside the norm (predominantly votes on remuneration and board composition). This form of activism can be viewed as a dramatic or disruptive form of protest—even more so in the era of in-person AGMs, where resolutions are spoken to and/or accompanied by visible protest (Piven and Cloward 1977). A second iteration of the action-reaction model relies on persuasion. Here scholars posit that protest can benefit from the support of powerful third parties. Once sympathetic third parties side with protesters they may enter the site of contestation, changing the balance of power (Lipsky 1968). In the case of shareholder activism, if activists are able to garner the support of proxy advisors, institutional investors, or other significant shareholders, their protest will be magnified beyond its original reach. By building internal networks of supportive actors, ESG activists can develop a shared identity as a basis for collaboration. This model highlights the process by which activists more closely resemble interest groups and are likely to use less disruptive tactics, such as lobbying, in order to persuade decision-makers (Andrews 2001). This access-influence model, as it is known, can be most easily seen where shareholder activists have long-running relationships with ethical funds, whose support is valuable in campaigns to improve companies' environmental and social performance. ESG activists use both approaches: engaging in disruptive claim-making while also building internal networks amongst shareholders, and even within firms themselves.

Social movements increase their effectiveness by changing "the number and level of coordinated contentious actions leading to broader contention involving a wider range of actors and bridging claims and identities" (McAdam et al. 2003, 331). Known as scale shifts, through this process claimants change the scale of the debate, resistance, and/or impact of particular movements using ideational and discursive linkages. They do this by shifting their target, or focal point. "In these processes, contentious claim-making transcends specific places, drawing in a wider range of actors, issues and places" (Boudet 2011, in Neville, 2021). This is the case with shareholder activists, who use their resolutions to target not only firms but also entire industries and their effects on environment, workers, and Indigenous land rights. Scale shift can be upward or downward, and can be used to examine the range of focal points, or targets, of activism (Soule 2009). For example, movements can (and often do) target firms themselves, holding them to account for certain actions or inactions. However, activists can also target industries, such as coal-fired power production, through the resolutions raised at individual corporate AGMs, designed to signal to the industry key societal concerns, and threats that this form of protest will be replicated. Activists can also scale shift beyond domestic companies and industries to transnational political institutions, including international organizations. They do so using frame bridging, matching disparate issues through identification of shared concerns, symbols, and values (Boudet 2011). By linking with transnational advocacy networks (TANs) activists can pressure multinational companies through their examination of local practices, reflecting these onto the global stage (Pye and Bhattacharya 2013).

Activists also create new political and social communities as part of the claim-making process. Brokerage refers to the relationship formation that occurs when organizers link otherwise disconnected people and places through contentious and private politics (McAdam et al. 2001; Boudet 2011). In the case of ESG shareholder activism, disparate activist groups work together, co-filing resolutions where one group cannot do this alone. Activists also rely on brokerage with other actors in this ecosystem, including proxy advisors, institutional investors, and shareholder associations (Elbra et al. 2025). This coalition-building can lead to further coordinated action, in turn developing new understandings of place, in this case AGMs, as sites of connection (Della Porta and Fabbri 2016). The internal constraints explored here are key constraints and motivations for activists. Also key to understanding anti-corporate politics are the external drivers, or opportunity structures available to SMOs. These are explored in the next section.

Opportunity Structures

The external environment, or range of opportunity structures, is also key to determining the formation and success of social movements. Opportunity structures exist at all levels of analysis, including the political (transnational and domestic), industry, and at the level of the corporation. The majority of the extant social movement literature focuses on the original level of analysis, that is political opportunity structures (POS), or the consistent "dimensions of the political environment that provide incentives for people to undertake collective action by affecting their expectations for success of failure" (Tarrow 1994, 94). Put another way, these are the factors that decrease or increase the cost of undertaking collective action, therefore making this more or less likely, while also determining the likelihood of success (Ancelovici 2021). Opportunity structures have traditionally been used to explain the context in which movements emerge, however there is an increasing body of work that utilizes the concept to explain policy outcomes, or a movement's success.

While the social movement literature has focused heavily on the political factors that drive the emergence and success of movements, more recent scholarship has expanded to include the multilevel analysis referred to earlier. In this vein, Soule (2009) argues that contentious and private politics operate at all levels of opportunity structure, from the transnational to the corporate, augmented by the various legal regimes in place from the local to the transnational (McDonnell et al. 2015), and that these levels may produce joint and interactive effects.

Transnational opportunity structures reflect the conditions under which mobilization against institutions of global governance, such as the United Nations, World Trade Organization, and World Bank, occurs (Keck and Sikkink 1998; Tarrow and Della Porta 2005). Like the political opportunity structure explored above, studies of transnational opportunity structures examine the context, strategies, and outcomes of mobilization directed toward international organizations (Shawki 2010). Multinational corporations are one part of what Sidney Tarrow (2005) refers to as "internationalism" or the "triangular structure or relations among states, nonstate actors, and international institutions" that provides opportunities for actors to engage in collective action at all levels of the international system. As treaties, norms, and agreements emerge from international cooperation, listed companies are bound by commitments at the global level through their investments, shareholdings, and customer base. It is on this basis that large-listed firms are governed by both domestic and international opportunity structures (Soule 2009).

Transnationality also impacts SMOs at the micro level. SMOs have borne witness to the growing professionalization of activists, reflected in their ability to move between organizations and across borders. Leonard Seabrooke and Duncan Wigan (2024, 3) provide evidence of this in the case of multinational corporate tax avoidance, where they identify "identity fixing," or the "professionalization and tightening of organizational strategy." Identity fixing at the SMO level relies on individual "issue professionals" who leverage their expertise, personal connections, and specialization to steer issue selection within SMOs (Seabrooke and Henriksen 2017; Eilstrup-Sangiovanni and Breen 2024). Similarly, Onna van den Broek and Robyn Klingler-Vidra (2022, 1307) demonstrate actors' power to diffuse the meaning of sustainability discourses such as those projected by the UN Sustainable Development Goals, arguing they have been transformed into a set of generalized principles, which can then be molded to meet SMOs' "preexisting organizational identities and practices." This work suggests that while salience is important, successful

SMOs are relying on professional activists who move between organizations and have the capability to steer transnational advocacy networks in directions of their choosing. In doing so, it highlights the micro-level drivers of global civil society.

Opportunities for effective SMO mobilization have also been identified beyond the political realm, at the industry and corporate level. Industry opportunity structure can be defined as "economic, organizational, cultural, and commodity-related" factors that facilitate or effect movements, and their effectiveness in relation to corporate targets across a wider industry basis (Schurman 2004, 251). Determinants of industry opportunity include competition between firms (Raeburn 2004), the supply chain characteristics of an industry (Schurman 2004), and the presence or effectiveness of industry regulatory bodies (Bartley 2007). For example, emissions-intensive energy production is now widely considered a harmful activity. Industries exposed to this, including energy production and financial services firms that lend to and insure emissions-intensive power projects, provide significant openings for social movements to gain traction. ESG-conscious investors are targeting companies across an industry within their portfolio where they see issues that have a sector- or economy-wide impact (Condon 2020; Coffee Jr. 2021). Anti-corporate activists may succeed in reforming industry behavior if there is significant competition between key players who can leverage a transition to clean energy to benefit their company's bottom line. Or, if an industry regulator has significant power over companies within that industry, activists may work more quickly to reform the industry by targeting the regulatory body in their lobbying efforts.

Finally, the level of analysis can be narrowed to corporate opportunity structures (COS)—or the openness of a firm to anti-corporate politics (Soule 2009). This is a key level at which we can analyze the likelihood of success for anti-corporate activists (Soule et al. 2015; Berenschot et al. 2022). This is because some companies remain hostile to activist claims, while others acquiesce relatively easily (Zald et al. 2005). COS explains the firm-level attributes that we might assign as important indicators of potential success for activists, and those that the activists themselves may use to select targets (B. King and Pearce 2010). Corporate characteristics found to influence the outcome of campaigns include a firm's past engagement with activism (McDonnell and King 2013), size and reputation

(B. King and McDonnell 2012), and the ideological position of key leadership within a firm (Briscoe et al. 2014). These characteristics are not static, and may evolve over time through changes in leadership, advances in technology, and in response to persistent activist pressure.

COS, including a firm's reputation for dealing with activists, is an important consideration for social movements' choice of target. Activists consider attributes of COS when selecting target companies, or those that they believe may be more receptive to ESG activism (Acharya et al. 2022). Over time, companies develop a reputation based on how they interact with activists, and this history may influence which companies are targeted in the future (Zald et al. 2005; Briscoe and Safford 2008). It is also argued that companies more frequently targeted develop an increasingly sophisticated repertoire of responses to anti-corporate activism, part of which may include not only defensive moves, but also reformed corporate behavior and improved communication of the company's ESG practices (McDonnell et al. 2015).

It is assumed that activists are constrained by a scarcity of resources, particularly in the NGO sector, meaning they must take into consideration the likelihood of success when deciding which companies to target in their campaigning (Soule 2009; B. King and Pearce 2010). This is even more true for shareholder activists in jurisdictions such as the UK and Australia, where corporations law requires activists to hold either a 5 percent stake in the company or represent one hundred individual shareholders before a shareholder resolution can be filed. Where hurdles to engagement are high, social movements are more likely to take COS considerations seriously as part of their strategy. In selecting targets of anti-corporate politics, Abhijith Acharya et al. (2022) argue that activists are likely to target firms that meet two criteria: firstly, firms that have demonstrated a willingness to engage with stakeholders (particularly activists), and secondly, firms that are perceived as legitimate in their field and whose reform may lead to other non-target firms voluntarily acquiescing to activist demands. The latter overlaps with the political economy scholarship on private authority, which is explored in the next section.

Private Authority

International relations scholarship has traditionally focused on the nation state as the principal actor in global politics. However, it is increasingly clear that non-state actors possess political power, and that the exercise of this power should be of interest to scholars of international relations and politics. This is highly evident in the field of international political economy, where non-state actors such as civil society and multinational corporations have been shown to exercise significant power (Cutler et al. 1999; R. B. Hall and Biersteker 2002). This exercise of power has been described as "a new source of global governance, that is mechanisms to reach collective decisions about transnational problems with or without government participation" (Haufler 2001, 1). When non-state actors, such as firms, possess private authority, they can engender new norms of behavior, set standards that others follow, and ultimately influence the direction of government regulation (Elbra 2014).

The ability of multinational corporations (MNCs) to engender new rules and norms hinges on their private authority, or their perceived legitimacy. Unlike power, actors respond to authority, not because they are coerced but because there is an "understood right to command" (J. F. Green 2013, 40). In the same sense, private actors with perceived legitimacy are able to set the rules of the game. These rules may be adopted by peers who, in perceiving competitors as authoritative, accept new norms of behavior as industry standards. We can observe the private authority of large corporations, for example, when a market leader develops and implements a new code of conduct that is adopted by other companies as a new norm of corporate behavior in a given area (Mikler 2018). These rules are sometimes then adopted by governments as regulation, in large part due to the private authority possessed by the corporate rule-setters (Elbra 2020). The private authority of large firms amplifies the efforts of ESG shareholder activists and makes these firms attractive targets for claim-making. At their most successful, ESG shareholder activists can lobby for change at the company level, which can lead to new industry practices, and potentially the regulation of such practices by governments. The extant literature on corporate power reflects this potential and suggests that firms can be the catalysts for regulatory change (Haufler 2006). Standards and norms can emerge from business, be adopted more widely throughout industry, and, in some cases, be co-opted as government regulation (Elbra 2017). The literature on private authority recognizes the links between corporate social responsibility and the potential for business behavior to shape states' interests (Newell 2001; Vogel 2006). This is particularly the case for firms with significant private authority, or high levels of perceived legitimacy (Cutler et al. 1999; Büthe and Mattli 2011). For example, in 2017, Australian iron ore miner BHP Billiton was targeted by shareholder activists over its memberships in the following industry bodies: the Minerals Council of Australia (MCA), the World Coal Association (WCA), and the US Chamber of Commerce. Activists argued that these groups' pro-coal lobbying activity was incongruent with BHP's own climate stance (Davies 2017). Ultimately, BHP withdrew from the WCA and was able to force the MCA to add an endorsement of the Paris Agreement to its existing focus on reliable and cheap energy (BHP 2019). The MCA, as Australian mining's peak industry body, has influence over other mining firms, suggesting that this activism went beyond simply forcing change at the corporate level.

The effectiveness of ESG shareholder activism does not rely on the private authority of firms alone. Activists also possess a certain level of legitimacy, evidenced by their ability to influence corporate decision-making. Changes to corporate behavior, policies, and procedures do not emerge from shareholders simply airing grievances in a forum such as an AGM. For such concerns to be given serious consideration the actors involved must possess private authority, which gives their actions legitimacy, or "acceptance of a shared rule by a community as appropriate and justified" (Bernstein and Cashore 2007, 348). This means that their claims are taken seriously by firms and their boards and executives. This may be supported by a genuine recognition of a problem or fear of material financial risk and reputational damage if an issue is left unaddressed (B. King and Soule 2007; McDonnell and King 2013). If companies are forced to respond to these claims and address the issues of climate and land rights, then activists too must possess private authority and legitimacy.

The private authority held by this wide range of actors has led to the emergence of a raft of transnational governance initiatives that are often multi-stakeholder in nature. Sometimes referred to as non-state market driven (NSMD) governance systems, these have emerged in an attempt to address cross-border challenges that appear unresolvable by traditional means such as multilateral or inter-governmental approaches (Cashore 2002; May 2006). The intractability of global challenges, such as climate change, have encouraged new actors, including international organizations, intergovernmental organizations, MNCs, and activist groups, to cooperate at the transnational level (Cutler et al. 1999; Avant et al. 2010; Hsueh 2017). The development of multi-stakeholder governance represents a move to more complex governance structures and broader global frameworks in order to respond to some of society's most pressing challenges (Falkner 2003; Ruggie 2004; Pattberg 2007). Examples of transnational governance that address non-climate issues include the UN's Guiding Principles on Business and Human Rights, and the Extractive Industries Transparency Initiative, which govern human rights and corruption, respectively.

During the late twentieth century, international non-governmental organizations and international organizations devoted to addressing environmental matters proliferated. This was due to what organizational ecologists refer to as "mutualism," where collaboration, rather than competition, between governing actors occurred due to the increase in funding for environmental causes from the 1970s onwards. As Jessica F. Green and Jennifer Hadden (2021, 1809) observe of this era, "the more people and governments care[d] about the environment, the better it was for organizations of all types." As a result, multi-stakeholder governance involving various combinations of private actors, international organizations, and governments became a key feature of environmental and, later, climate change politics.

Turning to the twenty-first century, while multi-stakeholder governance initiatives continue to emerge, their growth has slowed, alongside that of international non-governmental organizations. Increasingly, there is a trend to more single-issue-focused, or specialist, organizations, as seen in the cases of Market Forces and ACCR. In populations where the organizational ecology is less dense (as it is in Australia, where there is little influence from ethical or religious investors), these single-issue-focused activists have been shown to cooperate more than in comparable jurisdictions where the population is dense (Bush and Hadden 2025).

The mutualism that buoyed the environmental movement in the 1970s and the growth in environmental NGOs in the period since has led to a plethora of transnational governance initiatives focused on addressing climate change. This is also due to the intractability of climate change, the lack of incentives for states to act alone, and a warming climate's impact on trade, development, and security (Bulkeley et al. 2014). During the first era of climate change governance, international relations and environmental politics scholars assumed states would be the key actors responsible for reducing global emissions. However, in a post-Kyoto era, with clear evidence that states had minimal incentives to cooperate to set and implement rules to reduce emissions, transnational climate change governance emerged, opening up the possibility for innovation and experimentation by a much wider cast of actors (Hoffmann 2011). This includes MNCs, which make decisions about how and to what extent to engage with private governance regimes based on the interactions between firms and the multilevel governance structures in which they operate—including domestic law, regulators, customers, and investors (Hsueh 2019).

The importance of global corporations in leading the transition to a low-carbon economy has been recognized by the United Nations Framework Convention on Climate Change (Hsueh 2017). Unlike in the case of more localized environmental challenges such as air pollution or water system degradation, mainstream businesses and their industry bodies in finance, technology, and energy have frequently supported broader climate goals (Hadden and Prakash 2024, 18). The pro-climate positions taken by some business leaders, despite the anti-ESG backlash in the US, represents a "discontinuity in environmental politics" that deserves scholarly attention (Hadden and Prakash 2024, 18).

Going beyond business to investors, multi-stakeholder initiatives that involve ESG activists, including CERES and the ICCR, are key vehicles of ESG anti-corporate activism and lobbying. Michael MacLeod and Jacob Park (2011) refer to these coalitions as investor-driven governance networks (IGNs). As networked instruments of governance, IGNs are attempts to reorient and "regulate" the behavior of business by holding corporations accountable via mechanisms of information sharing, monitoring of environmental impacts, and disclosure of activities related to the corporate climate footprint. However, unlike in the case of NSMDs, IGNs or ESG shareholder activists include investors in the accountability process. Other scholars have compared ESG shareholder activists and their coalitions to TANs, where groups work together as vehicles of principled persuasion but in the case of IGNs, seeking to maximize profits whilst disseminating values (MacLeod and Park 2011). Emily McAteer and Simone Pulver (2009) extend the concept of TANs to shareholder transnational advocacy networks, or STANs, which include investors but represent a more ad hoc engagement than the organizations described as IGNs, and those examined in this book. While debate continues over the conceptualization of these networks, what is common amongst all the terms described here is that these groups redirect the dictates of the market (either with or without investor input) and seek to transform it by using the power of socialization within the structure of shareholder rights and responsibilities.

There is evidence that transnational governance drives change. Calvin Thrall (2021) shows that MNCs that are signatories to the UN Global Compact are 15 percent more likely to respond publicly to ESG concerns raised by other stakeholders, suggesting that membership of public–private governance initiatives drive improved ESG responsiveness and potentially outcomes. While initiatives such as the Global Compact do not provide a toolkit for solving all ESG issues, they can lower the reputational cost of engaging with stakeholders and can encourage firms to address negative externalities created by their business model (Thrall 2021).[1] This research acknowledges that markets are socially embedded. And, as Harriet Bulkeley et al. (2014, 45) note, "the economic or market processes that shape or change actors' calculations of costs and benefits" are central to our understanding of the role of private actors in addressing climate change and other ESG concerns.

Acknowledging a growing role for the private sector in addressing climate change, and the use of markets and market-based mechanisms to do so, reflects the prevailing view that climate action, if it is to be generally accepted, must be paired with the maintenance of the liberal economic order. Liberal environmentalism rejects more radical and revolutionary approaches, and instead reinforces a transition to a carbon-neutral world through established market mechanisms (Hoffmann 2011). This approach has been criticized by many for lacking the urgency required to address climate change. Yet, advocates of more moderate, market-based approaches highlight that these mechanisms allow stakeholders such as civil society to "express their demands to moderate the excesses of global liberalism and to 'embed' markets in broader societal goals" (Bernstein and Cashore 2007, 348). The expression of these goals through a market lens has led to significant buy-in by corporate actors, international organizations, and governments. The question remains, though, whether this buy-in reflects a genuine commitment to real and lasting change around emissions reduction, or an attempt to control the regulatory agenda by proposing private governance solutions to ward off public regulation.

Liberal environmentalism highlights the potential for cooperation between business and civil society. This brings into question the appropriateness of the term anti-corporate politics, which is often used to describe ESG shareholder activism. Anti-corporate politics suggests an ever-present antagonism between activists and their targets. Yet, there is evidence, for example in the proliferation of transnational governance initiatives, that the relationship between business and civil society around ESG issues is shifting from adversarial to cooperative. It has been argued that there is increasing scope for cooperation between civil society and business firstly because other approaches have been trialed and failed, but also in recognition of the growing power and influence of business in shaping the future (Parker 2003). In this sense, the interactions between activists and corporations are not always unidirectional. The motivation for this cooperation can be derived from a logic of appropriateness, where the corporation and its leaders now see an issue as salient to their business model and seek to address it with the support of activist shareholders. Or, it can stem from a logic of consequences, where companies recognize the structuring of power and ideologies and how these interact with legitimating discourses, and in turn fear activist attention and pressure and acquiesce to claim-making, or attempt to placate activists through evasive measures (Yadin 2023). In the case of the latter, "power-holders can co-opt the language and tools of claim-makers [and] respondents can make concessions to curtail resistance" (Neville 2021, 49). While it is clear that there is an opportunity for cooperation between activists and their target companies to achieve shared goals, there is also the risk that this form of insider lobbying reflects a generalized trend to the increasing professionalization and corporatization of protest. According to Peter Dauvergne and Genevieve Le Baron's (2014, 144) analysis, NGOs have been "nudged . . . toward supporting market-friendly strategies, tactics and goals" representing a shift toward "system-conforming activism." In this sense, activists may find themselves the victim of large corporates' public relations departments, encouraged to water down demands or take their claim-making out of the public sphere. This critical approach to the professionalization of activism suggests that activists lose their effectiveness as they move closer to business. It also suggests that the power of corporations remains such that they can minimize the work of activists who attempt to rein in poor practices.

The AGM as a Site of Political Contestation: A New Framework for Analysis

This chapter has explored the literature on social movements and private governance. In doing so, it places ESG shareholder activists and firms at the center of the analysis, recognizing the power of these actors in shaping political outcomes. By synthesizing these two distinct fields of study, it is argued that anti-corporate politics, as a social movement, has the potential to leverage the private authority of corporate actors in order to instigate change. While much of the social movement literature splits activism into two distinct paths, either contentious politics aimed at the state (or some level of government), or private politics directed at reforming corporations, here, it is argued that these goals can be mutually sought. While activists principally target corporations over ESG issues such as climate change, Indigenous land rights, workers' rights, and corporate governance, they are simultaneously attempting reform at multiple levels. By relying on the private authority of firms that have a strong reputation, are market leaders, and have access to policy makers, activists consider the possibility of reforming whole industries and encouraging regulatory reform. In this sense, their activism is highly political; it is not simply about improving the ESG performance of a singular firm. Activists seek to push firms, or cooperate with progressive companies, to contest the *politics* of issues such as climate change, Indigenous land rights, workers' rights, and corporate governance. They do so by leveraging the private authority of big business to influence norms of behavior.

The choice of the corporate AGM, as opposed to other sites of political contestation, represents a strategic decision by actors. Public policy scholarship offers insights into venue shopping, including the characteristics SMOs take into consideration when choosing where and how to engage with targets. Policy venues differ in "respect to their rules of access and participation, their decision-making procedures, their constituencies, and the incentives facing institutional actors," offering venue shopping strategies to activists who can leverage these differences (Pralle 2006, 122). SMOs are likely to select forums for engagement where they perceive a greater chance of getting their issue onto the political agenda, and having subsequent input into the formation and implementation of policy (Pralle 2010). Similarly instrumental rational choice theories suggest that in the presence of imperfect information, actors will select venues that they perceive offer the greatest benefits for the costs incurred (Weible 2007; Weible and Sabatier 2007). Where resources allow, SMOs will engage across multiple venues concurrently, to benefit from the many decisions being made simultaneously across the range of sites (Lubell et al. 2010; Lubell 2013). In doing so, activists must mold their framing of a particular issue to the receptivity of the chosen venue, often describing the same issue in multiple ways in order to appeal to a broader array of actors (Baumgartner and Jones 2010). When selecting venues, actors learn lessons from prior unsuccessful strategic decisions, adapting and applying these learnings to new venues where they are more likely to achieve the goal of policy change (Ley and Weber 2015). Policy venues also evolve to accommodate new or previously unwelcome actors. As contestation develops, activists gain access to key decision-making venues that they had previously been excluded from. They also become more sophisticated over time and feel more comfortable in these forums (Pralle 2006, 230). As explored in this book, the professionalisation of activists across a broad range of issue areas suggests that SMOs are increasingly gaining access to new policy venues. Activists are increasingly comfortable choosing to engage in contestation at AGMs and in corporate settings more broadly. Similarly, some corporations have evolved to willingly invite engagement with activist groups that were previously considered vexing.

Using the venues available to them, ESG shareholder activists harness the strategies of SMOs and anti-corporate activists to lobby large, listed corporations to reform their behavior. They recognize and target opportunity structures from the transnational down to the corporate. Activists use both noisy, disruptive claim-making tactics as well as coalition-building and cooperative approaches that include market-based actors, such as proxy advisors, institutional investors, and ethical funds, as well as forming relationships with target companies themselves. The choice of tactic largely depends on the openness of the corporate opportunity structure. As is explored in the following two chapters, each of these approaches (i.e., disruptive versus cooperative), has produced desired outcomes for activists.

By lobbying large industry players, ESG shareholder activists attempt to produce wider societal change. The goal is not simply to decarbonize mining company BHP, for example, but to push an industry leader to make significant changes to its business model, in the hope of influencing the policies and decarbonization strategies of competitor firms. Activists are not necessarily looking for a "win" each time they make a claim on a firm; instead, they are looking to engage in noisy politics, drawing continued attention to an issue to maintain momentum (Galanter 1974; Pralle 2010). In this sense, activists resemble Helen Callaghan's (2018) "challengers," or outsiders opposing established business interests, such as those of large shareholders or "incumbents." The power held by challengers and incumbents varies between different corporate governance models. By paying attention to the political economy of corporate governance, we can observe a wide variety of distributional impacts stemming from different regulatory settings (Gourevitch and Shinn 2005). In this case, the goal of challengers is not to reform only the target company, but to take aim at incumbents more generally, by generating new norms of business behavior that established business interests must respond to. The research in this book intervenes in debates over the political economy of corporate governance by uncovering a case where challengers have little legal power yet have managed to succeed in generating pro-social outcomes.

ESG shareholder activists contest norms of business behavior through market-based mechanisms. The aim of these contestations is to engender new norms of behavior that influence other industry players, whether this occurs through formal industry associations or informally through peer pressure. Activists have also called on companies to directly lobby governments to strengthen legislation. While this is a direct form of influence, it is also the case that once business has adopted a new norm (e.g., say on climate votes), legislating such requirements becomes much easier. In order to fully understand the strategies, effectiveness, and outcomes of ESG shareholder resolutions, we need to move moving beyond the dichotomous understanding of activists' attempts to lobby business *or* government and instead widen our scope of analysis to envisage successful activists co-opting business actors to push for broader change, particularly in jurisdictions or issue areas where governments have lagged. Climate policy and the recognition of Indigenous land rights are two key areas where Australian government regulations have failed to keep up with societal expectations. They have also been the target of ESG activist claim-making and, it is argued in this book, with some success.

Research Design

The analysis in this book relies on data collected on shareholder proposals filed at eight Australian company AGMs between 2017 and 2022.[2] The author analyzed seventy-one shareholder resolutions on ESG issues and triangulated their findings through analysis of corporate responses to the resolutions, shareholder voting records, and interviews with key actors.[3]

Firstly, the author developed a rich database tracking all ESG shareholder resolutions filed in Australia. The database draws on the open database developed by ACCR and published on its website. Using this as a starting point, missing and updated resolutions, additional details about secondary filers, links to voting records, and links to the AGM notice—which includes the claim as framed by the filer and the response as presented by the company—were added in. Secondly, the author conducted interviews with representatives of activist organizations, institutional investors, service providers, and shareholder organizations. These interviews took place in 2021 and 2022, when ESG shareholder activism in Australia was at its peak. Given the concentration of activist, proxy advisor, and investor populations in Australia, the interviewees remain deidentified, yet the interviews cover all organizations involved in ESG activism and most proxy advisors as well as large shareholder organizations. The interviews were conducted on the basis of anonymity, although some interviewees were happy to be named. Because not all agreed to be identified, none have been. Thirdly, using the database of ESG shareholder resolutions, the author analyzed proposals and corporate responses through the notice of AGM of the eight mining, oil and gas, and financial services companies most heavily targeted by ESG shareholder activists from 2017 to 2022. This resulted in a dataset of seventy-one resolutions, excluding the "dummy" resolution calling for a change to the company's constitution. These were then compared with shareholder voting records over time. Lastly, the researcher attended AGMs of all target firms in 2020 and 2021, undertaking participant observation. These AGMs were all webcast due to the impacts of Covid-19 and associated travel bans and lockdowns. The participant observation provided the chance to watch how Chairs and CEOs responded to activist claims, and although the remote nature meant there was little opportunity for questions from the floor from activists or visible protest in or outside of the AGM, the author did observe interactions between boards and ESG shareholder activists.

As has been done before in scholarship on social movements, the research focuses on the language and discourse of claim-makers and their targets. Discourses can be defined as "set of linguistic practices and rhetorical strategies embedded in a network of social relations" (Litfin 1994, 3). These strategies are employed by both claimants and counter-claimants in order to either progress or stall the movement's aims (Neville 2021). The successful use of discursive strategies is central to the repertoires of collective actions that groups use to achieve their goals, or to resist change (Tarrow 2013). In order to unravel these competing discourses and the embedded narratives employed by actors, the researcher conducted document analysis, through the use of qualitative thematic analysis of written texts. This analysis requires the systematic ordering of the text around major analytical themes in order to extract meaningful insights from the large amount of text (Tillotson et al. 2023). The identification of themes allows the capture of the overarching claims (and response) by activists and their target companies. It also examines the sequencing of these claims over time, and the manner in which activists' demands grew as public opinion and firms' responses changed.

CHAPTER 3
Wildfires for Activism

IN SEPTEMBER 2021, THE board of Australia's largest single carbon emitter, AGL Energy, faced a hostile AGM at which shareholders gave a resounding warning to the company over its approach to emissions reduction. The company had recently proposed to separate its emissions-intensive business from its retail business, in an attempt to downplay its contribution to the country's emissions profile (Toscano 2021a). At the meeting, Chair Peter Botton was forced to defend the proposal, as well as the company's otherwise lackluster attempts at reducing emissions. Ahead of the AGM, ESG shareholder activists ACCR filed a resolution proposing to tie company directors' remuneration to emissions targets. This resolution secured an unprecedented 53 percent shareholders' support, reflecting the fact the majority of investors were dissatisfied with the company's plans and wished to see individual board members take responsibility for the direction of their company (AGL 2021). Voting at this AGM sent the clearest signal yet to Australian companies that there was no time to wait for action on climate, and that investors were not content relying on government to regulate large emitters, such as AGL. Six months later, AGL was the target of a hostile takeover bid from Australian technology entrepreneur and philanthropist Mike Cannon-Brookes in partnership with Canadian asset manager Brookfield Corporation. While the takeover bid was ultimately unsuccessful, it led to the election of four directors backed by Cannon-Brookes to the board in 2022 (Hannam 2022). In 2023, Brookfield launched another unsuccessful takeover bid for AGL's rival coal-fired power generator, Origin Energy, which is itself grappling with how to reduce its direct and indirect emissions while ensuring a profitable future for the company.

Coal-fired power generators, such as Origin and AGL, have been the target of ESG shareholder activists since 2015. Alongside oil, gas, mining, and financial services firms, they have been the principle focus of investor activists. The emissions output of Australia's largest carbon majors is on average equivalent to that of 25 million Australian households, making these corporations obvious targets for climate activists (Moss and Fraser 2019; Yadin 2023). Simultaneously, awareness amongst non-activist investors of the risks their companies face is growing. A company that relies on the exploration and extraction of oil or gas, or one that provides coal-fired power in a world racing to renewable energy, faces legal, financial, and strategic challenges including the risk of a balance sheet littered with stranded assets. The rise in Australian ESG shareholder activism follows successful campaigns against oil majors overseas, including Shell in the UK, in the mid-2010s. After witnessing these successful campaigns and establishing a method for circumventing Australia's regulation aimed at stymying this form of activism, ESG shareholder activists began pressuring companies with the worst environmental records. In one sense, selecting target companies in an economy dominated by mining, oil, and gas companies is a relatively straightforward task. Yet, simultaneously, there is a plethora of large emitters in these industries and activists' resources are limited, making strategic decisions necessary.

This chapter explores the evolution of environmental shareholder activism in Australia. This activism took place against a backdrop of increasingly frequent and severe natural disasters, linked to climate change, and in a country where there remained little government action on emissions reduction. Taken together, this is one explanation for the heavy skew toward climate resolutions in the Australian context, when compared to other jurisdictions (say the UK and US) where there is a much wider range of issue areas covered by shareholder resolutions. The chapter begins with a discussion of the critical junctures that took place around the time of the Black Summer megafires, an event that catalyzed the minds of many Australians to a new era of natural disasters brought on by a lack of climate action. Such events helped activists to frame their claim-making and encouraged non-activist investors to take climate risks into their investment considerations. Several themes emerge from analysis of activist claims, including calling for emissions disclosure, and then reduction, questioning the membership of industry organizations, and finally asking powerful firms to lobby governments to incentivize emissions reductions. Corporate responses provide insights into the effectiveness of activism, and here it is demonstrated that a genuine consensus emerged amongst large, listed corporates that in the absence of government action, these companies would be required to address their climate risks. And in the case of large players such as BHP, this led to an industry-wide acknowledgment that emissions reduction was a core part of strategic planning. The success of activists is evidenced through the story of Australia's aging coal-fired power fleet and its increasingly under-pressure owners, who were forced to bring forward the closure date of their coal-fired power plants. It is shown that while activists were able to force change within the industry, starting by pressuring the largest corporations and then influencing smaller companies, there is little evidence of success in affecting policy outcomes, where government response continued to fall short of societal expectations. The chapter concludes by turning to the case of Australia's oil and gas majors, which were able to resist activist pressure to limit exploration and production by leveraging government discourse of a gas-led transition to green energy and a gas-led post-Covid economic recovery. The analysis demonstrates that market-based activism has the power to generate change within companies and industries, and that ESG shareholder activism, used alongside other tactics such as hostile takeover bids, is an effective form of claim-making. However, the chapter also shows that even when social movements are successful, recalcitrant industries and regulators may stymy change. In the cases explored in this chapter, governments have provided cover for gas exploration and extraction companies to continue their contribution to global warming. These companies have used the discourse of governments and transnational organizations, such as the International Energy Agency, to defend their business interests despite the well-understood urgency to transition away from emissions-intensive energy sources, such as gas.

Australia's Black Summer Megafires: A Critical Juncture

Described as "cataclysmic" and a "landmark in Australia's environmental history," the country's Black Summer megafires represent a key moment for environmental activism (Rumpff et al. 2023). The megafires began in June 2019, notably winter in the southern hemisphere, and peaked in December of that year and into the following January. The fires burned for almost an entire year, in what remains an unprecedented display of the consequences of human society's impact on the climate. The fires burned 243,000 square kilometers (24 million hectares) of land. The poor air quality associated with the blaze caused the deaths of approximately four hundred people, and another thirty-three lost their lives as a direct result of the fires (Pickrell 2020). The fires also decimated the country's fauna. It is estimated that three billion terrestrial vertebrates were lost, including many endangered species and animals yet to be documented by Western scientists (Rumpff et al. 2023).

The pervasiveness and all-consuming nature of the disaster remain difficult to reconcile with the temporal aspects of the fires. After all, some part of Australia was burning for a continuous eleven months. Every state in the country experienced large-scale fires (McDonald 2021). The impact of the fires was felt well beyond their immediate proximity. Those not directly impacted by the destruction caused by this natural disaster felt it all too acutely. Air quality in Australia's cities significantly deteriorated, particularly in Sydney and Melbourne. Each day for weeks and months would begin with the acrid smell of burning bush, the health impacts and impending sense of danger impossible to ignore. The everyday lives of Australians hinged on the state of the fires surrounding the country's major cities. Summer, traditionally a time for holidaying and celebration, was instead punctuated by media images of children piloting their families to safety in small dinghies and crowds of holiday makers and residents seeking shelter from fires on beaches, where they awaited instructions to enter the ocean, deemed the last safe place of refuge.

This time in Australia's history represents a critical juncture for the environmental movement. In many ways it represents what the political science literature tells us is a shift between continuity and change, between normal and intense times (Della Porta 2020). Australians have a long, lived experience with bushfires, floods, and other natural disasters. However, the 2019 and 2020 megafires were unprecedented in scope, scale, and intensity. One of the few positive outcomes of this disaster was that environmental activism had a wider and more receptive audience. The "valence" of climate change, or the emotional quality of an issue that makes audiences more receptive, was elevated by the pervasiveness and extent of the Black Summer bushfires and their impact on the population (R. H. Cox and Béland 2013). ESG shareholder activists were already experienced in filing environmental resolutions at corporate AGMs. However, after these megafires, their concerns were increasingly shared by a growing number of investors, institutional shareholders, and proxy advisors who had reached a realization that their company's reputation, and financial performance, were linked to its environmental credentials.

While social movements were gaining traction with corporations, increasingly aware of their reputation amongst broader society, governments (particularly the Australian Federal Government) remained laggards. *Nature* (2020, 449), the world's preeminent scientific journal, editorialized, "Australia's leaders have known for many years that climate change would make bush fires worse . . . but as *Nature* has frequently reported, the country's politicians delayed meaningful action through a wasted decade of arguments over whether human activities are causing climate change—in the face of overwhelming scientific evidence that they are." In what many saw as a dereliction of duty as well as a reflection of his commitment to addressing climate change, Australia's then Prime Minister Scott Morrison secretly flew himself and his family to Hawaii at the height of the megafires. According to this worldview, a well-deserved vacation took precedence over the heroic efforts of volunteers to try to rein in these fires. The firefighting efforts led to the tragic loss of life of three Rural Fire Service members, unpaid volunteers who train to be ready for such disasters, as well as three American firefighters who had traveled to assist in the blazes (Australian Institute for Disaster Resilience 2020). Beyond the immediate optics of a leader absconding, there was also the question of why Australia had failed to implement policies that would lead to emissions reduction, and why governments continued to subsidize coal, oil, and gas producers to the value of A$11.1 billion in the years 2022 and 2023 alone. This amount is fourteen times greater than the budget for dealing with natural disasters, and these subsidies are expected to grow to A$57.1 billion over the period of the forward estimates (Campbell et al. 2023).

These questions can partially be answered by examining the discourse of the ruling Liberal-National (LNP) coalition, whose parties traditionally represent conservative, center-right, and rural voters. The prime minister under the LNP coalition until 2022, Scott Morrison, was a vocal supporter of Australia's gas-led recovery from the economic effects of Covid-19 lockdowns, as well as a gas-led transition to renewable energy. The prime minister noted, "gas has a critical role to play as a backstop to our record investment in renewable energy generation. It helps to ensure we can keep the lights on when the wind isn't blowing and the sun isn't shining," in his reference to utilizing Australia's large gas reserves as a domestic source of power (Morrison 2020a). He also emphasized the country's role in exporting its gas reserves, explaining that his government would "work with industry to . . . ensure households and businesses enjoy the benefits of our abundant local gas" and describing gas as a "critical enabler of Australia's economy" (Morrison 2020b). Morrison's language was central to debates around a transition to green energy. The LNP argued that the path to a just transition required the extraction of more gas in order to reduce reliance on coal-fired power, while keeping Australian workers employed and ensuring continuity of energy supply. While the environmental benefits of this push for greater liquid natural gas (LNG) exploration and extraction were questionable, the economics remained inexplicable. Subsidies and tax concessions to oil and gas companies totaled A$1.35 billion in 2022 and 2023 (Campbell et al. 2023). Yet, the gas-led transition captured not only the minds of government, but also those companies who would benefit from such a focus. This included, and is reflected in the statements of, various gas suppliers and banks, who financed these projects.

This chapter explores the claims and counterclaims made by activists and corporations, leading to a discussion of the impact of this activism on government policy. Activists were able to work with or pressure many large Australian energy producers and miners into disclosing emissions, making commitments to reduce these, exiting and reforming industry peak bodies policy, and influencing peers to undertake these same activities. There was, however, less success in the oil and gas sector, which leant into the government rhetoric emphasizing the economic and strategic importance of gas extraction. It is also argued that while there was considerable progress at the company and industry level, this failed to translate to the level of government policy. The next section explores how activists undertook their claim-making against Australia's largest corporations, and in doing so it examines the discourse and themes used to engage companies and non-activist shareholders.

Activist Claim-Making

ESG shareholder resolutions are frequently crafted in an insider's voice. The reasons for this are twofold: one is that activist shareholders are in fact investors and therefore they speak the language of their non-activist peers through corporate governance mechanisms such as AGMs. The second is that increasing the "yes" vote on these resolutions hinges on convincing non-activist investors that these claims will be beneficial for their company. Given the motivation of non-activist investors is maximizing financial returns, "asks" on companies are often worded to enhance the value proposition to other shareholders. Activists utilize self-referential terms such as "our company's commitments" in their supporting statements, signaling to non-activist investors and management that these requests come from other shareholders, rather than outsiders. The motivation for this strategy was confirmed by a non-activist interviewee for this project, who noted that ESG shareholder activists and their resolutions are expressed "in the language of investors because it focuses the mind of the company in some ways on the issue . . . you can imagine if there was a high vote on an issue, well that would be an important issue to investors. And that's only going to happen if it aligns with the kind of the investor language and their approach to these things and the financial materiality." By framing their asks in terms that appeal to other investors, activists maximize their chances of recording higher support. Emphasizing the financial drivers of climate change emerged as a key strategy in the analysis of shareholder resolutions. In attempts to appeal to investors and companies, activists relied most heavily on claims that a failure to address emissions would impact the business's profitability. The most common rationale provided by activists to encourage emissions reductions included highlighting to companies and investors that failure to reduce emissions could lead to erosion of shareholder value, greater risk of stranded assets, increased costs devoted to capital expenditure and maintenance, and threats of litigation.

While activist shareholders aim to recruit non-activist shareholders in support of their resolutions, it was noted by one non-activist interviewee that the percentage support for resolutions does not need to be particularly high for claim-making to serve as an effective signal to boards and management. Shareholder resolutions in Australia are non-binding, and the *Corporations Act* does not require any action from companies even in the rare event of a majority vote. However, as one interviewee suggested, "even support in the high teens for a resolution can be much more meaningful" and it can "be the subject of quite a lot of discussion" and "prompt quite a lot of thinking in the boardroom and from investors." This suggests that the precise percentage of support for resolutions is less important than it appears, and that any level of material support from proxy advisors or institutional investors may cause boards and management to pay careful consideration to shareholder asks and the broader issues being raised by activists. This is particularly the case where representative shareholder associations are involved. Australia's two key shareholder associations ACSI and ASA represent pension funds and retail shareholders, respectively. Both organizations are committed to holding companies to account over issues that pose a material financial risk to their members' investments. They are explicitly noncommittal on ESG issues on a stand-alone basis, but may consider these where they have the potential to impact a company's profitability. This is not to say that the individuals in these organizations are unaware of or not concerned with ESG issues, but that as shareholder organizations their key drivers are financial materiality and the performance of their members' investments. These organizations are representative of their members, including the pension funds that administer Australia's sizeable pension holdings. An interviewee from a shareholder association noted,

> If [pension funds] do have a shareholder resolution before them, then they take it seriously, it's not, you know oh well, another box to tick. They actually really want to understand the merits, they want to understand the company's approach. They want to understand the effect on value. They do prompt discussions, and that's probably more important than the numbers [voting percentage] attached to them.

In instances where ESG activists can convincingly link claim-making to issues of material financial risk, ASA and ACSI can be helpful allies in pressing companies to reform their environmental and social records. As this chapter will discuss, financial materiality was a key driver of the success of activists targeting coal-fired power producers in Australia. The cost of maintaining aging power plants represents a material financial risk to investors, and this was leveraged by activists to encourage companies and their shareholders to shutter these plants earlier than planned.

In addition to demonstrating material financial risk, activists are also more likely to secure the support of proxy advisors and shareholder representatives where their asks are less onerous. One of the first asks that ESG activists placed on companies were calls for greater public disclosure of emissions. In this case, shareholder groups and proxy advisors found this a reasonable request to support, and well-resourced companies found it relatively easy to acquiesce to. As a result, this was readily agreed to by most companies over the course of 2017 and 2018, while companies were simultaneously being pressured to meet the Financial Stability Board's Task Force on Climate-related Financial Disclosures (TCFD) reporting requirements. The TCFD was developed to harmonize corporate reporting of emissions, which was seen as an easy win for companies attempting to address investors' climate concerns. The ease with which large listed companies can comply with requests for transparency and disclosure was confirmed by an interviewee who noted that their organization's approach "has typically been additional disclosure [of emissions] for large multi-billion dollar companies is something that they can afford [and] implement and is of value to shareholders who are concerned about managing what exposure they have to climate change, to see what exposure they have to regulations governing emissions." In this sense, the provision of information is a relatively simple ask of a company, and one which improves investors' ability to track their company's exposure to the financial risks of emissions-intensive activity.

Yet, as this chapter demonstrates, calls for disclosure and increased transparency led to a stronger focus on emissions profiles and eventually pressure on companies to share plans to reduce emissions with investors and activists alike. By 2018 activist claim-making had moved beyond calling for emissions disclosure, which was by now a generally accepted practice for large corporates, onto highlighting lobbying and membership of industry bodies that advocated for policy positions contrary to Paris Agreement targets. Activists identified multiple instances of companies that had announced credible emissions reductions targets and transition plans but remained members of industry bodies that actively lobbied policy makers to resist regulatory change. An early target of activists was one of the world's largest mining companies, and Australia's largest company at the time, BHP Limited. ACCR began filing shareholder resolutions at BHP's AGMs in 2017, and they did so again (along with a single Market Forces resolution) in 2019, 2020, and 2021. These resolutions were a mix of climate asks, with a heavy focus on the company's membership in industry groups Minerals Council of Australia (MCA), the World Coal Association (WCA), and the US Chamber of Commerce. ACCR argued that these groups' pro-coal lobbying activities were incongruent with BHP's own climate stance (Davies 2017). Unlike climate laggards Origin and AGL, BHP took a conciliatory approach to engaging with ACCR. Meetings between the company, its activist shareholders, and other parties such as proxy advisors were described by an interviewee as "regular" and "rich." The strategy employed by ACCR yielded results. In 2018, BHP exited the WCA, on the basis that it could not reconcile the industry body's position on climate change with its own. BHP then forced the MCA to include support for the Paris Agreement targets to its existing commitment to lobbying in favor of reliable and cheap energy (BHP 2019). By extracting this commitment from the MCA, BHP had effectively bound other industry players who were members of the MCA to a more rigorous approach to addressing climate change. Yet, activists continued to lobby the company. This led to the extraordinary move by the BHP board to encourage all shareholders to support ACCR's 2021 resolution, which called for BHP to convince all industry bodies of which it was a member to advocate for policy settings congruent with limiting climate change to 1.5 degrees. The backing of BHP's Board for this resolution led to a 99 percent vote of support from all shareholders, something never before seen in Australian corporate history.

The lobbying of BHP has impacts beyond the company, given its significance in Australian political and economic history, and its global contribution to mining. The company possesses a significant amount of private authority and legitimacy, so its actions are seen as sector-leading both in Australia and globally. This leadership and authority are driving factors behind activists' decisions to target large, influential companies such as BHP. In this instance, as one interviewee noted, "the accountability of BHP is to its shareholders, then the accountability of the Minerals Council is to BHP . . . There is this kind of cascading responsibility or a ripple effect." Large businesses that are seen as legitimate political actors are considered highly authoritative in their industry and capable of setting standards that other companies see as appropriate. Added to this, BHP has significant influence over the industry peak body, the MCA, which in turn has influence over other mining firms, suggesting that this activism went beyond simply forcing change at BHP. One interviewee suggested that gaining compliance from BHP "to do something like that, make some net zero commitment, make some disclosure" makes it "more likely you are to get the mid-caps put that on their radar." They continued, "A lot of what the market expects and what the market looks for is about benchmarking to market practice. And the big end of town market practice seems to count for a lot." BHP's private authority and leverage over industry associations and other competitors suggests targeting large companies yields increasing returns. As one interviewee noted, "there is no doubt that companies watch what happens in other companies and take their policy signals from that."

During this period, activists placed significant pressure on large companies to exit industry associations, like the WCA, whose policies were seen as barriers to achieving Paris-aligned emissions targets. This is because not only do these associations influence members, but they are also highly active lobbyists, with direct access to legislators around the world (UNPRI 2022). Activists' strategies were aimed at companies that had made credible emissions reductions targets of their own and were committed to changing their business practices in response. Activists aimed to delegitimize these industry associations and to defund their lobbying activities through reduced membership contributions from large companies. On this measure, activists can claim some level of success. While groups such as the MCA still play a powerful role in Australian politics and society, as one interviewee noted, "within the Australian market and beyond is now an expectation that companies will monitor, report on, and to an extent we're approaching accountability, but to an extent be accountable for the activities of their industry associations and their shareholder money that's been spent" on membership in these organizations. Furthermore, this expectation has disseminated transnationally, with the European investor peak body the Institutional Investors Group on Climate Change publishing its own investor expectations on climate change lobbying. The issue also now forms part of the global Climate

Action 100+ benchmark (Climate Action 100+ 2024). The assessment of companies' industry association memberships represents a "ripple effect" whereby the group can claim success as the issue has taken on a life of its own and does not require constant attention from activists.

Anti-corporate politics focuses on the manner by which activists can target companies in order to change corporate behavior, often in the absence of regulatory oversight. As one interviewee noted, in targeting issues "where the government policies seem to have lagged" activists believe that "the easier lever, or the more effective lever, would be at corporate." In this case, there was an expectation that BHP could and *should* do more than was legally required as a leader in its field. This was confirmed by a fund manager interviewed for this research, who noted, "We expect companies to act in the spirit of the law . . . we would expect a good company would be ahead of the Government," and "it is directors' job to actually be ESG literate to move this along, to be prepared at a much higher level than is required at this stage by the government." ESG activists achieved more than simply a revision of BHP's internal policies on industry associations. They accomplished change at the industry level, through BHP's ability to influence the MCA, and saw a more stringent set of standards on membership of industry associations embedded in global standards.

Social movement theorists argue that there is greater scope for change when targeting powerful corporate actors. One of the rationales for targeting large corporations is their recognized pathways of influence to policy makers. This again can be seen in the case of BHP, a corporation with significant private authority globally. In a 2022 ESG shareholder resolution, the company was accused by filer ACCR of playing a key role in the 2010 ousting of former Australian Prime Minister Kevin Rudd over plans to introduce a price on carbon. This is a serious accusation, and its inclusion in the AGM notice serves as evidence that activists see large, influential corporations as capable of leveraging their power to achieve political aims, in this case removing a prime minister who supported a carbon trading scheme. By 2022 ACCR was claim-making against a more climate-aware BHP, asking the company to leverage its influence and "proactively advocate for Australian policy settings that are consistent with the Paris Agreement's objective of limiting global warming to 1.5°C." This resolution goes further than any other shareholder resolution filed against an Australian company and recognizes the power of BHP and its associated influence on government policy. Interestingly, BHP concurred, noting the company "already advocate[s] for good climate policy where it aligns with our published Global Climate Policy Standards and is in the best interests of BHP. We intend to continue to adopt this approach to our advocacy going forward" (BHP 2022, 20); and that the Board believes it "can best support climate policy development by ensuring we meet our own climate targets, goals and commitments, continuing to make the case for the economic opportunities arising from the energy transition, and focusing on those policy areas where we are likely to have the greatest ability to influence change" (BHP 2022, 21). This extension of claim-making from company, to industry, to policy-making demonstrates the private authority and political power of large companies like BHP. It also evidences the power of anti-corporate politics in pushing for significant social, political, and economic change beyond the level of the firm.

Following activists' success in campaigns for greater disclosure and the reform of industry peak bodies, from the early 2020s their attention turned to pressuring firms to develop detailed transition plans outlining how their company will exit fossil fuel–intensive business activities. Activists demanded companies make their transition plans public by presenting them at AGMs and allowing activists and investors to vote on these plans, a practice known as "say on climate." The push, from 2020 onwards, for these resolutions to be part of companies' AGMs was led by ACCR and other transnational shareholder activist organizations, who were supported by the Children's Investment Fund Foundation to establish the practice of say on climate (Say on Climate 2024). When these transition plans form the basis of a board-proposed resolution, there is a requirement that they be made available to investors and the general public as part of the AGM notice. This process gives activists and investors an insight into transition planning ahead of the AGM, and an opportunity to signal their approval, or disapproval, to boards and management. ACCR, through its Say on Climate coalition, has targeted the largest and most authoritative industry players, calling for them to allow shareholders to vote on their transition plans. These companies have then influenced others to do the same. An interviewee noted that companies were increasingly agreeing to activists' asks to adopt an investor "say on climate," and that this informal standard spread to other heavy emitters that had not yet been targeted, with "other companies that [they] had considered putting the resolution to, now considering it." Overall, this campaign has also been successful with large companies including AGL, Origin, Woodside Petroleum, and Rio Tinto publicizing their transition plans in a similar way to earlier calls for disclosure of emissions. In this sense, success can be measured not by a supportive vote on an activist-filed resolution calling for transition plans to be made public, but by the preemptive meeting of an activist shareholder's ask, avoiding, as one interviewee phrased it, "a threat of contest at their AGM about something that they don't want to have a contest about."

In the five years following 2017, which included campaigns over greater disclosure, membership of non-Paris-aligned industry associations, and the publication of transition plans, support for environmental claim-making has trended upward. This upward trend, shown in Figure 3, has been amplified by the ten resolutions where more than 50 percent of shareholders supported activist claims. All of these were related to climate change, and all occurred from 2020 onwards. As noted above, we cannot observe the number of resolutions that were never put to AGMs as activists

FIGURE 3. Support for environmental shareholder resolutions. Source: Author's database.

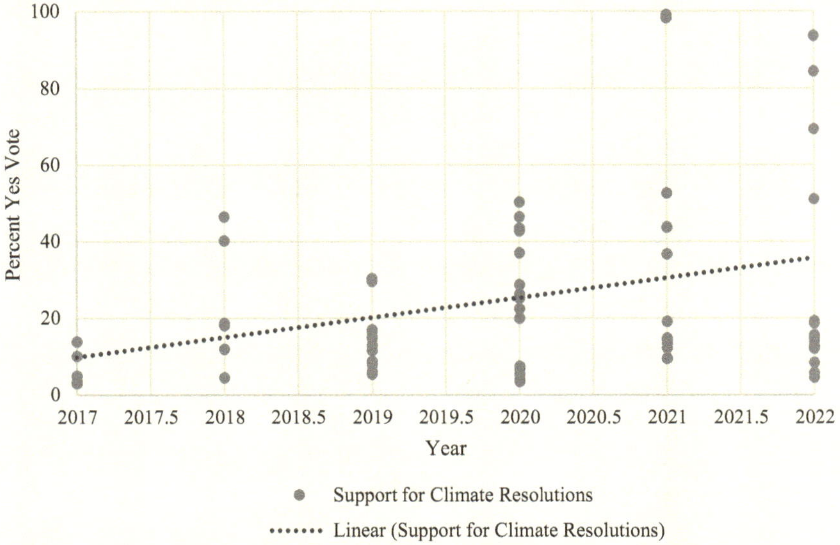

and companies were able to reach an agreement ahead of time. What this does demonstrate, however, is more instances where non-activist shareholders, proxy advisors, institutional investors, and even corporations themselves have coalesced around a push for greater climate action on behalf of Australian companies.

Corporate Responses: Consensus and Climate Laggards

Corporations have a right of reply to shareholder resolutions. These responses are publicized in the company's notice of AGM, alongside activist claims. This section explores these corporate responses to activist claim-making. Companies' responses to shareholder resolutions are comprised of the board's voting recommendation and a narrative justification for this position. In regards to climate, there was a unanimous consensus amongst all companies in the period studied (2017 and onwards) that climate change was a human-induced threat to planetary health and that all interested parties should be working towards reducing emissions so as to limit global warming to 2 degrees, and then later, 1.5 degrees. What varied between companies, industries, and over time was what role boards claimed their business played in the reduction of emissions and transition to renewable energy. In particular, while all companies took responsibility for their scope 1 and scope 2 emissions, most were at least initially reluctant to make any commitment to disclosing, and later reducing, their scope 3 emissions, citing a lack of control over how their downstream customers operated. Some companies, such as BHP, saw the divesture of emissions-intensive businesses as a legitimate way to reduce emissions. BHP sold its heavy-emitting petroleum assets to Woodside Petroleum in 2021. Activists were heavily critical of this approach, noting that the only result from such divestures was to shift carbon liabilities from one company to another, doing nothing to reduce overall emissions. Lastly, the response to anti-corporate claim-making varied by industry. While coal-fired power producers changed their business model under significant pressure in the early 2020s, gas companies remained shielded by the then federal government's promotion of a gas-led transition to renewables, and later, by the need to provide reliable power in Australia and the region, particularly in light of contemporary geopolitical events.

Over the period studied in this research, Australia's emissions-intensive energy producers underwent a significant change in strategy. Until the early 2020s, coal-fired power plant owners steadfastly reiterated their centrality to a just transition. In 2019, for example, AGL argued in its AGM notice that

> while AGL agrees with the sentiment expressed in this resolution about the importance of managing carbon risk, AGL considers that any approach to decarbonization should be based on a just transition process for customers, employees, shareholders and communities. In particular, ensuring system reliability and improving affordability are key priorities that must be met within any decarbonization strategy.

In 2019, AGL was able to leverage the interests of its wide variety of stakeholders, including employees, governments, and customers, to justify its plan to operate coal-fired power plants well into the 2040s (see Table 2). Just two years later the company was facing the circumstances detailed earlier in this chapter, where the board found itself under pressure from activists and investors, and the target of an attempted hostile takeover bid, which resulted in a successful board overhaul and a realigning of the business to decarbonize at a more rapid rate.

From the early 2020s onwards, Australia transitioned to renewable energy at a pace that took policy makers and industry by surprise. No substantial government incentives had been introduced to reduce emissions-intensive energy production, yet advances in technology and greater individual household uptake of solar power saw renewable energy grow an average of 15 percent per year to make up 32 percent of all energy production in 2022 (Department of Climate Change 2024). This rapid uptake, combined with an expensive and aging coal-fired power fleet, provided a window of opportunity for companies to engage with criticism from ESG shareholder activists, and others, in relation to the extended operation of coal-fired power generators. As they aged, these power generators required extensive capital expenditure and frequent shutdown periods to maintain their functionality. This expense and unreliability added weight to ESG activists' claims. ESG shareholder activists drew on these significant costs to business, lower return on investment, and a moral and scientific imperative that Australia transition away from emissions-intensive power generation in their appeals to investors.

One example of this multifaceted framing by Market Forces appeared in the AGL 2019 AGM notice in reference to its Victorian coal-fired power plants:

> The age of AGL's coal power stations also presents financial risks. The extended outage of one of Loy Yang A's four units is expected to reduce FY20 underlying profit after tax by $60 million to $100 million. Since December 2017, Loy Yang A has experienced 29 breakdowns, more than any other Australian power station. Liddell has had 13 breakdowns and Bayswater five. Further capital expenditure to keep Loy Yang and Bayswater operating until 2048 and 2035 respectively risks becoming stranded due to technological, market and regulatory changes required for a Paris-aligned energy transition.

While Cannon-Brookes and Brookfield's 2022 hostile takeover of AGL was unsuccessful, it did lead to board renewal through the appointment of four new climate-focused directors, all of whom prioritized reforming the company's balance sheet in the face of the pressures outlined by Market Forces and other investors (Hannam 2022). The backlash against AGL by both institutional and retail shareholders sent a clear message to Australian companies that their response to climate change could not wait for regulatory reform. This was a critical moment in AGL and rival Origin's history, with both companies subsequently succumbing to activist and investor pressure to close their coal-fired power stations earlier than planned (Packham 2022). Table 2 compares the original and revised closure dates of both companies' coal-fired plants.[1] Both companies have brought forward closure dates on some of Australia's most emissions-intensive power sources. The remainder of the industry has followed, with "up to 20 GW of the 23GW currently existing coal-fired electricity generation" likely to be withdrawn by 2030 (Australian Energy Market Operator 2022; Sharma and Loginova 2024). Moreover, estimates for coal-fired power

TABLE 2. Coal-Fired Power Plant Closure Dates. Source: Company websites.

Company	Power Plant	Original Closure	Revised Closure
Origin	Eraring	2032	2025
AGL	Loy Yang A	2045	2035
AGL	Bayswater	2035	2030–2033

phaseouts have been consistently brought forward since the early 2020s (Hannam 2021).

The story of coal-fired power can be contrasted with that of gas exploration and extraction in Australia. Where activists were able to pressure AGL and Origin to shutter their coal-fired power plants earlier than planned, gas companies (some of which were also coal-fired power station owners) benefited from the full support of the Australian Federal Government in their continued exploration and extraction of gas. This government support was used by corporations in response to activist claim-making calling for companies to cease gas exploration and extraction, an argument that weakened the effectiveness of this activism.

Australia is the world's second largest exporter of Liquid Natural Gas (LNG). In 2021 to 2022, the country exported 83.2 millions tons of LNG worth A$90 billion, representing 14 percent growth per annum over the preceding ten-year period (Geoscience Australia 2024). The country's four largest LNG producers, by market capitalization, are included in this research. In 2022, BHP divested its oil and gas portfolio to competitor Woodside, making it Australia's largest oil and gas company. Woodside's ESG engagement is analyzed here alongside other top Australian LNG companies, Santos, Origin, and AGL, and two of the banks that financed their exploration activities, ANZ and NAB.

Throughout the period studied, Australia's gas majors and their financial backers performed a mimicry of the government's promotion of a gas-led transition to clean energy. This is despite scientific evidence that increased reliance on LNG in place of coal-fired power is inconsistent with Paris targets (Morton and Murphy 2020). When ANZ, one of Australia's largest lenders, was pressed on its continuing support for gas companies in 2019, the company noted "to achieve the goals of the Paris Agreement it is critical to shift to more renewable and low carbon sources of energy." The bank argued, "For natural gas to fulfil its role as a transition fuel, resource development, additional pipeline capacity and market integration are critical." The bank repeated this line of argument in its 2020 communications to shareholders. At the same time, LNG producers were also guarding their balance sheets, Woodside defended its proposed development of new natural gas fields at its 2020 AGM, suggesting that "the proposed Browse and Scarborough projects can contribute to an overall reduction in forecast greenhouse gas emissions globally by displacing higher emissions fuels." The company argued that increases in LNG production should not be compared to clean energy, as while renewables "may offer the cheapest form of electricity," they "can also face physical constraints and grid stability issues." Instead, "LNG is therefore competing with other storable and transportable energy sources, offering a significantly less carbon intensive alternative to coal and oil." John Mikler and Imogen Ryan (2024, 20) argue that the gas sector contributes little in the way of employment, taxes, or investment in the country, but exercises significant "power though extensive lobbying, large donations, and appointments of politicians, their staffers, and bureaucrats." The politics of climate transition was such that companies continuing to explore and extract carbon-intensive forms of energy were able to respond to activist claims to cease these operations by relying on the Australian government's discourse of a transition to renewables that placed gas at the center of energy reliability, affordability, and employment. In return, the Australian Federal Government proactively supported the gas industry, providing subsidies and political cover.

In 2022, Australians voted in the federal Labor Party, a center-left government that had campaigned on a commitment to achieving net zero by 2050, and to implement policies that would support this goal. Many hoped that a change of administration would signal the abandonment of the country's gas-led transition strategy and the shield it provided companies engaged in gas exploration and extraction. However, these companies soon entered into in a new round of discourse, similar to that which had supported their earlier efforts. Instead of focusing on the reliability of the *Australian* energy supply, they highlighted the country's central role in supplying gas to the region. Companies put forward both economic and development arguments for the continuation of gas exploration and extraction in order to continue exports to Australia's largest Southeast Asian trading partners. For example, Woodside noted in its 2021 AGM notice:

> In the Asia Pacific region, only around one third of natural gas is used for power generation with the majority used in other uses, such as industrial, residential or transport applications which can be harder to abate or substitute. For these reasons . . . LNG is expected to remain strong in the Asia Pacific even in Paris-aligned scenario outcomes.

Woodside added, "The governments in Woodside's primary target markets in Japan, China and Korea have all set net-zero targets. We, and their respective governments, consider that the continued use of natural gas forms an important part of their decarbonization pathway."

Woodside also emphasized LNG's role in improving development outcomes in the region. In the same year, the company noted, "In the Asia Pacific region where energy demand is expected to continue to grow strongly, LNG can provide the energy to sustain and advance living standards, with lower emissions of greenhouse gases and local air quality pollutants than other fossil fuels." Despite various companies' counterclaims describing LNG as a transition energy source, vital to development, and in increasing demand, Australia's key gas export markets are all committed to net zero by 2030, or 2050 in the case of China (Hillman 2022). No major export market has announced plans to reduce coal-fired power by replacing it with gas. Instead, demand for gas in Australia's key export markets, including Japan, is predicted to decline rapidly as these countries increase their production of and reliance on green energy. At current rates of extraction, it is predicted that Australian gas producers could face crowding out in key export markets by the mid-2030s (Simmonds and Donnelly 2022).

Other gas majors looked beyond the immediate region for justification to continue LNG exploration and extraction. In 2022, when Russia escalated its military campaign in Ukraine, the International Energy Agency (IEA) released a ten-point plan to reduce global reliance on Russian gas supplies (International Energy Agency 2022). As gas-importing countries looked for alternative markets following the invasion of Ukraine, Australian LNG exports tripled from A$30.5 billion in 2020–2021 to A$92.3 billion in 2022–2023 (Office of the Chief Economist 2023). Santos, one of Australia's largest oil and gas companies, highlighted this in its 2022 notice of AGM, referring to the IEA report's directive to "reduce Europe's reliance on Russian natural gas supplies, including maximizing gas supplies from other sources" as a rationale for pushing back on activist shareholder demands that the company cease developing new oil and gas projects and instead provide a credible commitment to achieving the company's goal of net zero emissions by 2040. Instead, geopolitical instability resulting in Europe and the UK's search for new gas stores lent support to Santos's and Woodside's ongoing gas exploration and extraction plans.

Oil and gas companies were also the only corporations included in this study to dispute the accounting measures used by activists in their responses to claim-making. While other firms may have disagreed with the path to reducing emissions, they publicly supported the scientific basis of activist claims around emissions intensity and reduction. Opposition to claims from LNG majors included Origin refusing to set its "business strategy or emissions targets based on a high-level non-peer reviewed paper" as referenced by activists in their claims on the company. Santos argued activists drew on only one of the IPCC 1.5-degree scenarios in their claims on the company, ignoring those which took into account "any contribution from carbon capture and storage, bioenergy with carbon capture and broader agriculture, forestry and other land use abatement." Santos also included in its 2022 AGM notice its "rejection" that the company had attempted to weaken the methods used to measure methane emissions, and that instead it disagreed with the methods advocated by the Australian Department of Industry, Science, Energy and Resources, nothing that they "lacked accuracy." The Australian government, at the time, was also supportive of companies purchasing carbon offsets and relying on carbon capture and storage to reduce emissions, practices that have been widely criticized as having minimal to negative impact on Australia's emissions reduction (Macintosh et al. 2024). Woodside and Santos leant on this discourse, highlighting their use of carbon offsets and engaging in capture and storage as a central component of emissions reduction.

The gap outlined in this chapter between companies that have responded to activist claims through transparency and credible commitments, and those that remain steadfastly committed to the expansion of emissions-intensive activities continues to widen. As outlined in the section on activist strategies, much of the ESG focus in AGMs is now on the provision of detailed transition to net zero plans. In cases such as Origin, where a company has filed its own resolution detailing a viable and credible transition to net zero plan, investors have been supportive. In 2022, 94 percent of Origin's shareholders supported their company's transition plans. In the same year, a newly revamped AGL board secured the support of 69 percent of shareholders over its climate transition plan. Conversely, Woodside Energy's say on climate vote, explored in the opening chapter, failed to secure majority shareholder support and led to a significant protest vote against Chair Richard Goyder's re-election to the board. Companies that are responding to activist calls for greater transparency and accountability are demonstrating their ability to set a path forward for their companies, and in turn influence the transition to green energy in Australia. Those that resist, of which there are increasingly fewer, are missing an opportunity to set this agenda and thus are more likely to find themselves the subject of either market pressure to reform or a lack of willing financiers or insurers.

Assessing the Effectiveness of Environmental Shareholder Activism

This chapter has explored the evolution of environmental shareholder activism since 2017. It began by highlighting critical junctures in Australia's environmental history, including the 2019 Black Summer megafires and Northern NSW floods. These events lent urgency to the claims activists were making against corporations, that is without government action companies must be responsible for limiting their emissions. These claims were made in both financial and moral terms, in an attempt to target non-activist investors whose concerns are primarily financial. Similarly, any support from proxy advisors or shareholder associations would only materialize in response to material financial risks, of which there are many to heavy emitters, including potential fines, legal action, and the risk of stranded assets. Activists noted in interviews that there was a significant shift in corporate responsiveness over the latter part of the study. One suggested companies began to increasingly engage with them, often in a meaningful way. In a 2020 interview, this respondent noted that there had "certainly been a noticeable development in the last 12 months that there are, there's an attentiveness to what we're asking." Social movement scholars argue that political (and corporate) opportunities change through slow and sticky institutional reform (Kriesi 1995; McDonnell et al. 2015), or through abrupt processes (Della Porta and Kriesi 1999) akin to critical junctures in institutional political theory. Similarly, policy scholars have highlighted the power of valence, or the attractiveness of an idea or concept (R. H. Cox and Béland 2013). The widespread impact of the Black Summer bushfires enhanced the valence of sustainability and pro-climate policy. This chapter argues that this period in Australian environmental and corporate politics was one of rapid political change that saw significant alterations to climate policy by firms, including bringing forward coal-fired power plant shutdowns. This was in spite of a lack of government action on climate change.

Shareholder representatives also noted that their expectations of corporations went beyond adhering to weak or nonexistent regulation. Referring to the spate of natural disasters afflicting Australia, one noted, it is the directors' job to understand these risks and "now we're actually seeing real world costs." They went on to suggest that company directors should be aware that with these disasters comes an increased risk that Australia would move to a mix of energy production that relied less on heavy emitters, noting that they frequently tell corporates, "you should have been able to see that that was happening, and the risk of stranded assets and all that sort of thing. So, we're saying that it is an economic imperative as well."

Ultimately, the framing of issues as presenting a serious risk to corporate profitability led to some successes on the part of activists. From the start of their campaigns, they were able to extract a commitment to greater disclosure by large corporates, predominately because this was a relatively easy ask to meet. As it turns out, this has now been adopted more widely as standard business practice. Activists can also claim some credit for pushing for large corporates to reform industry associations, and at least make attempts at reducing the number of pro-coal and other lobbyists wandering the halls of Australia's parliament. While there is considerable work to be done on bringing all industries along, activists can also claim to have achieved significant success in changing the business model of coal-fired power station operators. In this space, a maelstrom of factors coalesced on the two main players in this area, AGL and Origin, at the same time as Australia was moving to a greener composition of energy production. Both companies were forced to agree to move ahead with plans to close power stations, which in turn offers the potential to significantly reshape the emissions profile of the country. Yet, this success has been tempered by the reluctance of governments to allow this to occur; in the state of New South Wales, the government has intervened to demand power stations be kept online for longer, in turn resorting to underwriting the power station operator, Origin, in order to assist with the inevitable maintenance costs of this prolonged transition. In this sense, the influence of activists is noticeable within the industry, but fails at the level of policy translation.

Lastly, it should be acknowledged that not all industries are experiencing the same combination of economic and societal factors that have made "going green" an appealing model for coal-fired power producers. Oil and gas majors in Australia remain keen to expand their projects, extract new reserves, and generally make the most of the geopolitical situation that has buoyed their industry in the face of climate concerns. Although the "gas-led recovery" rhetoric is no longer being used by the Australian government, gas firms are using similar discursive tools to claim that the world needs Australian gas, in order to develop and to cover the shortfall generated by Russia's invasion of Ukraine. This suggests that activism alone is not sufficient to reform industries, but that when profitability also appears to be threatened through the risks of litigation, fines, and stranded assets, change is indeed possible.

CHAPTER 4
First Nations Voice in ESG

IN 2012, AN EXTRAORDINARY general meeting (EGM) was called by Woolworths Limited in response to a request from activist group GetUp! that the company reprogram its gaming machines to reduce the harm to users by limiting potential losses. At the time, Woolworths, although better known as one half of Australia's supermarket duopoly, held the country's largest share of gaming machine licenses. For context, Australians lose more per capita to gambling, and through gaming machines, than any other nationality (Di Stefano and Hutchinson 2023). The resolution aimed at reducing the persistent harm caused by gaming machines, or "pokies" as they are colloquially known, attracted the support of only 2.5 percent of investors, indicating a lack of non-activist investor interest in the company's social license. It wasn't until five years later, in 2017, that ESG shareholder activists filed another resolution on an Australian listed company calling for action on social, rather than environmental, issues. In that year, ACCR filed resolutions at the AGMs of Oil Search and Woolworths, both over human rights concerns stemming from their operations. From this point onwards, ESG shareholder activists filed few, but regular, resolutions calling for their companies to ensure supply chains free of forced labor, obtain free and prior informed consent from First Nations landowners, and guarantee the rights of workers. Workers' rights were the subject of some of the earliest shareholder activist claims globally, as well as in Australia, where trade unions called on organizations to ensure worker health and safety was seen as central to corporate governance, for fair pay and conditions, and to head off redundancies. Over recent years there have been some notable attempts to hold companies to account over social issues using tools of political investorism including boycotts and divestment campaigns.[1] Yet, when compared with climate change, there have been far fewer attempts to draw the attention of boards, management, and investors to the social issues facing their corporations using the mechanisms of ESG shareholder resolutions (see Table 3).

The experience outlined above aligns with extant scholarship on ESG shareholder campaigns over social issues globally. The literature affirms the fact that social issues are being integrated into business models at a remarkably slower rate than environmental concerns (Pelosi and Adamson 2016). As such, social issues are often referred to as the neglected factor in ESG activism. Since 2017, just eighteen shareholder resolutions have been filed at Australian listed companies' AGMs on social issues. While this shows some activist attention to this broad range of issues, it is significantly less than the number of resolutions filed on the sole challenge of climate change during the same period. Nine of these resolutions relate to the protection of Aboriginal cultural heritage or FPIC, while the remaining resolutions relate to modern slavery or workers' rights, such as wage theft and worker health and safety. Prior to the destruction of Juukan Gorge, the majority of claim-making was focused on workers' rights and human rights. Predictably, following the destruction of the Juukan Caves, from 2020 onwards there was a distinct shift and mining companies BHP, Origin, and Fortescue Metals were all targeted over their engagement with First Nations Australians. Origin Energy, also the subject of multiple climate change resolutions, was the focus of this claim-making with six resolutions filed at its AGMs from 2020 to 2022, all over cultural heritage concerns. Overall, claim-making over the many social issues facing Australian corporations has been minimal when compared to claim-making over climate change. This heavy focus on climate change has shielded companies from scrutiny over relations with their employees and First Nations Australians, cohorts that are heavily impacted by corporate behavior, particularly where mineral, oil, and gas extraction intersects with Indigenous communities.

The lack of attention to social issues is somewhat puzzling, when one considers the origin of ESG shareholder activism and political investorism more broadly. The earliest campaigns waged by investors against their companies were over social issues such as civil rights in the United States, the use of Agent Orange in the Vietnam War, and, most notably, in attempts to isolate the South African Apartheid regime through campaigns for disinvestment and boycotts (MacLeod 2009). Moreover, Australia remains beset by complex social issues, some of which are shared with other liberal democracies, others of which are more uniquely characteristic of the country's settler-colonial history and economy dominated by extractive industries. In addition to companies' need to fully engage in obtaining FPIC, corporate social licenses also hinge on companies' guaranteeing the protection of human rights both in the workplace and in their supply chains (Wilburn and Wilburn 2011). As is occurring elsewhere globally, Australian companies are increasingly being scrutinized over modern slavery and their responsibility for the protection of human rights at all levels of the supply chain (Dinshaw et al. 2022). This issue moved beyond one of private governance or soft law, to public regulation, with the introduction of Australia's *Modern Slavery Act 2018*. As a result of this legislation, large Australian companies are now required to report on their efforts to inspect supply chains at all levels.

This chapter explores ESG shareholder activist claim-making over social issues in the Australian context. Given the country's economic base is heavily reliant on mining, oil, and gas, and that much of the exploration and extraction of these resources takes place on or near First Nations Australians' land, it is unsurprising to see the majority of social claim-making has occurred in this area. The chapter begins by exploring the patterns of social claim-making in Australia, describing the issues, actors, and infrequency of such activism. This then moves on to analyze two cases of ESG activism over FPIC: the first in the Beetaloo Basin, where licenses to extract shale gas have led to a great deal of contestation over the rights of Traditional Owners to stop fracking from occurring; and the second, the more prominent case of the destruction of the Juukan Caves. The latter represents a case where FPIC was not acquired, and it was not until after the event had occurred that the Traditional Owners were joined by the wider community, including investors, in punishing Rio Tinto. The chapter goes on to examine the impact of these cases on regulation, noting in both case studies explored in the chapter that companies are within their legal rights to both commence gas extraction and, in the case of Rio Tinto, destroy these sacred sites. The chapter concludes by examining why social issues are so poorly addressed in ESG activism, with findings that are applicable to settler-colonial societies like Australia as well as more generally. Using the evidence gathered through interviews, analysis of ESG shareholder resolutions, and corporate responses, this chapter argues that while ESG shareholder activism in Australia is undertaken by just two organizations, it is likely that the concentration on climate will continue. Additionally, companies' engagement with Indigenous Australians, and others impacted by their operations, is likely to remain unscrutinized. The narrowness of the Australian market-based activism landscape shields companies from negative attention over social issues. It also leaves the many companies that the two key activist groups do not target free from this form of inquiry. The funding sources of these organizations, their employees, and, importantly, the demographics of the non-activist investors that they target in their campaigns result in an outsized focus on climate change. It is argued that this is because climate change is a predominant and universal issue, whereas First Nations heritage, modern slavery, and asylum seeker rights, whilst well understood, are unlikely to affect this group of activists, their funders, or institutional investors and retail shareholders, and are thus less likely to gain traction with market-based activists. The result is that these important social challenges remain subject to the governance gap discussed in chapter 2 of this book, leaving them deprioritized by investors and proxy advisors who might otherwise have their attention drawn to these issues through market-based activism.

Social Claim-Making in the Australian Context

Social claim-making against companies in Australia originated with attempts to protect workers' rights. As detailed in chapter 1, the early 2000s saw a small series of shareholder resolutions filed by employees and trade unions over the rights of workers. During a period of declining workers' rights, trade unions saw shareholder activism as one way of claim-making against their employers in order to enhance working conditions (Anderson et al. 2007). Claim-making by trade unions included questioning the legality of proposed job losses, seeking the right to collective bargaining, and demands that worker health and safety be considered a core tenet of corporate governance. The latter of these, prioritization of worker health and safety, has been subsumed as a norm of corporate governance. This reflects what was demonstrated in the previous chapter in regards to emissions reporting, whereby activists succeed in pushing an issue onto the political agenda, after which point this norm of behavior becomes an accepted part of "doing business." Similarly to emissions reporting, it is now unthinkable that a corporation would see employee health and safety as anything but central to corporate governance and risk management.

Later in the decade, activists moved beyond claim-making over workers' rights to highlight concerns about companies' human rights records, the potential for modern slavery to permeate supply chains, and, in the case of Qantas, Australia's national airline, complicity in the country's offshore detention regime. In 2017, activists drew attention to Oil Search Limited's (now part of Santos) operations in Papua New Guinea due to concerns about the impact of the company's operations on local communities. ACCR filed a resolution asking Oil Search to guarantee compliance with the United Nations Guiding Principles on Business and Human Rights and the Voluntary Principles on Security and Human Rights (ACCR 2017). Both of these soft law instruments operate as private governance initiatives, whereby companies sign up and self-report under the guidelines provided. They are both part of the transnational ecosystem of market-based activism and provide an opportunity for local activists, such as ACCR, to leverage the membership of these initiatives to pressure companies on their human rights records.

Concurrently, ACCR began filing resolutions at the AGMs of Australia's supermarket duopoly, calling for these companies to examine their supply chain for instances of modern slavery. Forced labor is particularly rife in agricultural and food supply chains, and these two large companies were the subject of claim-making on this matter, where activists viewed a governance gap and the potential for these large companies to lead the way in addressing the issue. In evidence that a deficit existed between societal expectations and regulation, the federal government saw a need to remedy this, consulting widely on a proposed modern slavery law. The Modern Slavery Act (2018) formalizes these requests for large companies operating in Australia to guarantee the absence of forced labor in their supply chains.

In 2018, Australia's largest airline and national carrier, Qantas, was the subject of a uniquely Australian shareholder resolution. Since 2001, the Australian Federal Government has implemented a policy of deporting individuals seeking asylum in the country, sending them to third-party states.[2] This policy, known as "offshore detention," has bipartisan support, despite the known harm caused to detainees and widespread condemnation from human rights groups, civil society, and the United Nations (Barnes 2022). Médecins sans Frontières describes offshore detention as an "undeniably harmful policy with devastating mental health impacts," while Amnesty International says that "detaining asylum seekers offshore is a dead-end policy of cruelty" (Medecins Sans Frointieres 2020; Amnesty International 2024). Yet, the policy has retained support in Australia throughout multiple changes of governments. At various stages it has been promoted by politicians claiming to be "hard on borders," including center-left Prime Minister Kevin Rudd, who strengthened existing rules in 2013, telling those seeking asylum, "If you come by boat you will never permanently live in Australia" (Rudd 2013). The policy has proven appealing to other island nations, with the conservative United Kingdom government battling the country's judicial arm in proposing offshore detention centers be opened in Rwanda to house those seeking asylum in the UK (United Kingdom Home Office 2024). In Australia, offshore detention centers are operated by private and listed companies, and the model has relied on transporting asylum seekers via aircraft to Nauru and Manus Island in Papua New Guinea. Both the detention center operators and the country's national airline, Qantas, have been the targets of ESG claim-making over their culpability in this legally and morally questionable approach to the treatment of those seeking to escape war and political persecution. ACCR filed a shareholder resolution at Qantas's 2018 and 2019 AGMs, calling for the company to cease assisting the Australian government in its policies of offshore detention, which activists argue contravenes international human rights law (Qantas 2018, 2019).

Augmenting this limited claim-making over modern slavery, workers' rights, and offshore detention, the majority of social shareholder activism has been directed at companies and their operations on unceded Indigenous land. Mining's harmful impact on Indigenous communities is well documented, and in Australia, this is where the majority of social shareholder activism has been focused. Many of the social shareholder resolutions filed in Australia mirror the concerns raised by international bodies such as the United Nations, including calling for mining companies to ensure ongoing FPIC for their operations. The United Nations Permanent Forum on Indigenous Issues notes that

> extractive industries, such as mineral, oil and gas extraction, have proven especially problematic and continue to disproportionately impact indigenous peoples. . . . The impact of such projects includes environmental damage to traditional lands in addition to loss of culture, traditional knowledge and livelihoods, often resulting in conflict and forced displacement, further marginalization, increased poverty and a decline in the health of indigenous peoples.

This is clearly seen in Australia, where mining's direct impact on cultural heritage, water security, and dispossession all add to the cumulative harms of colonization that see Aboriginal and Torres Strait Islander Australians worse off than the remainder of the population across almost all measures of health, socioeconomic status, employment, and living standards (National Institute of Health and Welfare 2024). In 2017, the UN Special Rapporteur on the Rights of Indigenous Peoples reported that "it is woefully inadequate that, despite having enjoyed over two decades of economic growth, Australia has not been able to improve the social disadvantage of its Indigenous population. The existing measures are clearly insufficient as evidenced by the lack of progress in achieving the 'Closing the Gap' targets."[3]

While the existing scholarship and the common use of the acronym ESG suggest a clear delineation between environmental and social claim-making, it is worth noting that these issues are not always easy to separate. In many instances it is difficult to partition environmental concerns from social issues. And often, environmental claims accompany those made in regards to FPIC and the protection of cultural heritage. One interviewee noted that while their organization's key focus was on climate change, their remaining "attention was on Aboriginal heritage considerations which happened to be the heavy [carbon] emitters anyway." They went on to give the example explored in this chapter, opposition to Origin Energy's plans to expand its shale gas extraction operations in the Northern Territory, which takes on both an environmental and social dimension. As the interviewee noted, "Given that the consequence of the asks in regards to Aboriginal heritage would be to cease fracking activities it becomes a little bit hard to separate the Aboriginal heritage and the environmental goals." Similar examples exist in relation to protecting water quality from mining activities, which serves to limit environmental impacts but also protects the cultural heritage of surrounding Indigenous communities where water is a central part of culture and spirituality (J. Green and Moggridge 2021). It is thus possible to argue that many environmental claims are simultaneously social claims, however the number of these pales in comparison to the number of claims made on companies solely over emissions disclosure and reduction plans. This is even more striking because social claim-making has been mostly limited to questions of FPIC, which indicates very little attention being paid to other pressing social challenges such as modern slavery in supply chains, workers' rights, and human rights.

Table 3 outlines the social claims made on Australian listed companies between 2017 and 2022. Although it is difficult to draw any conclusions from such a small number of cases, there is a clear emergence of resolutions on cultural heritage and FPIC post the 2020 destruction of the Juukan Caves. With the exception of two resolutions filed at the Scentre Group and Woodside AGMs, all post-2020 resolutions have related to cultural heritage or FPIC, and all were directed at mining companies. Prior to this point in time, resolutions were more heavily skewed toward human rights and modern slavery risks to business, some of which may have been alleviated by the introduction of the 2018 Modern Slavery Act, which, although it only applies to large Australian corporates, captures all companies included in this study.

One of the key differences between the environmental activism studied in the previous chapter, and the social activism outlined here is the presence of GetUp!, an activist organization. GetUp!'s lobbying of Origin Energy over its interactions with First Nations communities is particularly noteworthy given that the other key player in ESG shareholder activism, Market Forces, has a solely climate change remit and does not participate in claim-making on social issues. While Market Forces and ACCR filed 91 percent of all ESG shareholder resolutions in Australia between 2017 and 2023, only ACCR engages with companies on social issues. GetUp!, who in 2020 acquired sufficient shareholdings in Origin Energy to meet the threshold of one hundred individual shareholders, has joined ACCR in lobbying the company over these issues. This follows their 2012 resolution filed against supermarket giant Woolworths, discussed in the introduction to this chapter. Origin's failure to properly consult Traditional Owners over the company's plans to explore and extract shale gas from the Beetaloo Basin was the catalyst for GetUp!'s campaign against the company, which has also faced significant pressure from activists over its emissions profile and the pace of its plans to transition away from coal-fired power. GetUp! has targeted the business on the basis of its impacts

TABLE 3. Social Resolutions. Source: Author's database; ACCR, 2025.

Year	Company	Industry	Content	Lead Filer	Yes Vote (%)
2022	Origin Energy	Oil/Gas	FPIC	GetUp!	6.7
2022	Origin Energy	Oil/Gas	Cultural Heritage	GetUp!	4.4
2021	Scentre Group	Property	Wage Theft Protection	ACCR	withdrawn
2021	Fortescue Metals	Mining	Cultural Heritage	ACCR	15.6
2021	Origin Energy	Oil/Gas	FPIC	GetUp!	11.0
2021	Origin Energy	Oil/Gas	Water	GetUp!	8.4
2021	Origin Energy	Oil/Gas	Cultural Heritage	GetUp!	6.2
2020	Origin Energy	Oil/Gas	FPIC	ACCR	11.8
2020	BHP	Mining	Cultural Heritage	ACCR	7.5
2020	Woodside Energy	Oil/Gas	Corporate Reputation Advertising	ACCR	2.7
2019	Qantas	Aviation	Human Rights	ACCR	23.6
2019	Coles	Retail	Modern Slavery	ACCR	12.8
2019	Origin Energy	Oil/Gas	FPIC	ACCR	5.5
2018	Woolworths	Retail	Modern Slavery	ACCR	14.9
2018	Origin Energy	Oil/Gas	FPIC	ACCR	7.7
2018	Qantas	Aviation	Human Rights	ACCR	6.4
2017	Woolworths	Retail	Modern Slavery	ACCR	15.6
2017	Oil Search	Oil/Gas	Human Rights	ACCR	6.2

on Indigenous communities, culturally significant sites, and access to basic rights such as clean water. As shown in Table 3, ACCR has taken the lead role in social resolutions in every other case since 2017.

The Intersection of Mining and Indigenous Land Rights

Australia's relationship with its First Nations communities remains fraught. As explored in this chapter, the country is still well behind on addressing the gap between Indigenous and non-Indigenous communities in economic, social, and health measures. Globally, attempts to reduce harm from mining and bring benefits to Indigenous communities impacted by mining have been led by international organizations such as the UN. The most widely adopted instrument governing Indigenous rights to emerge from the UN is the United Nations Declaration on the Rights of Indigenous peoples (UNDRIP), which was formalized in 2007. Australia, along with New Zealand, Canada, and the United States, originally refused to support this declaration at the time of its adoption. Australia and other settler-colonial states expressed concern about Article 3 of UNDRIP, which states that "Indigenous peoples have the right to self-determination. By virtue of the right they freely determine their political status and freely pursue their economic, social and cultural development." The concern of some member states was that Article 3 "was a mask intended to legitimize and enable potential secessionist movements or to create new Indigenous states" (Lightfoot 2021, 972). These concerns prevailed despite the UNDRIP guaranteeing that self-determination could not impact the territorial integrity of member states, such as Australia, which has since expressed support for the instrument but has not ratified it domestically.

FPIC is a "specific right granted to Indigenous Peoples recognized in the UNDRIP, which . . . allows Indigenous Peoples to provide or withhold/withdraw consent, at any point, regarding projects impacting their territories" and "to engage in negotiations to shape the design, implementation, monitoring, and evaluation of projects" (FAO 2024). The UNDRIP and its embedded definition of FPIC was adopted by the UN in 2007, but it was slow to spread to the private sector. The International Finance Corporation first included FPIC in its Environmental and Social Performance Standards in 2012. This approach, which seeks the consent of Indigenous peoples while respecting internationally recognized human rights, has since been adopted by the International Council on Mining and Metals (ICMM) and by large mining companies such as those studied in this book (Kemp and Owen 2017). It is generally considered best practice to seek FPIC prior to the commencement of projects and to then update it throughout the mine lifecycle. However, due to the historical lack of FPIC in Australia, many companies find themselves playing catch-up. This is a challenge, particularly because companies that have not sought full and proper FPIC are at risk of losing their social license to operate. Companies face many challenges in obtaining FPIC, including avoiding the exclusion of subsections of the community whose rightful access may have been omitted from records, a mismatch between project and community timelines, as well as methods by which rightsholders can resolve dissenting positions. Many of these problems have arisen in the Australian context and form a large part of the claim-making that takes place at AGMs. They are explored in this chapter.

As noted earlier, the ability of activists to frame social claim-making in financially material terms in order to resonate with investors is key to generating engagement from the investor community. This is particularly the case for social claim-making (as opposed to environmental claims), where the financial risks may need to be more explicitly spelled out to investors. In an interview, a representative of a shareholder association was asked about instances where an activist ESG claim resonated with their organization as also representing a material financial risk to investors. In response, they noted that there were "lots of overlaps" where they had found themselves indicating ESG issues as posing a risk "on a particular investment, or a sector, or even something that's market wide." The same interviewee compared social claim-making to climate change, which they highlighted "started as an issue that NGOs were involved with, and then the financial materiality became apparent." They went on to say that climate change is now systemically recognized as a threat to profitability—and in turn, share price—and that they are seeing this replicated in other areas. Comparing this to activist claims around Indigenous land rights, they highlighted the growing scrutiny companies are under over relations with First Nations Australians. They noted, "There was an ethical outcry in relation to the destruction of the Juukan Gorge but also, you know, actually, it's really clear that that is a financially material issue, not just for that company, but for where there's poor practice across the market," and that this represented a risk to companies' profitability and shareholder returns "if that approach to consultation with First Nations people is continued." As outlined by the interviewee, the intersection of social claim-making and financial impact on firms is the space in which they are most likely to garner the support of institutional investors, including pension funds, and non-activist investors, as well as proxy advisors and shareholder associations. Where activists can demonstrate a threat to returns on investment from a company's failure to meet societal expectations on ESG issues, they are most likely to get a receptive hearing from other actors in the shareholder ecosystem. It is at this point that campaigns for ethical investment gain traction and potentially force change in firms' behavior.

Some challenges to companies' social license to operate, particularly in regards to social issues, are more observable than others. For example, while climate change remains an existential threat to humanity and drastic action is required immediately, there remains a tendency to think of climate change as a long-term problem. Through this lens, we deceive ourselves into thinking we have more time to slow down emissions intensity than we do, and that a technological miracle may allow us to reduce emissions without impacting economic growth and quality of life (Gills and Morgan 2022). This thinking also applies to some social issues, including human rights questions, which can seem existential and too difficult for individuals to solve. Take, for example, the continued popularity of fast fashion amongst consumers, despite its known human rights impacts (Joergens 2006; Stringer et al. 2020). However, there are some issues that cause more immediately visible impacts, such as Rio Tinto's destruction of the Juukan Gorge caves. Here, the decisions of a mining company led to the significant destruction of cultural heritage and evidence of First Nations Australians' long-standing connection to place. The impact of Rio Tinto's actions was highly visible and very immediate. When discussing the destruction of the Juukan Caves, one interviewee highlighted that activism was more effective in these instances of sudden and observable effects, as companies were more receptive to the damage such catastrophes caused their corporation. This was even the case for companies not responsible for the disaster but operating in the same sector. The interviewee noted, "There's nothing like a catastrophe to focus the mind and put resources into these issues." This sense of urgency allows activists to amplify their claim-making on an industry-wide basis, as other firms feel the pressure of the increased attention to their ESG practices and socio-environmental relations. The same respondent went on to compare corporate responses to social issues, such as what occurred at Juukan Gorge, to trying to gain traction over climate change; the latter, they argued, is "a different kind of an issue, because the harm's so cumulative." The interviewee suggested, "Controversy definitely makes our engagements more relevant and immediate for corporate boards and executives." In this sense, while recognizing the enormity of the damage caused by catastrophic events, it is clear that they serve to buoy ESG shareholder activism and turn companies' minds to such issues where activists may have struggled in the past to get these issues onto the corporate political agenda.

Damaging and impactful disasters such as that which occurred in the Juukan Gorge can do more than just encourage industry peers to take ESG issues seriously; they can also catalyze action on other, unrelated issues. When companies are under intense public scrutiny in instances where corporate reputation, legal action, financial penalties, and consequences for the board and management are all possibilities, they may be more likely to acquiesce to activist demands over unrelated concerns. For example, in the immediate aftermath of the Juukan Gorge disaster Rio Tinto was the subject of two climate change shareholder resolutions, one filed by Market Forces and the other by ACCR. In this case, Rio Tinto decided to recommend a vote in favor of the activists' ESG shareholder resolutions, arguing that the company itself saw room for improvement on emissions reduction targets and the need for a review of industry association memberships and their alignment with Paris goals. Activists were not entirely convinced that this sudden support for the company to take more responsibility for its contribution to climate change was borne of internal reflection. As one interviewee noted, the unprecedented decision to support activist claim-making "was a result of the controversy with Juukan George and them [Rio Tinto] just wanting to avoid any scrutiny." Whatever the motivations, this shareholder activist tactic was successful: at the 2021 AGM, 99 percent of shareholders voted in favor of the two resolutions calling on Rio Tinto to implement improved emissions reduction targets. The historically high level of support for these resolutions not only reflects the company directing votes in this manner, but also a feeling amongst non-activist shareholders that their investments were at significant risk of diminished returns due to the actions of the company. One commentator described these as an attempt to "strengthen its environmental, social and governance credentials with investors following a bruising year," after which the company and its investors saw an improvement in approaches to sustainability as fundamental (Toscano 2021b).

While there have been far fewer ESG shareholder resolutions filed over social issues in Australia since 2017, most of these have been aimed at improving the rights of Indigenous communities in relation to corporate activity. This is particularly prescient in cases where business operations overlap with cultural heritage concerns of First Nations Australians. According to industry peak body the Minerals Council of Australia, 60 percent of operating mines are located near to Aboriginal and Torres Strait Islander communities (Minerals Council of Australia 2024). As we shift to a less emissions-intensive future and rely increasingly on renewable energy sources, we are experiencing greater demand for the metals and minerals required for renewable energy production and storage (Kramarz et al. 2021). Critical minerals are central to this transition, and in Australia 58 percent of critical mineral projects lie within formally recognized Indigenous lands, while another 19 percent are subject to open Native Title land claims (First Nations Clean Energy Network 2024). These figures are evidence that the mining, oil, and gas sectors operate at the intersection of social claim-making and the drivers of Australia's economic growth. These relations are explored in this section. The first case, attempts to stop shale gas extraction in the Beetaloo Basin, represents a preemptive attempt to protect cultural heritage in an area where relations between extractive companies and communities have changed over time. The second is the Juukan Caves, already introduced in this book. This case demonstrates the reaction to the wanton destruction of culturally significant sites, which resonated globally and, in the process, highlighted Australia's fragmented legal protections for Indigenous sacred sites, as well as the country's fraught relations with its First Nations inhabitants.

Indigenous Australians and Resource Extraction

Until the mid-twentieth century, relations between Indigenous peoples and mining firms were governed through national or sub-national legal systems. Following the end of World War II, an international legal regime emerged, focused on the guarantee of universal human rights and self-determination, including for Indigenous and colonized peoples (Lightfoot 2021). The component parts of this regime include the Universal Declaration of Human Rights (UNDHR) (1948), the International Covenant on Civil and Political Rights (ICCPR) (1966), and the International Covenant on Economic, Social and Cultural Rights (ICESCR) (1966). All of these aim to provide all peoples with the "right of self-determination" and to "freely pursue their economic, social and cultural development." Yet scholars such as Ciaran O'Faircheallaigh (2023) have detailed how in the decades after these instruments were introduced, Indigenous rights globally were routinely trampled by the interests of corporations, particularly mining firms. This occurred through forcible removal of communities, desecration of sacred sites, exploitative negotiations, and denial of access to basic needs such as clean water (Greaves 2018).

It is against this backdrop that Australia's complex history of poor relations with Indigenous land holders, most of whom have only had their rights recognized in more recent decades, can be explored. It was as recently as 1993 that the Australian Federal Government passed the country's Native Title Act, which recognized that the lands and waterways of the country belonged to its original inhabitants (*Native Title Act* 1993). Thirty years later, in 2023, a referendum that proposed recognizing First Nations Australians in the constitution as the land's original inhabitants and enshrining an advisory voice to parliament was overwhelmingly rejected by Australians, failing to win a majority "yes" vote in any state or at the national level (Parliament of Australia 2023).[4]

While relations between First Nations Australians and the remainder of society remain difficult to reconcile, it is the country's overwhelming reliance on mineral extraction to fuel its strong economic growth that forces this issue to the center of ESG debates. The intersection of the country's mining-led economic growth and the rights of its First Nations peoples now sits at the forefront of corporate governance strategies. This is because Australia's mineral wealth is largely held in rural and remote areas of the country, many of which lie out of sight of most Australians, who reside in its cities and regional areas. The location of mineral reserves and operating mines frequently intersects with First Nations' land and, often, sites that are deemed sacred to Indigenous Australians. The governance of these lands is also complex, and it is sometimes the case that

Aboriginal Land Councils, the legally recognized representatives, do not represent all of the Traditional Owners of a particular site or location. When a company claims that it is consulting with Traditional Owners, this can have multiple meanings. It can mean liaising with either the local Aboriginal Land Council or the many groups of Traditional Owners who have cultural links to a specific site. Potentially, it could mean a combination of both. In fact, best practice FPIC would adhere to this last definition by engaging with the legal rights holders through the Aboriginal Land Council, but also other Indigenous peoples with links to culturally significant sites. This definitional gap, and varying views held by Traditional Owners inside and outside land councils, has been exploited by mining firms aiming to secure permission to mine on Indigenous lands. This is despite the Native Title Act's recognition that Traditional Owners have a "right to negotiate," a right that is often practiced by one group over all others (*Native Title Act 1993*). Furthermore, as Australia has not legislated FPIC by incorporating it into a legal framework, as outlined in UNDRIP, it relies on domestic jurisprudence to implement international best practice to ensure that genuine inclusion and consultation with First Nations Australians is sought prior to decisions being made about Indigenous land (Southalan and Fardin 2019). As this chapter will explore, the divisions in groups over who can provide consent and what occurs when the "right to negotiation" fails to produce a satisfactory outcome to all parties are issues that have attracted the attention of ESG shareholder activists.

Fracking in the Beetaloo Basin

The Beetaloo Basin is located 500 kilometers south of Darwin in the Northern Territory in an area that encompasses Aboriginal land, pastoral leases, cattle stations, and remote Aboriginal communities. The basin sits on an enormous known gas reserve estimated to contain 500 trillion cubic feet of gas, comparable in volumes to the Marcellus Formation in the US (Northern Territory Government 2024). Exploration of the basin began in the 1980s and fracking, or shale gas extraction through hydraulic fracturing of rock, has been planned in the Beetaloo since 2004. Prior to 2022 gas was described by the federal government and industry as a reliable path to transition away from coal-fired power, while simultaneously being pushed as a post-Covid lockdown economic recovery tool. The government of the day frequently referred to Australia's "gas led" or "gas fired" economic recovery, or "gas led transition," as justification for ongoing support for the industry. However, local Traditional Owners and pastoralists, as well as activists, have been vocal in their opposition to shale gas extraction. They have argued that fracking will harm waterways, and in turn agriculture, whilst also impacting local First Nations peoples' connection to country. One Traditional Owner, Ned Jampijinpa Hargraves, described the proposed gas extraction as akin to "digging up my body" and "breaking my Tjukurpa (dreaming)" (R. Pepper 2018, 266).

Beetaloo's Traditional Owners have been negotiating with gas exploration companies since the early 2000s. At the time, community representatives formalized agreements allowing fracking to go ahead. As greater scientific knowledge of the dangers of fracking and the extent of mining that companies planned to undertake this emerged over time, opposition to fracking has grown. Traditional Owners now argue that their elders signed agreements to allow fracking without being provided with information about the potential damage it can cause to waterways and the environment; instead, these risks were downplayed compared to promises of economic opportunity and employment (L. Cox 2023). Community advocates have also noted that in the early stages of negotiation "the nature of fracking projects had been vastly understated" and that when agreements were signed Traditional Owners could "never have imagined fracking on Country would occur at such an enormous scale" (D. Butler 2023). In 2018, the Northern Territory commissioned the independent Pepper inquiry into the socio-environmental impacts of fracking, chaired by the Hon. Justice Rachel Pepper, whom the inquiry was named after. While the response to the report was being prepared by the government, a five-year moratorium into fracking was put in place. This was lifted by the Northern Territory government in May 2023, on the basis that it had satisfactorily responded to all the report's recommendations. This then allowed companies with existing permits to begin extraction. Yet there remains widespread anger about both fracking in the Beetaloo itself, as well as the Northern Territory government's response to the Pepper inquiry. Climate activists have referred to the Beetaloo as a "climate bomb" (Market Forces 2024). At the same time, Traditional Owners have reiterated their claims that permits were not negotiated with fully informed parties, nor were they renewed on an ongoing basis, hence pointing to a failure of companies to engage in FPIC. Recent negotiations with Traditional Owners in the Beetaloo Basin have also been beset by evidence of failure to engage in FPIC as well as the presence of conflicts of interest (L. Cox 2025). Compounding these concerns are the fact that Traditional Owners do not have a veto right over the projects, and that there is significant contestation about who can speak for the multitudes of groups affected by potential fracking in the Beetaloo (Fitzgerald and Spina-Matthews 2023).

Two of the companies included in this study, Origin Energy and Santos, held the permits to explore and extract gas from the Beetaloo. Origin has since sold its interest in the Beetaloo to US-based Tamboran Resources Corporation (Tamboran), in a move that received a mixed response. Critics highlighted that on-selling its interests to Tamboran simply shifted the potential destruction and environmental damage to a third party, and potentially one less receptive to calls for recognition of the need for FPIC due to it being an unlisted, foreign-owned company (ACCR 2022b). On the other hand, supporters of the move noted that this represents an admission by Origin that while they will still negotiate guaranteed offtakes from any production to fuel the company's own needs, the future of gas and fossil fuels more generally is in decline, and the economic viability of the Beetaloo is impacted by the need to protect cultural heritage and the climate (Dick 2022).

The local land council responsible for the Beetaloo Basin, the Northern Land Council (NLC), holds the right to negotiate with gas exploration companies on behalf of local First Nations communities. Yet, as has occurred elsewhere (see Kelly and Behrendt 2007), the NLC has failed over time to capture the breadth of community sentiment in regards to fracking (see the views presented in Australian Senate 2021). The wide-ranging Pepper inquiry found that submissions from Aboriginal people from regional communities almost universally expressed deep concern about, and strong opposition to, the development of any onshore shale gas industry on their country (R. Pepper 2018). While the NLC has been engaged in negotiations for fracking to go ahead, many other Traditional Owners have opposed shale gas extraction. There is a considerable divergence of views between the at least sixty affected Aboriginal nations, within communities and even families. One spokesperson suggested most groups were opposed to gas extraction and believed that the NLC was "just a handful of people that want to frack" (D. Butler 2023). Between 2018 and 2020, Native title holders wrote repeatedly to the NLC and gas exploration companies, highlighting that earlier agreements were not signed in full knowledge of the impact of fracking on the environment and cultural heritage. Eventually, Traditional Owners and Native title holders, who felt their interests were unrepresented by the NLC, attempted to intervene legally in 2020, but were warned off by the NLC, which reminded them that they could be forced to absorb the legal costs of both parties (L. Cox 2023).

These power imbalances are reflected elsewhere globally. Colin Jerolmack's (2021) *Up to Heaven and Down to Hell* narrates similar stories of local landowners' struggles against powerful fracking interests in rural Pennsylvania. Here, powerful companies exploited economic disadvantage and divisions between parts of the community, including between "locals" and city interlopers to develop a booming fracking industry in spite of significant community apprehension. Fracking interests were so successful that even the most ardent opponents found themselves signing over rights to drill on their properties, only for the companies and all the associated financial promises to vanish when the industry went into sharp decline in 2021; this left behind scarring environmental impacts and damage to the area's social fabric inflicted throughout the negotiating process, which pitted community members against one another (Jerolmack 2021).

Underpinning negotiations over fracking in the Beetaloo is the legal reality that Australia's federal Native Title Act does not give First Nations peoples a veto right over mining projects on Aboriginal Freehold Land. Instead, it provides Indigenous landowners with "Right to Negotiate" provisions, which can lead to amendments of conditions in their favor (O'Faircheallaigh 2021). If these negotiations fail to produce an agreed outcome within six months, companies can appeal to the Native Title Tribunal to go ahead with the proposed extraction. These decisions overwhelmingly find in favor of the mining company (O'Faircheallaigh 2021). This incentivizes companies to stall negotiations or offer up sub-satisfactory options in attempts to have permits granted through the legal system. This lack of legal recourse combined with the variation of views amongst Traditional Owners, and between these parties and the NLC, leave windows to opportunity for companies to move ahead with operations that are potentially damaging to cultural heritage, whilst being able to simultaneously claim they have met community demands.

In 2018, ACCR brought these tensions to the attention of Origin, through the company's AGM. As part of this claim-making, ACCR noted that Origin held exploratory and fracking permits on Aboriginal land, in the Beetaloo Basin. Yet, that the 2014 Hawke Inquiry into Hydraulic Fracturing in the Northern Territory and the 2018 Pepper inquiry both found that most, if not all, mining permits in the Northern Territory were obtained without FPIC. In speaking to non-activist shareholders, ACCR framed these concerns in investor-friendly language, noting the potential for reputational risk as a by-product of protest and media attention. Their ask, in this instance, was an internal company review of FPIC by Origin and, if it were found not to have been obtained, a fresh commencement of discussions with Traditional Owners over Origin's rights to frack in the Beetaloo (Origin Energy 2018). ACCR chose to refer to the landholders as Traditional Owners, which reflects the diverse range of concerned parties, in preference to the NLC, a narrower group of representatives that does not appear in its claim-making.

Origin's response to these claims took the form of conflating the Traditional Owners of the Beetaloo Basin with the NLC, something that has been widely disputed and has emerged quite clearly in the opposition to the project (L. Cox 2023). In doing so, Origin attempted to close the corporate opportunity structure available to ACCR by reaffirming its commitment to the rights of Traditional Owners, as negotiated through the "statutory representative body, the Northern Land Council" (Origin Energy 2018, 12). The company went on to list examples of its continuous engagement with the Traditional Owners "undertaken through the NLC." In doing so, Origin noted compliance "with the relevant national and jurisdictional laws" and that the company "goes further and genuinely works towards contributing to regional economic development in the communities" (Origin Energy 2018). It concluded by noting the list of company priorities, which include the protection of human rights, respect and preservation of culture, and avoiding adverse impacts. It is on this basis that Origin refuted the claims made by ACCR.

The disjuncture here between claimant and company is the consultation with local groups over whether these priorities are being met. According to some Traditional Owners, the NLC's priorities are to proceed with fracking albeit whilst also protecting cultural heritage. Other Traditional Owners see their views as being left off the table in this political negotiation.

In 2019, Origin was again petitioned by ACCR, although this time activists focused on the methods by which permits to frack were obtained, highlighting the "substantial length of time which has passed since the permits were obtained by our company's predecessors . . . and the developments in scientific and community understandings of fracking since that time" (Origin Energy 2019). In its response, Origin again emphasized its relationship with the NLC and its tripartite agreement with the Northern Territory Government and the NLC, granting it the rights to undertake exploration in the Beetaloo. The company also highlighted "seven on-country meetings with Native Title holder families," although it is not clear if these families were part of the NLC or those who had raised concerns about the potential for fracking in the Beetaloo (Origin Energy 2019).

In 2021, the company was targeted by activist group GetUp! as well as ACCR, again over the socio-environmental impact of its planned fracking of the Beetaloo Basin. GetUp!, in departing from the approach taken by ACCR and Market Forces, avoided the language of investors in its statement to Origin, instead using the words of Traditional Owners to highlight the impact that fracking would have on Indigenous communities. These shorter, first-person accounts included statements such as "our connections to country have been established and proven time and time again by the white man's law. We hold Native Title and Land Rights—a system that is meant to protect and enforce our rights. These have been denied to us" (Origin Energy 2021). By including the statements provided by affected Traditional Owners, GetUp! introduced previously unheard voices to challenge Origin's claim that its engagement with community represented FPIC.

As it had done in the past, Origin responded by noting its relations with the Northern Land Council, and in 2021 it also acknowledged its compliance with the Northern Territory *Aboriginal Sacred Sites Act 1989*, which states that the company must obtain permission from Traditional

Owners to install fracking wellsites. The company argued that it was abiding by both federal and territory regulation, by consulting with the NLC as well as Traditional Owners over sacred site clearance prior to exploration. The company argued,

> Under our Exploration Agreements, prior to undertaking any activity, work programs are shared with Native Title holders. Native Title holders can choose (and have done so in every case so far) to undertake a sacred site clearance and avoidance survey to understand what work is proposed and where it is located. The purpose of the survey is to allow Native Title holders to be part of decision-making about where activity can or can't take place so the work proposed will have no impact on sacred sites or objects. (Origin Energy 2021)

A year later, the company attempted to clarify why it saw engagement with the NLC as legally sufficient by responding to activist claims with the following statement:

> The Federal Court of Australia has made Native Title determinations over the entire Beetaloo Exploration Project area. The Federal Court determinations set out the Native Title holders, decision makers and the decision-making process for those areas in accordance with the Native Title Act 1993. Native Title holders are those people referred to in the Federal Court determinations who have both the legal and traditional rights to make decisions for those areas. This is distinct from Traditional Owners, who may have decision-making authority under traditional law to their respective Country, but not with regards to the project (Origin Energy 2022).

In its 2022 report to shareholders, Origin noted that as part of its "robust cultural heritage framework" it applied a definition of FPIC that aligned with global governance standards, namely "the definition of FPIC set out in the International Finance Corporation Performance Standard 7 (IFC PS7), which is now also reflected in the Equator Principles" (Origin Energy 2022). Yet, as shown throughout this section, the company relied on a narrow legal definition of rightsholders, engaging only with the NLC, which had long expressed support for fracking to go ahead. This approach provides a distinct section of the community with negotiation rights on behalf of all, in direct contradiction to best practice FPIC.

Adding to the complexity around obtaining FPIC to frack the Beetaloo Basin is the question of historical negotiations. Origin obtained the permits to explore for gas and to frack known reserves in 2014, through its purchase of Falcon Oil & Gas Limited's gas permits (Falcon Oil & Gas 2023). As discussed earlier in this section, these permits were negotiated with Traditional Owners in the early 2000s, when the potential extent of fracking and the damages posed by this form of shale gas extraction were less well known and potentially not effectively communicated to local communities. Under globally accepted standards of FPIC, rightsholders can withdraw their consent at any time, and as it is an evolving and continual process, it must be renewed regularly (FAO 2024). Origin alludes to a lack of renewal when it notes, "Origin carried out a due diligence process prior to acquiring its interest in the permits and was comfortable that written consent to the exploration activities was given by the Native Title holders and claimants" (Origin Energy 2021). Yet, it has become clear in the time since that these original negotiations have framed future engagements with rightsholders and that wide-ranging consultation has not occurred.

Over time, Origin's communications with investors and activists included more guarantees that it understood and was seeking FPIC from Traditional Owners, yet it continued to rely on negotiation in only the narrowest legal extent, and ignored the incomplete information provided to the original signatories to these agreements. Ultimately, a combination of market forces, sustained activist and media pressure, and an acceptance of changed societal expectations led to Origin selling its interests in the Beetaloo Basin. The company, however, did not fully reject Beetaloo's gas supplies. In order to guarantee future gas supply, Origin's sale included offtake guarantees from the new owner, Tamboran. Following the lifting of the Northern Territory fracking moratorium, Tamboran has indicated the company will commence extraction as soon as it reaches a final investment decision, and is granted approval from the Northern Territory's Environment Protection Authority (Fitzgerald and Spina-Matthews 2023). This follows a deal between the Northern Territory government and Tamboran to supply the Northern Territory's power generators with gas for the next nine years, through a contract that was not put to competitive tender (Morgan 2024). Tamboran remains under significant activist pressure to abandon these plans, which have been the subject of ongoing legal challenges (Fitzgerald 2024). However, with the full support of the

Northern Territory government and in the face of global gas shortages due to Russia's invasion of Ukraine, it looks unlikely that these concerns will be heeded.

Rio Tinto: A Missed Critical Juncture

In May 2020, Rio Tinto destroyed a series of sacred rock shelters in the Juukan Gorge, in Western Australia's Pilbara region, in order to expand its Brockman 4 iron ore mine. In doing so, the company desecrated a site that represented 46,000 years of continuous civilization for the Puutu Kunti Kurrama and Pinikura (PKKP) Traditional Owners (Wahlquist 2020). Rio Tinto simultaneously exposed the limitations of Australia's Native Title Act, namely its inability to protect First Nations Australians' culturally significant sites. Outrage at the incident was widespread, both locally and internationally. A parliamentary inquiry launched shortly after the incident labeled the destruction as "not just a loss for the PKKP peoples, but it is a loss for the nation, and the world as a whole" (Parliament of Australia 2020). Condemnation was swift, including from Federal Environment Minister Tanya Plibersek, who compared Rio Tinto's actions with that of the Taliban's destruction of the Bamiyan Buddhas in Afghanistan (McGuirk 2022). Yet, Rio Tinto had what its management viewed as a seemingly sound defense. The company's actions that day were legal; in fact, Rio Tinto had adhered to the requirements for consultation with Traditional Owners outlined in both Western Australia's *Aboriginal Heritage Act 1972* and the Federal *Native Title Act 1993*. While the Native Title Act had acknowledged the local PKKP peoples as the rightful owners of the land, with non-exclusive rights in 2015, this was trumped by earlier agreements based on negotiations between the company and the land council originally given rights over the area, the Yamatji Marlpa Aboriginal Corporation (E. Ho 2022). These agreements formed the basis of Rio Tinto's application under the *Aboriginal Heritage Act 1972* (Western Australia) to impact the rock shelters in order to expand the mine. Since 2015, the PKKP had been given the right to negotiation with Rio Tinto over the protection of culturally significant sites; however the decision to grant permission for the blasts occurred before this was recognized, and as such, it was overruled by the state's legal system, which in this case favored the interests of capital over the acknowledged First Nations land holders.

Widespread condemnation emerged from First Nations' advocates in Australia and beyond, investors, and the media. Australia's Indigenous Affairs Minister Ken Wyatt labeled the actions "incomprehensible" (Young and Toscano 2020). Among those outraged by these events were the company's shareholders, who not only held moral concerns about the actions of Rio Tinto, but also saw the potential for the reputational damage caused by the incident to impact the value of their investment. ESG shareholder activists saw a window of opportunity for mobilization, both at the industry and company level. Using their existing network of relations with shareholder organizations, proxy advisors, and institutional investors, ACCR shared its concerns in a briefing with "institutional investors accounting for well over $20 trillion in assets under management" (Australasian Centre for Corporate Responsibility 2020b). Together with pension funds AustralianSuper, HESTA, and Cbus Super, ESG shareholder activists voiced their concerns over not only the original incident, but also about Rio Tinto's governance structures that oversaw relations with First Nations communities, on whose land the company operates (Knight 2020).

Rio Tinto's initial response was to strip CEO Jean-Sébastien Jacques and two other senior executives of A$7 million worth of bonuses in recognition of their responsibility for the company's actions. This proposal was met with condemnation from investors, including large pension funds UniSuper, AustralianSuper, and HESTA, which threatened to vote against the re-election of key executives. These funds were joined by one of the two main proxy advisory firms, ISS, which also demanded a stronger response from the company (Ker 2020; Toscano 2020). Investors were encouraged by activists, such as ACCR, who were contributing to the debate both privately and publicly. ACCR's Legal Counsel and Strategy Lead James Fitzgerald noted that Rio Tinto's initial response of a Board Review represented "an appalling indictment of how Rio Tinto truly values cultural heritage. Investors who have condemned this destruction must continue to hold Rio to account. Tens of thousands of years of cultural significance get blown up and all that goes to show for it is A$7 million of lost remuneration" (ACCR 2020a). Indeed, shareholders did continue to pressure the company.

By September 2020, investor pressure had reached a tipping point, with Jacques, Head of Iron Ore Chris Salisbury, and Head of Corporate

Relations Simone Niven all departing the company by mutual agreement (Chau and Janda 2020). At the time, ACCR celebrated the coordinated efforts of various market actors in bringing about consequences for poor corporate behavior, with Fitzgerald noting, "Shareholder democracy and investor action is alive and well in Australia. Corporate captains may think twice before attempting to mislead investors, not to mention a Parliamentary Inquiry, in future" (ACCR 2020b).

The fallout continued into 2021 at the company's AGM, ahead of which it was revealed that the three departing executives were entitled to significant payouts, or "golden handshakes" as they are colloquially known. The company defended the payouts. Independent director Sam Laidlaw noted that "the board had to balance a number of factors including that there was no deliberate act or omission to act by the three executives" and that the executives could not reasonably be expected to "recognize and remediate systemic weaknesses in the heritage risk management process" (B. Butler 2021). Investors were not convinced. At the May AGM, encouraged by both main proxy advisory firms ISS and CGI Glass Lewis, 61 percent of all shareholders rejected the company's remuneration report, and in turn vetoed the departed executives' golden handshakes (Rio Tinto 2021). Although an ESG shareholder resolution was never filed at Rio Tinto's AGMs, activists worked together to pressure the company to respond to the destruction of this culturally significant site, the impact on First Nations communities, and the reputational damage caused to the company.

The impacts of this campaign were felt beyond Rio Tinto. In an example of scale shifting, activists mobilized around this destructive event. In 2020, ACCR filed a resolution ahead of the BHP AGM demanding the company avoid a repeat of Rio Tinto's actions. ACCR's ask of BHP was to go beyond its legal requirements under Western Australian law and the Native Title Act to adopt a moratorium on any activities that would damage cultural heritage sites and commit to nonenforcement of any contract that would not allow Aboriginal or Torres Strait Islander Traditional Owners the right to speak publicly about cultural heritage concerns (ACCR 2020a). This resolution was withdrawn ahead of the meeting, after BHP met activists' demands through an agreement with the First Nations Heritage Protection Alliance, a coalition of more than twenty Aboriginal and Torres Strait Islander organizations across Australia (BHP

2020b). Then, in 2021, ACCR filed a shareholder resolution at the Fortescue Metals AGM calling for the company to lobby the Western Australian government to enhance legal protection of culturally significant sites. At the time, the government was under significant pressure from industry to retain the legal status quo that had allowed the blasts to proceed.

In the weeks following the destruction of the Juukan Gorge caves, the Western Australian government came under immense pressure over the weakness of its cultural heritage laws. Criticism came from Aboriginal and Torres Strait Islander activists, the media, and the wider population. The *Aboriginal Heritage Act 1972* (Western Australia) had been the focus of criticism since its inception for its failure to protect culturally significant sites, and work had been underway to reform the Act well prior to the destruction of the Juukan Caves (Thomson and Dortch 2022). The government's "Avery Review," held between 2012 and 2014, called for three stages of public consultation over reform to the outdated 1972 Heritage Act. The first two rounds of consultation appeared meaningful in their approach. But a 2020 draft bill presented to the public attracted widespread criticism, after which the government reverted to "limited, selective, and opaque consultation" (Thomson and Dortch 2022, 22). In 2021 a final bill was presented to parliament just a few days prior to the vote (Towie 2023). The new legislation was notably varied from the one presented for public consultation and also appeared not to include the recommendations from the Juukan inquiry's interim report (Thomson and Dortch 2022). Yet it passed into legislation without opposition in 2021, briefly coming into effect in November 2023. In the intervening period, it became obvious that the reform was highly unpopular with stakeholders. The desecration of the Juukan Caves and the ensuing outrage had led to the rushed implementation of the *Aboriginal Cultural Heritage Act 2021* (WA); the speed and the associated lack of consultation with which this came about would ultimately spell the failure of legal reform in this area. The new act was described by the incoming West Australian Premier as "divisive, confusing and stressful for landowners" in a pre-election pitch to voters to repeal the law (Towie 2023). The laws were equally unpopular with Aboriginal rights groups, because the final determination over heritage rested with the state's Aboriginal Affairs Minister.

There had been growing concern about the new legislation from the time it passed parliament in 2021. Pastoralists described the laws as overreach that "paralyzed them with fear" over the requirement to engage in "costly cultural heritage checks prior to development" (Towie 2023). Farmers groups publicly lobbied for the repeal of the laws, calling them "poor and unpopular" and noting that the short-lived enactment should send a warning to other states considering similar legislation (Thompson 2023). Mining companies were more circumspect in their public announcements, instead preferring to lobby behind the scenes against the new laws, which they claimed would add significant costs to the development of new mines (Thompson 2023). It was on this basis that the Western Australian government repealed the legislation just five weeks after its implementation (Maloney 2024). While the updated legislation was described as a "basket case" and an unsurprising outcome of a government with near full parliamentary control rushing through poorly debated legislation, the decision to rescind the legislation failed to protect cultural heritage (Towie 2023). Much to the disappointment of Aboriginal advocates, the reversion to 1972 legislation once again plunged the state into a pre-Native title rights era, where Indigenous Australians are treated as second-class citizens and their cultural ties are deprioritized behind economic gain.

Prominent Indigenous Australians referred the Western Australian Government to the United Nations Committee on the Elimination of Racial Discrimination (CERD) over the failure to consult on the revised legislation, one of the reasons suggested for its short-lived nature (Maloney 2024). The referral also noted that the decision to reinstate the 1972 laws, which permitted the destruction of the caves, was undertaken without consulting Aboriginal Australians, in direct contravention with the federal government's commitment to the elimination of racial discrimination (Environmental Defenders Office 2020). Yet, the 1972 Act remains in place as the key regulatory mechanism to protect Indigenous sites in Australia's largest state. As the federal government inquiry into the destruction of the Juukan Caves notes, the Act, which continues to govern Indigenous relations in Western Australia, "played a critical role in the destruction of the shelters" and "failed to protect Aboriginal Heritage, making the destruction of Indigenous heritage not only legal *but almost inevitable*" (emphasis the author's own) (Parliament of Australia 2020).

It is clear that activist pressure on large, prominent corporations has done little to improve regulation of private economic activity and its impacts on culturally sensitive sites. The Northern Territory government, which agreed to an offtake deal with the new owners of Origin's gas permits, and the Western Australian government, which bowed to pressure from mining companies and pastoralists to roll back greater protection for culturally significant sites, have demonstrated that societal pressure is no match for economic reality and the power of Australia's mining sector. Yet, we do have evidence of this pressure forcing change at the industry level. In the aftermath of the destruction of Juukan Gorge, one of the companies that bore pressure from activists was BHP. Their response suggests that industry change may be possible in the absence of legal reform, as in the case of climate change.

> BHP agrees that legislative reform is required but it has not waited for such reform to occur. For BHP, the current legislative framework is only a starting point. BHP's policies, practices and agreements with Indigenous peoples well exceed the legislative framework. The Company's policies, practices and agreements focus on consultation, negotiation, partnership making and formal, mutually beneficial agreements. BHP's approach is to agree with Traditional Owners how cultural heritage is to be managed. One way that we achieve this is through land use agreements developed in partnership with Traditional Owners. (BHP 2020a)

Unlike Origin and Rio Tinto's approach, BHP consults a wider array of actors beyond simply the local land council and has agreed not to impact any culturally significant sites—and not to seek permission under existing heritage laws to do so. In 2020, BHP noted:

> All of BHP's Western Australian mining agreements with Traditional Owners identify the areas of special heritage significance to Traditional Owners (referred to as "exclusion zones"). These exclusion zones include areas where the parties agree that no mining activities will occur and other areas that are afforded special protections. BHP has never sought a government approval to impact an exclusion zone. The Heritage team is complemented by an Indigenous Engagement team, which is responsible for ensuring the right levels of engagement with Traditional Owners and other Indigenous stakeholders at all levels of the Company. BHP's approach has resulted in BHP's Western

> Australia Iron Ore business undertaking, in conjunction with the Traditional Owners, over 4,300 days of heritage field work covering 267,000 hectares. At the South Flank project, BHP has undertaken over 700 days of heritage survey work. (BHP 2020a)

The commitments made by BHP suggest there is room for mineral extraction and the associated economic benefits, alongside the recognition and protection of Aboriginal cultural heritage. It also indicates that companies can move beyond weak or outdated regulatory frameworks to develop their own governance procedures.

The response to the destruction of the Juukan Caves points to a governance gap. The widespread outrage was reflected by investors in the form of a campaign against the management of Rio Tinto, mirroring societal concerns over weak regulation governing corporate practices. The case also demonstrates the ability of ESG shareholder activism, and political investorism, to address serious concerns about corporate behavior with significant penalties applied to board members deemed responsible for the destruction. Until this point, there had been several shareholder resolutions filed in regards to companies' approach to human rights, modern slavery, and workers' rights, yet these were largely disjointed and ad hoc in nature. Very little social activism has taken place over FPIC and cultural heritage in the wake of the destruction of the Juukan Caves. The case of Juukan Gorge can be viewed as a missed opportunity for activists to shift toward a serious focus on social claim-making and a coordinated and sustained campaign of activism over First Nations land rights, akin to what took place over climate change. While activists had been lobbying companies, including through shareholder resolutions, for some years on their relations with First Nations communities, the widespread condemnation of Rio Tinto and the shock that this act had in fact been legal represented the potential for a turning point in the expectations of companies operating on culturally significant sites. Instead, the power of the mining lobby was such that only temporary law reform emanated from this activism, and a sustained campaign opportunity has been missed.

Explaining the Missing *S* in ESG

This chapter has explored two prominent cases of social claim-making in the Australian context, both concerned with matters of Aboriginal land rights and mining. In both cases, activists had targeted large, listed corporations over their engagements (or lack thereof) with the Traditional Owners of the lands on which the companies held mining permits or operated mines. Engagement with Australia's Indigenous population is a crucial and important issue for mining companies, business more generally, and Australian society—however it is far from the only social challenge to corporations. Recognition of the importance of these other social challenges is missing from the Australian experience. As this chapter has explored, there has been little sustained pressure on companies to improve their relations with workers or the communities in which they operate. Many issues appear to be missing from the investor-political agenda, and this section explores the potential reasons for these omissions.

As shown in Table 3, there have been a total of eighteen social claims made on Australian companies through AGM shareholder resolutions since 2017. Voting patterns on these, a reflection of non-investors' rating of the importance of these issues, closely resembles the voting outcomes on environmental and climate resolutions. In fact, remarkably so. The average support for all ESG shareholder resolutions filed since 2017 is 15.8 percent. Breaking this down into *E* and *S* resolutions makes no discernible difference; social issues have garnered an average "yes" vote of 15.1 percent, while environmental claims attract an average of 15.8 percent. This is even more surprising when you consider the only resolutions to have received the backing of the board, and as a result an extremely high "yes" vote, have been related to corporate approaches to the climate. As shown in Table 3, there are a handful of climate-related shareholder resolutions with high votes due to either widespread frustration with the company, or where the company has supported or filed the resolution themselves. There are no such instances over social issues. Support for social resolutions peaks in the wake of the Juukan Gorge disaster. This is not surprising. We would expect investors to be motivated by both moral and financial concerns over mining companies' relations with Indigenous Australians in the wake of the widely published destruction and corporate aftermath explored in this chapter. An investor's choice to vote "yes" on a resolution calling for their company to engage in full and proper FPIC may be a way for institutional investors and retail investors to protest what they saw as the unnecessary destruction of culturally significant sites. It also may be that investors see a material financial risk in their company repeating similar behaviors, leading them to demand that leadership demonstrate effective governance systems and a commitment to avoid this at all costs. It also may be a combination of both: an expression of moral concern accompanied by an acknowledgment of the potential for financial consequences.

As noted in the introduction to this book, the filing of shareholder resolutions is the end point of a spectrum of activism, much of which is not visible. In this sense, one could argue that the low number of social resolutions could be masking greater behind the scenes engagement (although the same thing could be said about climate change, which is still the overwhelming focus of most ESG shareholder resolutions). One rationale for fewer social resolutions, particularly over the issue of FPIC and cultural heritage, may be a reluctance of activists to speak for Indigenous populations by both ACCR and GetUp!, the two organizations active in this space. ACCR has a social impacts team that focuses on workers' rights; First Nations issues, particularly around extractive companies; cultural heritage and land rights; and other human rights issues, including race and gender and how those issues play out across major Australian listed companies. Yet, we see little evidence of this in the public claim-making that ACCR does. One potential driver of this is an organizational aim to create an opportunity for Indigenous voices to be heard. ACCR notes that it "seek[s] to create space for First Nations groups to effectively engage with companies and investors" (ACCR 2022a, 12). This represents a very different approach to ACCR's climate work, where the organization directly engages with companies as an active investor. This may be why so few FPIC or cultural heritage resolutions are filed, magnified by Market Forces' absence due to its sole focus on climate change. ACCR's approach allows First Nations groups the ability to work to protect country and their relationships with the mining companies that operate on their land. Unlike in the climate space, where a public campaign followed by a high non-activist investor vote signals success, examples of success in cultural heritage might mean a withdrawn or not-filed resolution, or an agreement between a Native title body or a group of Traditional Owners and a company to preserve a culturally significant place.

Similarly, GetUp!'s work on cultural heritage also demonstrates a recognition that activists' voices may not be the most appropriate vehicle for pressing claims over FPIC. In their submissions to Origin's AGM they take a very different approach to other professional investor activists, who speak the language of shareholders and companies in an attempt to place themselves on parallel with other financial actors, and appeal to their profit motive. Instead, GetUp! uses first-person accounts from First Nations Australians over the impact fracking would have on their connection to country, as well as the environment that they have been custodians of for tens of thousands of years. This approach uses emotive language in preference to more formal financial terms.

While this rationale for the lower-than-expected number of resolutions on cultural heritage may go some of the way to explaining the lack of attention from activists on social issues, it fails to fully explain the significant gap between the number of climate change and non-climate-change campaigns. As noted by one activist, "The issues that get the greatest attention from us are climate and environment issues, mostly climate, decarbonization related and lobbying, the effective corporate political lobbying on climate policy." This is reflected in the fact that 83 percent of all ESG shareholder resolutions filed in Australia between 2017 and 2022 were focused on climate change.

More closely examining the remit, funding, and personnel of activist organizations and, importantly, non-activist investors may shed more light on the lack of social resolutions filed in Australia. Significantly, Market Forces' remit is solely to focus on climate change. Its funders and personnel direct all of their resources to this particular social issue. Given the duopolistic nature of ESG activism, removing one key actor from the field leads to a significant loss of avenues for claim-making. Secondly, while the remaining organizations, ACCR and to a lesser extent GetUp!, do have First Nations representation in their organizations, they are on the whole more reflective of non-Indigenous, middle-class Australia. That is, most activists and financial backers are university-educated, white-collar professionals, for whom climate change is the most universal challenge society faces. This prioritization may be argued to be accurate, but there is no clear reason why climate change could not be addressed *alongside* social issues. By extension, while climate change is an ever-present threat, for most activists, modern slavery or workplace rights are not part of their lived experience. In this sense, it becomes difficult to prioritize these issues in the same way the climate is treated.

More important than the make-up of activist organizations and their funders is their target audience. Here again it is most likely that climate change is considered of great importance and an existential threat to humanity. Without disagreeing with this perspective, it is worthwhile to note that corporate executives, board members, representatives of institutional investors, proxy advisors, shareholder organizations, and ordinary investors are again less likely to feel personally impacted by modern slavery, workers' rights, or cultural heritage claims (PwC 2023; Diversity Council of Australia 2024; Governance Institute of Australia 2024). For example, when former Western Australian Treasurer Ben Wyatt was appointed to the Woodside board in 2021 (and the Rio Tinto board later that year), he was the only Indigenous board member of any ASX 200 company (Australian Institute of Company Directors 2023). As of 2024, there are just five Indigenous board members of ASX-listed companies. Given the lack of diversity in Australian corporate governance, it is unsurprising that climate change remains prioritized as the most significant societal challenge. However, what is notable is the *de-prioritization* of social challenges, which remain a central part of Australian political-social relations.

There are relatively very few social claims made on Australian companies, despite the myriad of issues faced by workers, asylum seekers, and First Nations Australians. Given the intersection between Australia's mining industry and its First Nations peoples, it is unsurprising that the focus of the few socially guided resolutions has been on cultural heritage and the acquisition and maintenance of a social license to operate. The cases of fracking in the Beetaloo and the destruction of the Juukan Gorge caves demonstrate that while there is some evidence of activist success in forcing change at the industry level, as in the case for the climate, regulation lags. This governance gap remains a key driver of social activism, particularly where Aboriginal heritage is concerned. Finally, the chapter provides some explanations for the lack of social claim-making in Australia, including activists' determination to make space for Indigenous voices but also the characteristics of activists, their funders, and their targets—for whom climate change remains society's greatest threat.

CHAPTER 5
A Global ESG Backlash?

THE FINAL CHAPTER OF this book examines the implications of the key research findings for other liberal market economies where listed companies face similar ESG challenges, including the US, EU, and UK. Unlike in Australia where systematic ESG shareholder activism has been short-lived, these jurisdictions have a long history of investor activism. As ESG activism is transnational in nature, many of the institutional investors and proxy advisors engaged in or responding to ESG claim-makin, operate globally. This chapter begins by sketching the transnational ecosystem of market-based actors engaged in ESG investing, highlighting the contestation around norms of business behavior. The chapter goes on to examine two areas in which the Australian experience provides lessons for other liberal market economies. The first of these is the impacts of attempts to legislate against investor voice, and the second is the challenges faced in settler-colonial states, where the intersection of environmental and social concerns is inescapable.

Around the world, listed companies face increasing pressure from shareholders, activists, and regulators to respond to ESG issues. Engagement, including through ESG shareholder resolutions continues to grow, with the number of resolutions increasing 4.6 percent globally from 2022 to 2023. Much of this growth occurred in the United States, where 550 companies were targeted by investor activists in 2023, representing an 8 percent increase compared to 2022 (McAllister 2024). Canada has also seen growth in ESG shareholder resolutions compared to previous years, whereas European countries have seen a decline, thought to be related to the war in Ukraine reprioritizing investors' focus (McAllister 2024). In these jurisdictions the majority of claim-making emerges from long-term stewards of capital, or investors who see themselves as universal owners. That is, they are first and foremost investing in companies for financial gain, however they also perceive opportunities for companies to improve their socio-environmental performance (Katelouzou and Klettner 2022). These large institutional investors, such as pension funds or sovereign wealth funds, hold diversified portfolios that are representative of a significant portion of the global economy. They are considered "universal owners" because their investments span multiple sectors, industries, and geographic regions. They therefore have no interest in one company increasing its valuation by risking bringing an entire industry into disrepute through, for example, poor environmental practices. This is very different to the Australian model, which emerges due to the difficulties in filing shareholder resolutions and the small ecosystem of investors, despite the relatively large size of the market. In this case, investors buy into companies in order to lodge ESG shareholder resolutions, becoming "unnatural insiders," a reference to the social movement scholarship that places actors as either insiders or outsiders for the purposes of collective action (O'Brien et al. 2023). Globally, claim-making on corporations addresses a broad range of social and environmental challenges facing society (Barko et al. 2022, 778). Given the much longer history of ESG claim-making and larger pool of investors and activists in jurisdictions such as the US, UK, and EU, it is unsurprising that companies operating in these locations are lobbied over a much wider array of issues, including climate change and human rights, but also animal rights, forestry practices, corruption, genetic engineering, and biodiversity (Barko et al. 2022).

The upward trend in ESG claim-making globally not only reflects growing demands by domestic actors on corporations, but is also driven by a transnational movement or ecosystem of diverse actors that "provide both normative and practical support for the global dissemination of ESG stewardship" (Bowley and Hill 2024a, 237). This ecosystem consists of non-state actors including institutional investors, NGOs, investor bodies, and service providers (such as proxy advisors) that support institutional investors, international institutions, and inter-governmental agencies. Contrary to much of the literature, which assumes institutional investors are reticent to involve themselves in the ESG affairs of companies, Tim Bowley and Jennifer Hill (2024a) find that institutional investors have instead been shown to work closely with other actors in this transnational ecosystem. This suggests a potential for greater convergence and harmonization of ESG stewardship and activism across global markets. This transnational ecosystem disseminates global norms of business behavior through its reach into multiple markets via private governance initiatives, standards, and cross-border anti-corporate activism. However, at other times it presents challenges to corporations attempting to meet competing demands from pro- and anti-ESG jurisdictions in which multinational corporations operate in simultaneously. The next section explores the transnational nature of ESG shareholder activism and its impacts on corporate behavior. The chapter then moves on to examine two areas in which Australian ESG shareholder activism provides potential comparative lessons for similar jurisdictions: firstly, by comparing regulators' attempts to legislate to limit investor voice in Australia and some US states; and secondly, by examining the similarities between settler-colonial societies and their relations with First Nations peoples, a common target of ESG activism globally.

Transnational ESG Activism

Investor ESG stewardship and activism is not solely a domestic phenomenon influenced by local market imperatives and regulations. While local factors certainly drive investor activism, ESG activism is also a by-product of a transnational ecosystem of market-based actors characterized by their interconnected nature. Institutional investors sit at the core of this ecosystem, operating alongside proxy advisors, activists, and shareholder organizations to engage with companies over ESG concerns. When companies are lobbied by particular institutional investors over ESG issues, it is likely that they are reckoning with not only that fund manager but "the outworking of complex, often unseen, interactions occurring among multiple organizations within the global ESG ecosystem" (Bowley and Hill 2024a, 251). As a result, it can be argued that the content of ESG claim-making is not limited to local market factors or company-specific issues, but is also reflective of global norms of corporate behavior projected onto companies through a range of global and local actors (Elbra et al. 2025). The intensity and extent to which global norms of behavior impact individual firms can be directly linked to levels of foreign ownership in a given market. In markets with significant offshore institutional investment it is more likely that companies will be exposed to macro-level claim-making, which reflects international trends, compared to smaller inward-looking markets with high levels of domestic ownership and investment (Bowley and Hill 2024a). ESG activism in one jurisdiction, such as Australia, has the potential to influence the global ecosystem of ESG actors through the projection of activists' concerns into other markets. As Ronald Gilson and Jeffrey Gordon (2013) note, there is ample evidence to suggest that institutional investors are willing to join activists and ethical funds in lobbying their companies to improve corporate behavior. It is clear that this is not limited by borders or geographical regions, as the examples provided in this chapter demonstrate.

The transnational ecosystem of ESG actors consists of global governance initiatives, institutional investors, professional activists, and proxy advisors with global reach. The first of these, governance initiatives promoted by international organizations, have played a central role in the spread of ESG standards, stewardship norms, and business practices. The most notable of these is the UN and its corporate sustainability initiatives, the Global Compact, and later the UNPRI. Launched in 2000, the Global Compact currently has more than twenty thousand corporate members who have committed to principles of sustainability in their business operations (United Nations Global Compact 2024). The Global Compact has been used strategically by the UN, which has leveraged its large membership "to involve the private sector in advancing human rights and global sustainability" (Bowley and Hill 2024a, 238). By calling on CEOs and business leaders to consider ESG issues in their business operations, the UN, through the Global Compact, disseminates new approaches to corporate conduct that prioritize sustainability and human rights alongside profitability.

Membership of the Global Compact also includes fund managers, who are encouraged by the UN to evaluate the ESG performance of their companies and push management to meet improved sustainability metrics. Drawing on the intersection between ESG concerns and financial materiality that is a consistent theme throughout this book, asset managers are reminded that unmet ESG challenges pose a risk to valuations (Pargendler 2020). The UN, through the Global Compact and later the UNPRI, has also formed investor alliances including the Net-Zero Asset Owner Alliance, and a parallel scheme for fund managers, the Net-Zero Asset Manager Alliance; membership in these alliances commits owners and managers of funds to achieve net zero in their funds through either steering capital (owners) or lobbying companies (managers) through ESG engagements. Although, as discussed later in this chapter, these initiatives have fallen afoul of the Trump-era anti-ESG rhetoric in the US and have since curtailed their activities. Nonetheless, these transnational initiatives were designed to pressure companies across the globe to reduce emissions and simultaneously influence regulation of ESG stewardship. Another area over which the UN has sought to influence fund managers is questioning existing definitions of fiduciary duty and their treatment of ESG issues. Fiduciary duty refers to the responsibility of boards, managers, and investors to act in the "best interests" of the company and its shareholders. Over time the concept of best interests has evolved through the types of contestation explored in this book, where there is tension between financial concerns and impacts on other stakeholders, or ESG issues. Traditional, narrow definitions of fiduciary duty, which consider only profitability and returns, are often relied on by anti-ESG advocates to argue that directors, investors, and managers are legally bound to focus only on financial metrics. This limited definition has been challenged by the UN, amongst others. In 2019, the UNPRI, the United Nations Environment Programme Finance Initiative, and advocacy group Generation Foundation released a report contesting the traditional interpretation of fiduciary duty, which focused on profit over all other concerns. The report concluded that institutional investors *are required* to take ESG considerations into account in their decision-making, dispelling "the all-too-common misunderstanding" that fiduciary duties are limited to value and profit maximization only (UN Environment Programme Finance Initiative 2005, 3). It also noted that "failing to consider long-term investment value drivers, which include environmental, social and governance issues, in investment practice" actually represents a "failure of fiduciary duty" (UN Global Compact, UN Environment Programme Finance Initiative, and PRI 2015, 9). The UN, through its governance initiatives, has intervened in debates around the role of the firm. In doing so, it has advocated for a broader definition of fiduciary duty and consideration of ESG issues by companies and their investors.

Shifting the focus beyond companies, to large, institutional investors, provides greater insight into the way in which norms of corporate behavior are disseminated globally through the market. This is because fund managers play a significant role in directing companies' responses to ESG issues through their significant ownership stake. In particular, the Big Three US fund managers (BlackRock, Vanguard, and State Street) play a central role in setting new standards of business behavior through their significant ownership stake in firms across the globe. This ownership stake across industries and markets allows them to serve as both a gatekeeper and ally of activists in their campaigns for more ethical and sustainable business practices. The Big Three's influence has grown due to a mass migration of funds into their products, as a result of the rapid growth in demand for passive investing. Passive investments are funds that mirror a given stock market index, as opposed to portfolios where managers actively select and deselect investments over time. The former are a growing and significant segment of financial markets in liberal market economies and are dominated by the Big Three (Fichtner and Heemskerk 2020). While historically index funds such as the Big Three typically held a small parcel of shares in a large number of companies, more recently growth in funds invested through passive investment strategies has meant these few firms now hold large positions in a larger number of companies (Davis 2008). The Big Three are now the largest single investor in 88 percent of S&P 500 companies (Griffin 2019). The average combined ownership stake of the Big Three in US listed companies as of 2021 was 22 percent (Lund and Robertson 2023). This significant ownership stake across sectors globally places these fund managers in a strong position to steer corporations' response to ESG challenges.

There is evidence that the Big Three operate as gatekeepers and supporters of ESG activism, despite rarely being the driver behind this claim-making. For example, in 2020 US activist hedge fund Engine No. 1 acquired a small shareholding in ExxonMobil, worth US$40 million or 0.02 percent of the company's total shares. Just weeks later the fund's founder, Christopher James, wrote an open letter to the board of ExxonMobil arguing that the company's historically poor returns were linked to its strategic denial of the impacts of climate change. It was on this basis that the letter called for the business model to be reformed, and as part of this process James nominated four new directors to the ExxonMobil board in an attempt to "purposefully reposition the company to succeed in a decarbonizing world" (Engine No. 1 2021). With such a small ownership stake, Engine No. 1 was unlikely to succeed alone; however, institutional investors had also been expressing some frustration with the company over its poor financial performance. Engine No. 1 and James leveraged this, garnering the support of BlackRock, Vanguard, and State Street, who together held 20 percent of the company's shareholdings. As a result, three of the four proposed candidates were elected to the board (Herbst-Bayliss 2021; Mufson 2021). The Big Three's widespread investments provide them a seat at the table at many large, listed corporations. At times of significant change for companies such as ExxonMobil the Big Three practice engagement through investor voice and material voting rights on issues such as who sits on the board of directors, whether remuneration is linked to incentives such as emissions targets, and on hostile takeovers. The Big Three have been called on to support all of these tactics as employed by shareholder activists, in addition to ESG resolutions, to steer companies to respond to environmental and social challenges.

The power of the Big Three and other large funds has not gone unnoticed. Concerns have been raised about companies within industries sharing a similar ownership profile due to the large shareholdings of managed funds. It has been argued that this could potentially lead to limited competition, antitrust issues, or worsened outcomes for consumers (Schmalz 2018; Backus et al. 2021). From a corporate governance viewpoint, this concentration raises concerns about the significant amount of corporate control residing in the hands of three US-based asset managers (Fichtner and Heemskerk 2020). There have also been suggestions that this concentration may also lead to "centralized voting strategies," although this has been dispelled in the literature, where it is acknowledged that investment strategies are at least somewhat diversified within each fund manager and across the three large players (Lund and Robertson 2023). Further complicating some of these claims, fund managers' support for ESG has also changed over time. For instance, despite BlackRock CEO Larry Fink claiming in 2018 that companies need to have a "social purpose," it took until 2020 for the BlackRock to issue a report stating that climate change posed an investment risk and to highlight the likelihood that climate-integrated portfolios may have better long-run returns (Sorkin 2018; BlackRock 2020). The following year, both BlackRock and State Street declared climate change to be at the center of their investment strategies, with Vanguard belatedly acquiescing in 2022 (Etchart 2022). In the decade prior to the acknowledgment of the material financial impact of climate change on business performance, BlackRock's ESG engagements grew 48 percent, leading to claims that the fund manager was playing a role as "a very powerful driver towards a more sustainability-oriented future in corporate governance" (Ringe 2022, 93). While ESG engagement by the Big Three has declined in 2024, much of this has been attributed to the funds refusing to support claim-making that was redundant, represented potential overreach, or was actually anti-ESG, suggesting the decline in sheer numbers of ESG votes may instead reflect a refinement of these managers' approach to sustainability. Nonetheless, large fund managers play a central role in determining businesses' prioritization of sustainability issues. Despite the shift to passive funds as a default investment strategy, institutional investors such as the Big Three possess the ability to reward or punish firms for their response (or non-response) to ESG claims, and can do so globally due to their large investment footprint, revealing a central role in transnational ESG activism.

Proxy advisory firms are another key actor in the transnational ESG ecosystem. This global duopoly of US-based proxy advisors is engaged by almost all institutional investors in the United States, the United Kingdom, Canada, and Australia (Sharfman 2020; Spatt 2021; C. Shu 2022). Advisors ISS and CGI dominate the shareholder advice sector through their coverage of listed firms on stock exchanges around the world. The majority of institutional investors outsource their decision-making to these two proxy advisors who are engaged by investors to "report and recommend" (Ertimur et al. 2018; Malenko and Malenko 2019; Boone et al. 2020). CGI and ISS possess significant influence over companies through their choice of which issues to report on and advice on how investors should vote at AGMs. This influence becomes political when the issues at hand include many addressed by ESG activists and ethical investors, who are targeting companies covered by CGI and ISS. This power is enhanced and concentrated when one considers the significant reach of the advisory firms, CGI alone advises a global suite of investment funds with a total of US$40 trillion in assets under management (Copland et al. 2018; CGI Glass Lewis 2023b). Much of the existing research on proxy advisors has focused on their ability to direct votes for and against shareholder resolutions. While this is a key role of advisors, more recent scholarship has highlighted their ideational influence, derived from their ability to not only direct significant capital to and from ethical investment, but also to establish norms of business behavior that have long-term political consequences (Elbra et al. 2025). The transnational ecosystem of market-based ESG actors includes international organizations and their governance initiatives, large fund managers with an eye to ESG concerns, and the proxy advisors that advise these investors. Together, these actors possess significant influence over the success and failure of market-based campaigns for ethical investment through their ability to guide institutional investors on which issues to prioritize and how to vote on contentious claim-making at AGMs.

This cross-border activity has led to a convergence of ESG standards through transnational claim-making, which has intensified in recent years. Australian ESG shareholder activist group ACCR has been particularly active in this space, targeting companies in overseas jurisdictions where they argue failure to reduce emissions is impacting overall planetary health. In 2022 and 2023 ACCR co-filed shareholder resolutions at the AGMs of one of Japan's largest coal power operators, J-Power. The resolutions were filed alongside institutional investors, including global banking giant HSBC, and garnered significant levels of investor support (ACCR 2024a). In response, J-Power agreed to close five coal-fired power generation plants by 2030, addressing the activist investors' concerns, which included the risk of stranded assets. Key activist investor ACCR highlighted the impact of their pressure on the company, noting that "collectively these five coal unit closures will prevent the release of 16.2Mt of CO2 per year" (ACCR 2024b). When announcing the rationale behind the closures, J-Power noted that activism by ACCR and other investors "deemed it necessary to demonstrate to shareholders our strategy for coal power plants on a site-by-site or unit-by-unit basis" (Reuters 2024).

In 2024, ACCR co-filed ESG shareholder proposals alongside Corporate Action Japan, at the AGM of Nippon Steel. The proposals called for executive remuneration to be linked to the company's GHG emissions reduction targets and requested the company disclose short- and medium-term GHG emissions reduction targets for scope 1, 2, and 3 emissions. In the same year, ACCR co-filed an ESG shareholder resolution at the AGM of Shell plc. ACCR worked with Norwegian pension fund KLP, Danish fund Sampension, and UK-based ShareAction to call for Shell to disclose its lobbying practices in developing and emerging economies. This claim-making followed the release of ACCR's report *In the Dark: Gaps in Shell's Climate Lobbying Disclosures*, which demonstrated that Shell's carbon reporting in these jurisdictions fell short of industry norms, suggesting that the company had successfully lobbied regulators in these countries to permit minimal disclosure. The shareholder resolution was withdrawn prior to the AGM, after Shell announced it would disclose its climate and energy lobbying activities in five to ten emerging and developing markets before its 2025 AGM.

There are also examples of institutional investors from overseas jurisdictions exercising their right to investor voice in Australia. This transnational activism has occurred where trade union and faith-based investors such as the Labour Union Co-operative Retirement Fund (LUCRF), Mercy Investment Services, and St. Columban's Mission Society have co-filed resolutions alongside Australian activist investors. In 2019, these investors partnered with ACCR to call on supermarket giant Coles to review its supply chains to eliminate any instances of modern slavery. While the company announced, ahead of the AGM, that it had signed an accord with three of the country's largest unions to ensure the protection of workers in fresh food supply chains and to consult with employees through regular meetings, the resolution was not rescinded. In the same year, a group of institutional investors, including UK ethical funds ACTIAM and Church of England Pensions Board, lobbied BHP over its continued membership of industry associations whose commitment to Paris Agreement targets was seen as inadequate. The group filed a shareholder resolution pointing to the company's own review, which committed to funding only industry associations that included a commitment to a just and orderly transition to renewable energy. The resolution attracted the "yes" vote from 22 percent of shareholders, with Church of England representative Adam Matthews noting:

> Regardless of the percentage of the vote achieved today, we know that over 50 climate aware institutional investors with over ten trillion US

> Dollars in Assets Under Management have indicated support—either publicly or privately for resolution 22. This includes Aberdeen Standard, AXA, AVIVA, BNP Paribas, CalPERS, Union Investments and LAPFF amongst many more. (The Church of England 2019)

The widespread support for this resolution from BHP's international investors highlights the pressure that emanates from the transnational dissemination of norms of business behavior. The coalition of investors, coordinated by the UNPRI, lobbied BHP over its industry associations, suggesting that global governance institutions have the ability to mobilize market-based actors to make claims against large multinational corporations.

The coordinated forms of activism outlined above can be juxtaposed with other examples, where the transnational ecosystem of actors has failed to converge on mutually agreed standards of corporate behavior. In these cases, divergence between jurisdictional attitudes toward a company's ESG commitments prevail. On occasion, this can prevent effective activism from materializing. An example of this can be seen in offshore investor responses to the destruction of the Juukan Caves, explored in the previous chapter. In this case, Australian pension funds, guided by their peak body ACSI, voted down reduced remuneration packages for the executives held responsible for the destruction of this site in 2020. These packages reflected reduced, but significant, payouts for the departing executives. Pension funds did so on the basis that the executives needed to be disciplined for the company's poor performance, rather than rewarded with hefty bonuses. These institutional investors were joined by their US counterparts, who also rejected the payouts. However, the US institutional investors did not vote against these penalties because they saw them as *insufficient*; instead, they perceived the reduction in golden handshakes as "dramatic overreach against three otherwise-excellent executives" (Toscano and Knight 2020). This sentiment was shared by European-based funds, which supported the retention of the executives despite strong calls within Australia for management to be removed. In the end, the tension was resolved in favor of the Australian pension funds, supported by the Chair of the country's Future Fund, and the country's former Treasurer, Peter Costello. These investors were joined by the UK Local Authority Pension Fund Forum, Aberdeen Standard Investments, and the Church of England Pensions Board in calling for the removal of the three executives with a reduced payout or golden handshake (Allam 2020; B. Butler 2020; Toscano and Knight 2020). In this case, Australian and UK investors in the dual Sydney–London stock exchange listed mining company perceived the material financial risk of the destruction of the caves differently to international actors, who perceived the loss of experienced management as a greater risk than the reputational damage from the destruction of the site.

This divergence in norms of business behavior poses a challenge to companies and investors globally. While in the case of Rio Tinto, the result was a difference of opinion in terms of management remuneration and retention. Elsewhere, there are much higher stakes at play for actors in this system. The next section explores attempts to limit investor voice through anti-ESG legislation in some US states and contrasts this with the requirements of jurisdictions such as the EU and UK, where ESG considerations are mandated. It points to the inbuilt tension and challenges for companies, investors, and proxy advisors, who operate transnationally in meeting these contradictory requirements.

Legislating Against ESG

The growth of ESG investing and the embedding of ESG stewardship norms globally has led to significant political backlash over the blurring of financial and ethical concerns. Nowhere has the right to investor voice over ESG issues been more intensely contested than in the United States, particularly in Republican-controlled states. This rhetoric has only heightened since the 2024 US presidential election campaign and subsequent re-election of President Donald Trump. Certain jurisdictions in the US, arguably the home of ESG shareholder activism, now represent some of the clearest examples of contestation between political actors, activists, investors, and their companies. In these states, the term "ESG" has taken on seriously partisan meaning, with critics of "woke capitalism" claiming these considerations have no place in the boardrooms of large corporations. Such sentiments have been backed up with attempts at regulatory reform. Prior to Trump's re-election, in 2023, 165 pieces of "anti-ESG" legislation were introduced to US state legislatures (Gibson and Sawyer 2023). These bills aimed to limit the power of state pension funds to make investment decisions based on ESG criteria, restrict funds' rights to express political or non-financial views to boards and management, and to blacklist investors who engaged in boycott and divestment campaigns (Gibson and Sawyer 2023). Most attempts at anti-ESG legislation in the US focus on restricting the rights of state pension authorities, proxy advisors, and service providers to make investment decisions based on consideration of long-term sustainability commitments, or to vote on this basis at AGMs (Malone et al. 2023). Proposed penalties for breaches of these rulings are significant. For example in Missouri, a company that violates this rule is obligated to pay the state an "amount equal to three times all moneys paid to the company [that is the proxy advisor] by the system for the company's services" (Missouri Senate 2023). These efforts to legislate against ESG activism were introduced after two successful attempts to tighten US Securities and Exchange Commission rulings in 2018 and 2019, which aimed to restrict the role of proxy advisors in providing judgments on matters deemed overtly political (Boone et al. 2020). Federally, the US House Committee on Financial Services recommended tighter constraints on the ability to file ESG shareholder resolutions and impediments on shareholders' rights to vote on such resolutions (S. Lewis 2023). Proxy advisors have also attracted the attention of regulators in other jurisdictions. In 2021, the Australian government attempted to constrain the power of proxy advisors by proposing strict new regulations (Frydenberg 2019). This attempt, albeit unsuccessful, came about despite the regulator's recommendation that no changes were required.

Trump's 2024 re-election intensified ongoing debates over the role of business in addressing ESG concerns. The president has publicly railed against ESG issues, specifically climate change and DEI initiatives, leading to suggestions that his re-election would lead to the death of ESG. During the campaign, right-wing think tank The Heritage Foundation released a policy manifesto calling on Congress to "oppose efforts to redefine the purpose of business in the name of social justice [including ESG]" and that what they term "racist" offices for DEI should be abolished in the name of equal opportunity and individual merit (Burton 2024). On the first day of the second Trump administration, the US withdrew from the Paris Climate Agreement in a concerted effort at undermining multilateral efforts at reducing global warming (The White House 2025). The administration then moved quickly to sign executive orders aimed at weakening state and local government climate laws, ending DEI initiatives in federal government agencies, and banning federal agencies from contracting to technology companies that use ideologically biased AI. The administration also plans to reverse the Biden administration's requirement that pension funds consider ESG factors in investment decisions. This rhetoric and the subsequent executive orders have led to a cascade of similar policies at the corporate level as companies work within the new political context.

In January 2025, the UN's Net Zero Asset Manager Alliance announced it would pause all activities after the departure of a number of high-profile asset managers, including BlackRock, JPMorgan, and Citibank, from the initiative. Asset managers' decision to leave the Alliance coincided with many fund managers retreating from positions on climate change and DEI in an increasingly hostile political environment. Citing recent developments in the US, the Alliance announced along with the pause in activities that it would launch a review of the organization to ensure it "remains fit for purpose in the new global context" (Peach 2025). Further evidence of anti-ESG rhetoric eroding shareholder democracy in the US includes Exxon suing its own investors for exercising "voice" over a lack of climate action (T. Smith 2024). Elsewhere globally, Trump's anti-ESG push has seen Dutch shareholder activist group Follow This pause the filling of ESG shareholder resolutions at major oil and gas company AGMs in 2025 due to the changing political landscape (Follow This 2025).

While anti-ESG rhetoric and legislation have altered the political investor landscape, particularly in the US, this shift is by no means universal. There is considerable evidence that globally, voting publics have rejected attempts at weaponizing divisive and harm-inducing language, and that ESG concerns are embedded in financial markets and corporate norms of behavior. During the period of Trump's second ascendancy to the White House, the results of a series of elections in liberal market economies worldwide suggested a rejection of this form of politics. In July 2024, the UK Labour Party was elected in a landslide defeat, representing the worst ever loss for the UK's Conservative Party. The following year in Canada, the Liberal Party won its first popular vote count since 2015, when it was returned to office. And in 2025, the Australian Labor Party was re-elected with a significantly larger majority than its previous term in what has been described by renowned psephologist Antony

Green (2025) as "one of the more one-sided results in Federal election history." All three elections represented victories for left-leaning parties, and a repudiation of Trump-style politics, including anti-ESG sentiment. In this sense, it can be argued that the US is somewhat of an outlier when compared to other liberal market economies, where the recognition of the need to address climate change and rectify social inequalities is more widely accepted. There is little evidence that Trump's divisive politics have found mainstream audiences in Australia and other comparable states. As such, Australia looks likely to continue down the path of a new system of carbonizing and decarbonizing corporate governance systems through market-based activism.

Beyond these election results there is ample evidence globally of support for enabling investor voice on ESG issues and requiring companies to publicly commit to meeting sustainability targets. Unlike the US, the EU has demonstrated a growing commitment to regulating *for* ESG stewardship as part of shareholders' responsibilities. The EU Shareholder Rights Directive includes a requirement that institutional investors will engage with their companies on a range of issues, including those captured under ESG (I. H. Chiu and Katelouzou 2017). The EU's Non-Financial Reporting Directive, Sustainable Finance Disclosure Regulation, and Taxonomy Regulation also contain clauses that promote sustainable investment and transparency around engagement between investors and their companies (Ringe 2022).

The Australian case explored in this book shows that attempts to regulate against ethical investing, ESG, or sustainable approaches to finance are unlikely to succeed in the long term. There remains demand for ethical finance, and investors are likely to continue to demand for ethical funds and the rights to express opinions on ESG matters. If attempts to limit these succeed, as is the case in Australia, where the regulatory environment is unfriendly to activists, activists are likely to work to circumvent these restrictions and in turn continue to make ESG claims against companies and industries. There is already evidence of anti-ESG legislation being rolled back in the United States, largely due to the difficulties and costs associated with compliance (Garrett and Ivanov 2022). In Indiana, a House bill requiring the state's public pension system to divest from funds that consider ESG issues in their investing was amended to exclude private companies, after opposition from the Indiana Chamber of Commerce.

This change alone is expected to reduce the cost of compliance to the state pension system from US$6.7 billion over ten years to US$5.5 million (M. Katz 2023).

Despite the UK's departure from the EU in 2020, EU regulation still impacts some UK firms, particularly those that do business on the continent and where EU law is extraterritorial. The UK itself has a range of disclosure regulations requiring companies to publish reports on climate targets, modern slavery statistics, gender pay gap, and other ESG measures. The UK Financial Conduct Authority (FCA), the regulator responsible for overseeing financial services firms and markets, also released new sustainability disclosure requirements in November 2023. These rules include anti-greenwashing provisions and investment product labeling to assist consumers in understanding the ESG commitments of funds (UK Financial Conduct Authority 2023). However, these rules are less proactive and relevant to investors than those in the EU, which place binding commitments on institutional investors to understand ESG issues relevant to their companies.

All of this suggests that ESG is now socialized as an investment norm, not simply a fringe issue for activists. Private research suggests that in the wake of the Trump administration's re-election, 80 percent of companies adjusted their ESG policies, however only 6 percent made any material change (Braun 2025). The material financial risks posed by stranded assets, reputational damage, and the threat of fines and penalties is only likely to further embed ESG considerations into business practices. As such, the debate between the vocal anti-ESG movement spurred on by the US president and his supporters and those who advocate for the consideration of ESG risk is unlikely to result in a zero-sum outcome. However, nor is the election of Trump likely to end the ongoing debate between these polarized ends of the spectrum. In the middle of this debate are firms, fund managers, and proxy advisors actively working in this space continuing to respond to ESG risks as they apply to their business or investment. These actors are required to simultaneously walk the line between jurisdictions that demand these considerations be addressed and those that regulate against any consideration of ESG issues, as though this alone will eliminate the risks associated with a rapidly warming climate, the dispossession of Indigenous landowners, and ongoing instances of modern slavery. The likely outcome is that firms and investors will continue to take ESG considerations into account, but their public commentary on this will be adjusted to the political settings they operate in. This is manageable for those operating in single jurisdictions such as the US or the EU, however it will remain a challenge for fund managers and businesses operating across divergent regimes, where the public response to ESG will need to be crafted for fiercely opposed audiences.

Non-regulatory governance mechanisms, such as stewardship codes, also guide business behavior in many jurisdictions. Known as "comply or explain" soft law, these corporate governance codes such as the UK Stewardship Code require companies listed on an exchange to either meet certain ESG targets or provide the market with an explanation as to why these cannot be met (Keay 2014; Klettner 2016; Klettner 2021). Advocates argue that while these codes are voluntary soft law, they remain a powerful normative precedent, communicating investor and societal expectations of firms (I. H. Chiu and Katelouzou 2017). Yet, there is considerable debate around the effectiveness of these voluntary codes, with some authors criticizing narrow coverage (Cheffins 2010), difficulty in enforcing the codes (Reisberg 2015), and their lack of specificity (I. H. Y. Chiu 2013). Others point out that ESG activism takes place in jurisdictions without stewardship codes like Germany and many emerging markets, or in the US where the stewardship code does not include ESG guidance (Bowley and Hill 2024b). The emergence of voluntary stewardship codes may reflect the convergence of expectations around corporate behavior, whereby ESG considerations are being integrated into corporate governance codes. While they remain a helpful guidance on the expectations of firms, it is clear that they are not codified hard law and that firms do internalize ESG norms without these codes as seen in jurisdictions as diverse as Germany and the US.

It is clear from this discussion of the regulatory push for and against ESG considerations that there is a growing likelihood that corporations will find themselves caught between the backlash to "woke capitalism" seen in the US, and pro-ESG regulation emerging from more liberal US states and in the EU. Companies and investors that operate transnationally, across jurisdictions, may struggle to meet these divergent regulations that demand both evidence of ESG awareness while simultaneously requiring that companies ignore ESG concerns in their understanding of financially material factors. Yet, as has been explored in this book, the key driver of ESG activism is investors' desire to understand company valuations beyond shareholder primacy. The most successful ethical investment campaigns have been those which have drawn in the support of institutional investors on the basis that unaddressed ESG risks are materially financial threats to corporate value. In this sense, the demand for ESG reporting, and corporate responses to challenges such as climate change, modern slavery, or the protection of culturally significant sites, is unlikely to disappear anytime soon. The latter of these is explored in the next section, which examines the challenges faced by mining companies operating in settler colonies.

Settler-Colonial Challenges

The circumstances explored in chapter 5 are not unique to Australia. The intersection of mining and Indigenous land rights has led to profound environmental and social impacts, and these have been keenly felt in other settler-colonial societies, such as the United States and Canada. Indigenous peoples in resource-rich regions globally have borne many of the costs, but have seen few of the benefits, of mineral extraction—and have thus been described as "victims of progress" (Bodley 2014). Indigenous peoples globally are subject to displacement through physical relocation, the harms accrued to First Nations' lands, and through the uneven distribution of the wealth generated from mining (Kramarz et al. 2021). This is only set to worsen as the world moves to a more mineral intensive future, whereby the development of renewable energy sources relies heavily on the extraction of critical minerals. Almost 70 percent of the minerals required for a transition to renewable energy are mined on Indigenous Peoples' lands (Owen et al. 2022).

Mirroring the findings in this study, it is apparent that globally, institutional investors and socially responsible investment funds tend to focus on environmental issues more so than social and governance-related investment criteria. William Nikolakis et al. (2014) agree with the conclusions in the previous chapter, that one potential cause of social issues being overlooked is the universality of climate change and its impact on investors, fund managers, and activists. Perhaps as a result, there is a relative lack of academic work that examines the relationship between First Nations peoples and investor engagement (Nikolakis et al. 2014). This is also reflected in the fact that North American funds that are engaged with First Nations peoples generally have a broader ESG mandate; here the *S* is often elevated alongside environmental concerns. These funds are also more likely to seek advice from First Nations NGOs—and use these relationships to build links with extractives firms, leveraging their networks to obtain better First Nations outcomes (Nikolakis et al. 2014). Furthermore, it has been shown that this approach is also more likely to be applied by the same portfolio managers in their offshore engagements, where they bring their awareness of First Nations issues, particularly FPIC, to new jurisdictions in an example of effectively leveraging transnational opportunity structures.

Faith-based investors in the United States have filed resolutions against major banks over their financing of projects that they claim have not sought and received appropriate FPIC. These include Citibank, Wells Fargo, and JPMorgan, which all faced claims in 2023 that they failed to meet international standards in regards to obtaining FPIC at various oil, gas, and coal projects (Hawser 2023). These organizations have partnered with various Indigenous activist groups from areas as dispersed as Chile, Peru, and the Tiwi Islands, off Australia. Activists, including a range of religious organizations represented by IGNs such as the UNPRI and ICCR, note that violations of FPIC under the UNDRIP can "adversely affect shareholder value, including reputation damage, project disruptions, and civil and criminal liability" (Interfaith Center on Corporate Responsibility 2023c). Moreover, they note that all three banks *were* committed to the Equator Principles, which banks use to measure the ESG risks of projects they finance, however they departed from the Principles at the beginning of 2023, further fueling speculation that their financing arrangements failed to align with international norms (Hawser 2023). First Nations communities affected by the proposed pipelines funded by these three banks argue that the planned projects will impact drinking water, ecosystems, and culturally significant sites, such as those used in customary ceremonies and where ancestors are buried. The banks deny that the loans they provided directly fund these proposed projects, however as one of the lead filers, The Sisters of St. Joseph of Peace, suggests, banking lines of credit are not always clear, and if these loans were to be rescinded, the companies would struggle to move ahead with the projects (Hawser 2023). Lessons from the case of Juukan Gorge should be heeded by mining companies operating on the land of Indigenous peoples globally. Full FPIC should be sought, and updated, throughout the life of a mine site. Failure to do so risks the sort of transnational activist campaign that Rio Tinto endured, and which resulted in the departure of three executives and serious damage to the company's reputation. More positively, there is evidence that IGNs can work together across an issue area to pressure companies to engage more fully with impacted communities.

While Australia and other settler colonies, such as the US and Canada, share similarities in their history and ongoing relations with First Nations peoples, their settler legal systems remain disparate. In the US and Canada, virtually all new mining projects emerge as a result of negotiations between Indigenous groups, mining corporations, and frequently the state (O'Faircheallaigh 2021). Complicating comparisons is the multilevel governance structures at play in federations such as Australia, the US, and Canada, where national and sub-national legal systems overlap to govern the rights of Indigenous landowners. While strictly speaking, these legal systems are not comparable, it remains that lessons can be learned from activism, such as those explored in this chapter. This also highlights the importance of a focus on "agreement-making," which is inclusive and represents the interests of First Nations groups broadly, rather than relying on a strictly legal interpretation that may be disputed by excluded parties and lead to the outcomes evidenced in chapter 5 (Mascher 2022).

This chapter has explored the transnational ESG activism space, highlighting the globally interconnected nature of the key players. These actors coalesce around campaigns for ethical investment as well as point-in-time responses to ESG breaches, as seen in the case of the Juukan Caves. While there is ample evidence to suggest the dissemination of norms of business behavior through these connections, there are also instances of divergence. In these cases, ESG activists, institutional investors, proxy advisors, and international organizations are unable to agree on a global ESG standard, or response, reflecting contestation over the norms of business behavior.

Divergent definitions and understandings of fiduciary duty drive much of this contestation. However, as these are increasingly being incorporated into hard law, many actors in the transnational ESG ecosystem will find themselves governed by conflicting regulations. Drawing on the example discussed in this chapter, while some US states are attempting to legislate against ESG, using very narrow definitions of fiduciary duty, it may be that offshore investors are simultaneously pressuring listed funds, and by extension companies, to consider exactly the issues that are being excluded from consideration. The reverse is also possible. Institutional investors from states in the US where ESG considerations are removed from decision-making may find it difficult to demonstrate to EU regulators that they have incorporated these risks into their calculations. The result may be unresolvable tension between the demands of investors and regulatory frameworks that govern local funds and management. This is most likely to emerge over the issue of climate change, which remains a universal challenge and one that many stewardship codes, pension funds, and shareholder organizations have declared central to investment decision-making, yet which has also attracted the ire of anti-ESG legislators in some Republican-governed US states.

CONCLUSION

THIS BOOK DOCUMENTS THE emergence of a particular form of anti-corporate politics, ESG shareholder activism, in Australia since 2017. The analysis and conclusions contribute to our broader understanding of social movements, market-based activism, and the role of investors and companies in addressing some of society's most pressing issues. Through the development of a database of claim-making, interviews with key players, and participant observation at AGMs, the book expands our understanding of anti-corporate politics. The analysis shows that, unlike other liberal market economies, Australian investor activism is embryonic and duopolistic. It also demonstrates that it is dominated by civil society actors rather than ethical investors, institutional funds, or other financially motivated actors. Market-based activism in Australia came to be dominated by two organizations, ACCR and Market Forces, due to the legal constraints placed on investors who wish to express views to boards and management. The same hurdles explain the late adoption of this form of activism, when compared to other liberal market economies, and the overwhelming focus on climate change at the expense of other pressing social issues. These findings provide insights into the potential unintended outcomes of legislating against shareholder voice, using a unique case study that allows us to understand how this emerged in a socio-legal system designed to stymy investor expression.

The two key actors studied in this book, ACCR and Market Forces, are likely to dominate the investor activist space in Australia into the future, due to their ability to work around legal efforts to limit investor voice. While they have been active, and successful, in lobbying companies over ESG challenges, their dominance comes at the cost of broader investor and civil society engagement as occurs in other liberal market economies such as the US or UK. Given their dominance now and likely into the future, their focus, tactics, and strategies should be of particular interest to scholars and practitioners interested in harnessing corporate power to address ESG challenges. This is particularly the case as pressure on regulators to limit investor voice intensifies in pro-business jurisdictions globally. Australian activist organizations are constrained in many ways. The legal requirement to control one hundred shareholdings means that they can file resolutions at only a small number of companies. Their mandates are defined by their founders, personnel, and financial backers, which in the case of Market Forces results in a sole focus on climate. ACCR, while given a broader remit, remains heavily concentrated on pressuring corporations to reduce emissions. The duopoly's narrow scope of engagement leaves important issues off the political agenda, allowing many firms to evade scrutiny over their ESG commitments. There is little to suggest this will change going forward, given the funding and remit of these two groups, as well as the barriers preventing new activist groups from engaging in this form of contestation. It also challenges the prevailing view in much of the political participation scholarship, which suggests that shareholder activism is a force for widening political participation. Even if one were to look beyond these two groups to other investors who could ally themselves in campaigns for ethical investment, the investor community remains unrepresentative of broader Australia. As demonstrated in this book, this matters. It goes some way to explaining the prioritization of climate above all other social and environmental claim-making—something not seen in other jurisdictions where a broader suite of ethical investors advocates for social issues. This book argues that despite attempts to limit investor voice over issues such as ESG based on a narrow definition of fiduciary duty, it remains that investors, fund managers, proxy advisors, and activists are concerned about these issues. And the various actors in this ecosystem take ESG considerations into account in their investment decision-making, making them critical to campaigns for ethical investment. While legal constraints may narrow the scope of anti-corporate politics, as is seen in the case of Australia, it is highly unlikely that ESG concerns can be separated from financial decision-making. This chapter explores the key findings of the book, including their theoretical and empirical implications. Finally, the chapter concludes with avenues for future research in this growing area of political economy scholarship.

This research confirms the literature that emphasizes the importance of financial materiality in sustainable and ethical finance. All actors in the Australian ecosystem, aside from activists, are driven by profitability and shareholder returns. Outside of Australia, where activists are also financially motivated investors, it is more so the case that financial materiality is key. It is insufficient for activists to highlight a company's contribution to greenhouse gas emissions alone as the rationale for divesting part of a business or exiting an industry. While investors may have personal concerns about ESG matters, as was often mentioned in interviews for this research, their role is to grow their portfolios, or to advise their members on how to do so in the case of shareholder organizations representing investors. As this analysis shows, definitions of financial materiality range from purely returns-based to those that place a higher priority on sustainability. It is through these evolving definitions of financial materiality and fiduciary duty that ESG concerns have been embedded in questions of corporate governance. ESG impacts may be expressed as risks to corporations' bottom line through adjacent issues such as reputational risk, potential legal challenges, or the risk of stranded assets. Activist investors have seen the greatest amount of success in influencing other market-based actors when they have been able to articulate these material threats to business profitability.

ESG shareholder activists are aware of the importance of financial materiality, and as a result, they frequently frame their claim-making in this way. The resonance of this discourse was evident when comparing the success of ACCR and Market Forces' campaigns with that of GetUp!, where the latter employed the language of affected community members in opposition to fracking in the Beetaloo Basin. Using the support of non-activist investors for these campaigns as a proxy for success, ACCR and Market Forces' approaches garnered far greater support. This finding points to the tension faced by activists who have competing goals of attracting non-activist investor support whilst avoiding speaking for Indigenous communities, and is a possible explanation for the low number of social resolutions filed in Australia. This tension is not unique to Australia, and ethical investors operating in settler-colonial states globally face similar constraints. In Australia, activists have filed far more resolutions lobbying firms to lower emissions, where it is far simpler to highlight the financial impacts of a failure to respond to climate change. This is particularly the case for energy-generating companies with significant infrastructure at risk of becoming stranded assets when compared with mining companies who are struggling to maintain a social license to operate or companies whose operations impact human rights. While these issues are important, it is much more difficult to calculate their financial materiality. The quantifiable risk of costly, aging, and potentially redundant coal-fired power stations can be leveraged to secure the interest of financially motivated investors. A remaining challenge for activists and ethical investors is to foreground the material financial risks in some of these more difficult to quantify cases, in order to elicit a corporate or investor response.

The financial materiality of ESG challenges is also a barrier to policy makers attempting to regulate against investor voice. It is increasingly unlikely that investors, proxy advisors, and corporations themselves can, or will, ignore their impact on the environment or stakeholders. As such, it is impossible to mandate that pension funds ignore ESG issues, on the basis of political overreach, as these issues are likely to impact the fund's returns. Anti-ESG regulators are unlikely to overcome the blurred line between profit and politics, which has been recognized by many market-based actors, from the activists explored in this book to the US Business Roundtable and the Big Three fund managers.

While support from non-activist shareholders is often touted as a measure of success, it is not the only guide to the importance of ESG issues to the wider investor community and even firms. Yet, the scholarship on shareholder activism is heavily focused on this as a quantifiable metric. Measures of investor support for activist resolutions are used in research as a procurator for the power of activists, proxy advisors, and investors. In some jurisdictions, such as the UK, binding resolutions that attract a more than 50 percent "yes" vote compel the corporation to respond in some way. This has occasionally led to a fixation with this threshold.

However, this research demonstrates that in order for an ESG shareholder resolution to gain traction and impact corporate behavior, the AGM supporting vote does not need to be excessively high. In Australia, where non-binding resolutions are the only option, or in other jurisdictions where they are the more common form of engagement, the presence of an ESG shareholder resolution and an indication that *some* shareholders find this relevant is enough to elicit a response from companies. This confirms the literature that highlights the "hassle factor" of shareholder activism, and which notes that even a small number of shareholders can force a company to devote a significant amount of energy to an issue. The effectiveness of ESG shareholder activism, even with low levels of support, also explains why companies might be willing to meet "simple" demands. This was evident in the calls for greater transparency around Australian companies' emissions in 2017 and 2018, which led to the publication of these metrics as an accepted norm of business behavior.

Companies' willingness to increase emissions transparency is an example of activists' success in leveraging corporate opportunity structures to claim-make on companies. As discussed, many firms found demands around emissions transparency relatively simple to acquiesce to, responding reasonably promptly to these demands in order to placate activists whilst providing more detailed information to investors. However, this then exposed these same companies to a cascade of related claims. Over this period studied in this book, companies began by willingly engaging with activists and concerned investors over transparency. Once this was seen as a business-as-usual approach, the greater detail of emissions available for scrutiny by activists, investors, and the media combined with the demonstrated capacity of companies to conform to claim-making set the scene for stronger demands from activist investors. Armed with more information about which companies were contributing to Australia's emissions profile, and knowing that corporations had met past demands, activists called for more transparency of emissions beyond the operations of the target company, including scope 3 emissions, as well as for stronger emissions reductions targets and commitments. This has played out in boardrooms of companies explored in this book, including most recently the example of Woodside's say on climate vote being rejected by shareholders, as well as the failed takeover of AGL that resulted in a board reshuffle that introduced four pro-climate directors. Other examples of sub-optimal outcomes for companies engaged with activists abound. While ACCR and BHP have a history of working together on ESG issues, ACCR has on occasion targeted BHP to call for more action on ESG issues than the company's board and management were willing to agree to. Despite, or perhaps because of, a history of meeting activist demands over lobbying, climate, and relations with First Nations Australians, when BHP put its say on climate to vote in 2024, ACCR declined to support the plan. Ongoing engagement and businesses' willingness to meet activist demands may not appease or reduce protest. Instead, companies may see increasing demands both in scope and frequency from activists who see a business willing to undertake ESG reform while at the same time keen to avoid public scrutiny.

This research builds on the scholarship noting that activist pressure on one firm can have industry-wide ramifications. This confirms the literature on opportunity structures, which suggests anti-corporate activists can have wide-ranging effects on industries through corporate lobbying, and that industry opportunity structures enhance activists' ability to target firms across a given sector, particularly in times of crisis. Activists' ability to leverage industry opportunity structures was explored in chapter 3, where anti-corporate politics was focused on Australia's largest coal-fired power generators, AGL and Origin. In this case, activists were successful in forcing the industry to shift focus from self-preservation via the status quo, to genuine engagement with decarbonization as a path for future viability. This was also clear in the issues discussed in the next chapter. Following Rio Tinto's destruction of the Juukan Caves, other mining companies proactively engaged with activists and investors to reassure them that they had examined their policies and procedures, and strengthened these where required in order to avoid a repeat of the incident. Rival BHP went as far as to engage a coalition of Aboriginal and Torres Strait Islander organizations to certify that their practices met community standards. BHP has also been called on to leverage its private authority to reform industry associations and to lobby governments. The company was the target of anti-corporate activists who highlighted that although it had divested its high-emitting petroleum assets to rival Woodside, the company remained a member of several industry associations that were actively lobbying against climate action in countries such as the US and Australia. Activists pressured BHP to reform industry associations and went further to demand the company lobby the Australian government to improve its response to climate change. Companies with significant political power, and private authority, such as BHP have the influence to cascade this approach through other firms in their industry. As such, they are more likely to be targeted by activists, as there is the clear potential for their actions to impact the broader industry, and potentially policy-making.

The role of critical junctures in anti-corporate activism and politics more broadly often assumes these punctuations are a necessary condition for activism to succeed and solidify a broader response. The two critical junctures highlighted here were the 2019 megafires and the destruction of the Juukan Caves. These two shocking events had the potential to catalyze action in response to the issues of climate change and the protection of culturally significant sites. Both were leveraged by activists and investors to pressure companies to improve their social and environmental performance, with mixed success. And while there was demonstrable change at the industry level in both cases, it was also shown that they failed to generate a regulatory response. In these cases, sub-national governments stepped in to prolong the life of coal-fired power stations, to support the fracking of the Beetaloo Basin through offtake agreements, and to quickly reverse laws that enhanced protection of culturally sacred sites. In the case of gas offtakes from the Beetaloo Basin and extending the life of coal-fired power stations, state governments underwrote these assets (and their emissions) even when companies themselves were attempting to shift away from carbon-intensive energy production. While corporate actors responded to calls for stronger environmental and social protections, activists have failed to secure meaningful policy change. This failure suggests the governance gap that drives much of the ESG shareholder activism is not narrowing. In fact, despite corporations increasingly taking on the responsibility of responding to some of society's most pressing issues, governments remain capable of destabilizing solutions to address these.

Australia is one of the world's most challenging liberal market jurisdictions for investor activists. This book represents the first attempt at understanding the drivers and implications of the limits to investor voice and assessing the extent to which activists can succeed in the face of legal barriers. The *Corporations Act* and its 2015 interpretation by the Federal Court are clear attempts to extinguish shareholders' rights to file advisory resolutions and, in turn, one of the key methods by which investors can express opinions to their board and management. Australia's legal regime is at odds with other comparable legal regimes globally. The mechanism by which investors can express voice under this ruling, that is, calling for a constitutional amendment or the removal of directors, has been described as "blunt and disruptive (and often futile)" (Bottomley 2019, 129). Unsurprisingly, it has had profound implications on market-based activism in Australia. Despite expectations that ESG claim-making on companies would cease, at least as far as the filing of resolutions and discussion thereof at AGMs, this did not eventuate. Instead, a duopoly of activists established a method to work around the legal constraints placed in their way. Since 2017, they have filed almost all ESG shareholder resolutions at Australian company AGMs, and where they have not been the lead filer (i.e., where GetUp! has filed) it has been their activism model that has been relied upon to move past the legal barriers. There is no other comparable jurisdiction that has produced such a narrow concentration of activists with the power to lobby companies through corporate governance mechanisms. And, unlike in other jurisdictions, these are not investor-activists, that is, long-term stewards of capital with a universal ownership mindset, attempting to grow financial returns through ethical investing. Nor are they ethical funds, where sustainability concerns are balanced with financial considerations. Instead, these two groups are what has been referred to as "unnatural insiders," or activist investors. By obtaining control of sufficient shareholdings in a handful of companies, these groups have gained access to boards and management. They do not, however, have any interest in companies' financial performance, and therefore their claims can be highly unappealing to institutional investors. Claim-making that goes beyond what investors perceive as reasonable remains a serious barrier to non-activist investor support. This is not the case in other liberal market economies where coalitions of concerned investors lobby their companies over ESG issues, but always with profitability as a consideration.

The emergence of ACCR and Market Forces demonstrates that avenues for the expression of investor voice do exist in otherwise hostile legal climates. This can be viewed as a positive outcome, as without these groups there would be little pressure placed on large companies through corporate governance mechanisms. However, it remains that this narrow duopoly of activists determines the ESG issues under consideration and which companies are targeted. As a result, they also decide which issues and target companies are left off the political agenda. While other actors such as institutional investors and proxy advisors influence companies' approaches to ESG, they do not file ESG resolutions. As a result, the small pool of funders and personnel that make up these organizations effectively determines the direction of anti-corporate politics in Australia. It is the objectives of the small group of activists and their donors that have then led to a predominant focus on climate change, at the expense of other non-climate environmental and social issues. If attempts to legislate against investor voice in jurisdictions such as the US succeed, we would expect to see a corresponding narrowing of the activist landscape, and a reduced number of companies and issues on which activists would engage.

While the decision of activists to target large Australian corporations over emissions reduction is justified by the fact the country has highly divisive climate politics, no market mechanism to reduce emissions, and an economy dominated by high-emitting mining, oil, and gas companies, it remains that only 17 percent of the ESG shareholder resolutions filed between 2017 and 2022 were focused on issues other than climate change. What is more striking is that often, social claim-making also includes calls for environmental protection, meaning purely social ESG resolutions are extremely rare. This enmeshing of social and environmental claims is partly an inescapable outcome of Australia's mining industry and its impacts on the environment and First Nations' communities, and has been seen in other jurisdictions where First Nations peoples' rights intersect with environmental degradation. For example, claim-making over Origin's plans to frack the Beetaloo Basin included accusations that this activity would negatively impact water supply. In this instance, the water supply is of both environmental and cultural importance. It is impossible to separate the two. However, it remains that the concentrated nature of ESG activism in Australia, and the focus of the two groups that have emerged as a result of limits on investor voice, are highly focused on the existential threat of climate change. As discussed in chapter 4, social issues are not elevated at anywhere near the same rate climate change has historically been. While the drivers of this include the ever-present threat of a warming climate, it is also a reflection of the organizations engaged in this work. Social issues, and non-climate environmental issues to an extent, are part of Australian anti-corporate politics, yet it is clear that restrictions on investor voice have limited the attention paid to these issues. This gap reveals a potential avenue for transnational governance over First Nations land rights. The universality of this issue, and the long global history of privileging of capital over Indigenous rights, suggests that market-based activism could be a potential avenue for justice. While First Nations groups have worked locally on boycotts, protests, and legal challenges to development that impinges on land rights, there is scope for greater cooperation at the transnational level for the use of shareholder activism to achieve these goals.

Missing entirely from the Australian case is claim-making over governance issues. There is no evidence of ESG shareholder activists targeting Australian companies over gender pay gaps, diversity of board composition, or other governance practices, despite all of these issues being recognized as challenges to good corporate governance. The closest example identified in this research on ESG shareholder resolutions was ACCR's ask that Woodside cease advertising its company on a prominent Australian Rules Football team's jersey, as a club sponsor. This claim sits fairly comfortably in the social category but could be argued to be an attempt to reform the governance of the corporation, in particular its community engagement strategy. However, there have been no other governance claims made on companies. This is despite the fact other actors in this ecosystem, such as proxy advisors, publicize policies on governance issues. An example of this is CGI's policy of refusing to vote up the nomination of board directors that dilute women's representation on boards below a set threshold, which is at least two women on a six-person board, and one on a five-member board (CGI Glass Lewis 2023a). When pressed on ACCR's commitment to governance, an interviewee did not directly respond. Instead, they referred to global standards, highlighting their membership in the UNPRI as one way by which they were bound to meet global norms around governance standards.

In addition to the strong focus on climate resolutions, there are other limitations that result from the concentrated ecosystem of activist investors. The legal requirement that resolutions can only be filed by investors representing one hundred shareholders places a resourcing constraint on activists. This barrier is significant and difficult for activists to surmount, even when they have derived a path around the legal challenges put in place. As a result, Market Forces and ACCR have the capacity to file shareholder resolutions at only a small number of Australian listed firms. While these companies face the breadth of ESG shareholder activism, their peers escape the scrutiny applied to the dozen or so firms that these organizations have selected as targets of anti-corporate politics. This includes other listed companies where activists have not sought to control one hundred shares, and unlisted companies where ownership is managed "off-market" or privately. These remaining firms, the majority of the actors in corporate Australia, are out of reach of ESG shareholder activists.

The lack of scrutiny applied to companies that are not listed on the ASX, and where activists have not sought to control one hundred shareholdings, has led to suggestions that companies may "go private" in order to evade this form of scrutiny and attention (Chuah et al. 2024). That is, companies may de-list, or privatize, based on their peers' experiences with ESG activists. While this is possible, it is highly unlikely that the large, listed companies studied in this book would de-list from the ASX on this basis alone. Any attempt to privatize these companies would be virtually impossible given the profit and valuation implications. However, there is a real risk that shareholder activism may dissuade some corporations from listing on stock exchanges in the first place (Fairfax 2019). This is particularly the case for companies engaged in the sorts of practices that have been the focus of activists, including heavy emissions, engagement with First Nations communities, and pressure on water and other valuable commodities. This is particularly relevant in the mining sector, where many companies' impacts on the environment and Indigenous Australians may remain unscrutinized without the corporate governance processes, such as public AGMs, that occur when a company is listed on a stock exchange. The global growth in ESG shareholder activism may dissuade companies from listing on stock exchanges as a way of limiting scrutiny over their operations. Or, where ESG reporting requirements are rigorous, this reporting may also encourage firms to remain unlisted. In this sense, pro-ESG jurisdictions may be avoided by the companies whose operations should be most closely examined. Anti-ESG jurisdictions, such as the US, may become a magnet for corporations that wish to ignore ESG concerns. Origin's sale of its Beetaloo fracking rights to US-based private firm Tamboran suggests this is a reality. On the contrary, firms that have an ESG mindset, or operate in the renewable energy industry, may find they too seek corporate governance regimes that support their business model, such as those in the EU.

Attempts to further tighten Australia's corporate governance laws failed due to a change of government in 2022. However, while in power, the Morrison LNP government sought to intensify the rules governing proxy advisors and legislate against secondary boycotts. The proposals were introduced in response to environmental groups targeting financial institutions that were financing the proposed Adani coal mine in Queensland (O'Brien et al. 2023). The Morrison government, a supporter of the mine, sought to extinguish the campaign against the mine, partly through the curtailing of market-based activism, including secondary boycotts. While the Australian Federal Government was following the lead of other pro-business regulators globally in an attempt to limit the ability of social movements to target corporations over their social record, it is possible that a government open to the concept of market-based activism and scope for investor voice may one day seek to instead expand shareholders' rights. The predominant manner by which interviewees suggested this could change would be to simply allow shareholders to file advisory resolutions, once a minimum parcel of shareholdings was met, as is the case in other comparable jurisdictions. The ability of investors to file non-binding resolutions was seen as something which would open up debate due to the non-consequential nature of the filing. One interviewee described non-binding resolutions as "an expansive discomfort rather than a narrowing discomfort" for companies, where their policies, approaches, and management could be challenged and subsequently negotiated without a resolution calling for the overthrow of the board, as is currently the case.

The research in this book confirms the presence of a transnational ecosystem of market-based actors who leverage systems of corporate governance to pressure companies, industries, and policy makers to respond to urgent issues of ESG concern. The emerging literature on this topic suggests a convergence of global norms of business behavior is possible, as activists target firms across borders and investors are increasingly required to take ESG considerations into account. It is clear from the examples presented in this book that convergence across some jurisdictions is taking place. There is evidence of what one interviewee described as a "ripple effect," that is, the dissemination of new norms of business behavior through activist pressure and the behavior of firms with significant private authority, as well as investors who increasingly take into consideration companies' ESG practices. For example, ACCR has been pivotal in developing the say on climate initiative, through its local demands that companies put their climate transition plans to vote. Working with transnational actors, this group has exported this initiative globally, and it is increasingly being absorbed into norms of business practice. The entangling of ESG with traditional financial metrics is further complicated by the introduction of EU and UK regulation obligating investors and proxy advisors to consider sustainability in their investment decisions and advice. As in other policy arenas, the legislating of mandatory ESG considerations may lead to convergence globally. Companies that operate transnationally and are required to meet these obligations in the EU and UK can disseminate these norms of business practice to other jurisdictions where this is not a hard law requirement but where firms and investors will report, nonetheless. The challenge may lie in instances where investors, companies, or advisory services operate in multiple markets, including those with anti-ESG regulation; here, they may find themselves unable to meet competing regulations. This tension is a reality for companies operating globally and may lead to convergence through the avoidance of markets with a strong anti-ESG stance. Again, this suggests that those attempting to regulate against investor voice may find the targets of their regulations unable to neatly and effectively separate profits and sustainability.

Convergence, however, is not universal. Global divergence on norms of appropriate business behavior remains evident. Australia's legal approach to the protection of First Nations' cultural heritage has lagged behind other settler colonies', and the powerful mining sector has been long resistant to accepting and promoting norms around the protection of First Nations' heritage, norms that had been readily accepted elsewhere globally. Resistance from local powerful interests, including mining companies, led to contestation and the emergence of a "fragmented norm," one that was internalized at the transnational level but not yet by local actors. Sub-national law also fails to compel companies to engage effectively with local communities, leaving the decision of when and how to engage to companies and their willingness to comply with international soft law. The implications of this weak regulation were evident when Rio Tinto destroyed the Juukan Caves, an action that was legal under Western

Australian law. Yet, when investors were asked to reach a consensus on consequences for the board and management, their response was highly divergent. Australian-based institutional investors, backed by their British counterparts, sought the dismissal of the Chair and senior executives and a reduced severance package, while US-based investors saw the loss of leadership as potentially damaging to the valuation of Rio Tinto and pushed for the executives to remain in their positions. While there is likely to be some convergence on ESG standards globally, particularly as legislation requiring companies, investors, and proxy advisors to incorporate ESG concerns proliferates, there remains significant room for not only divergence, but conflict. Where market-based actors engage across borders, they may increasingly find themselves unable to simultaneously meet the legal requirements of jurisdictions that are pro- and anti-ESG. Moreover, as the case of Rio Tinto shows, investors in the same company may not agree on ESG standards or appropriate responses to poor corporate performance.

Australian government action on ESG issues including climate change and the protection of First Nations' culturally significant sites lags behind societal expectations. Even where ESG shareholder activism has been successful and has led to change at the corporation and industry level, governments across the board have failed to translate this into policy and regulation, or have even reversed activist gains. It is argued in this book that Australia's ability to meet its Paris targets, and reconcile its fraught history with Indigenous Australians, hinges on the actions of corporations. Large, listed companies are under immense scrutiny over their ESG performance, and activists, investors, and other market actors have expressed a view that waiting for legislative guidance is an insufficient response. Instead, where regulation lags, companies that fail to meet societal expectations are likely to be punished by shareholders. This may be through overhaul of the board and a subsequent repositioning of the company, as occurred with AGL. It may be through forced departures of executives, as occurred at Rio Tinto. Or, it could be through a divestment of core business activities, as occurred with Origin in the Beetaloo Basin. A powerful duopoly of activist investors has harnessed shareholder support for more sustainable business, supported at various times by wealthy ethical investors, overseas pension funds, and proxy advisors. This buttressing of local activism is only likely to grow as funds that operate in the EU and UK are increasingly forced to report on their ESG considerations. It is the more responsive and engaged firms that will benefit from this foreign direct investment, rather than those that continue to ignore society's calls for the transition to clean energy, respect for workers' rights, and consideration of Indigenous Australians and their culture.

Avenues for Future Research

This book presents the first comprehensive study into ESG shareholder activism in a unique and interesting case, Australia. While it presents important findings, it also raises the potential for future avenues of research. Firstly, this research has focused on the rise of ESG shareholder activism in one jurisdiction, Australia. In doing so, comparisons are drawn between Australia and other regions where ESG activism has been the focus of scholarly work (i.e., the US, UK, and EU). There are valuable lessons to be learned from states outside these examples, and there is scope for greater comparative studies of market-based activism in liberal market economies. Missing from almost all of these discussions, however, are the voices and strategies of anti-corporate activists from First Nations' communities in settler colonies, as well as voices from the Global South. Indigenous peoples globally are at the forefront of the interplay between mining, the shift to renewable energy, and the protection of human rights, environment, and culture. For them, anti-corporate politics is nothing new. First Nations Australians have been actively resisting the destruction of culture and environment since their first interactions with Europeans. There is much to be written about the anti-corporate politics of First Nations peoples, both locally and at the transnational level.

While Australian ESG shareholder activists have demonstrated a record of success in lobbying companies over sustainability challenges, this form of engagement disappeared as rapidly as it emerged. In 2023 there were only six resolutions filed at the AGMs of Australia's largest corporations. As one interviewee hinted in their discussions for this research, activists had indicated this would be part of their strategy. While ESG shareholder resolutions remained a tactic that could be used, activists were now planning on targeting individual board members, particularly at the time of their re-election. This was visible during the high-profile campaign against Chair Richard Goyder's re-election to the Woodside board. In these cases activists are not required to file a shareholder resolution;

instead, they can focus their energy on mobilizing other market-based actors such as institutional investors and proxy advisors to protest director and chairs' re-election. This opens up the range of possible corporate targets, as activists do not need to meet the relevant ownership hurdle, meaning all listed companies could feasibly be targeted. This is in alignment with the strategy conveyed in personal communication with activists, who noted that they will continue to target companies but through the rights and responsibilities of board members, pressuring individuals to take responsibility for their company's ESG performance through the concept of fiduciary duty.

As noted throughout this book, the role of business in solving ESG challenges remains contested. The potential for greenwashing is often cited as evidence of the inability for society to rely on business to solve these issues. This argument is used by anti-ESG activists who argue business and politics should remain separate. It is also often touted by those who view corporate governance skeptically, seeing no reason to think business can be incentivized to "do good." This book does not explore the potential for greenwashing but acknowledges its existence, particularly in the area of passive investing. Funds under management in passive ESG funds, such as those managed by the Big Three, have grown exponentially over the last decade. Yet, these funds are frequently exposed by regulators for making misleading claims about their ESG credentials. For example, in 2024, the Federal Court of Australia fined Vanguard A$12.9 million for failing to properly apply ESG exclusionary screens in its Vanguard Ethically Conscious Global Aggregate Bond Index Fund. Noting that this is an area of concern for the Australian regulator ASIC, Deputy Chair Sarah Court stated, "Greenwashing is a serious threat to the integrity of the Australian financial system, and remains an enforcement priority" (ASIC 2024). While this work has focused on ESG shareholder activism, which does not suffer from the same exposure to the risks of greenwashing, there is much work to be done on ensuring ESG-focused investors are being protected in the high-growth space of passive investing.

Finally, this research has demonstrated a serious lack of attention paid by activists, investors, and other market-based actors to social and governance challenges. While climate change remains an existential threat, heightened by the shape of Australia's economy and its reliance on mineral extraction, the country also faces many other challenges that remain unaddressed. There is significant scope for research that seeks to understand how these issues can be elevated to the agenda of large corporations in the same way that climate change has. There is much work to be done globally on the rights of workers in opaque supply chains, the treatment of Indigenous rightsholders, and other social issues, particularly in settler-colonial states. An important future avenue for research is to examine how market-based activism can be leveraged to address a wider array of issues.

This book focuses on a period of great change in Australia's political economy. It was during this time that activists devised a method of exercising investor voice, giving them a seat at the table and a mechanism by which they could bring non-activist investors into discussions about the direction of their companies and their impact on society. Concurrently, and partly as a result of this voice, corporate Australia began to reckon with the impacts of a rapidly changing climate. Natural disasters were increasing in frequency and intensity, a fact not lost on insurers, financiers, and corporations in general. Suddenly, the federal government's refusal to formalize commitments to lower carbon emissions was peripheral. It was clear that it was not regulatory mechanisms that would drive change; corporations themselves began to understand the risks of being trapped with stranded assets. Motivated by profits, companies also saw opportunities in renewables. Mining and energy-generation companies were cognizant of the risks of losing these opportunities to new entrants or competitors. The resulting shift to renewable energy in the late 2010s was unpredicted and unprecedented. So much so that governments were not ready for the rapid uptake of renewables and the speed at which companies like AGL and Origin would redirect their strategies toward exiting emissions-intensive power generation. Activists and investors led the charge in reforming these companies, which are now being steered toward the path of transitioning to renewable energy generators. It was only through the underwriting of state governments that these companies were willing to continue to generate coal-fired power. Yet, there is a finite limit on how long this arrangement can last, given the age and condition of the country's coal-fired power stations. Corporate Australia continues to carry the burden of the shift to renewable energy.

While this rapid pace of change is occurring in Australia's race to renewable energy, the same cannot be said for the other issue central to the analysis in this book. Australia continues to struggle to reconcile its fraught history of relations with Indigenous Australians, as was evidenced by the failure of the 2023 referendum, which modestly proposed to recognize First Australians in the constitution and to provide an advisory voice to parliament. Sub-national laws, which regulate mining and its impact on culturally significant sites, have repeatedly failed to put the interests of capital behind those of the country's First Peoples. There is also little to suggest that companies have learned from Rio Tinto's corporate governance failures. While large competitors, such as BHP, have made moves to reassure investors, smaller companies remain free to abide by weak state regulation, ignoring the calls of international soft law instruments.

Corporate Australia is likely to remain a target of ESG activists, motivated by the lack of regulation governing emissions reduction and social issues. As explored in this book, there remains little to suggest national or sub-national governments will introduce a price on carbon or greater protection for Australia's First Nations peoples' culture. Those concerned about the country's contribution to climate change or the protection of vulnerable groups in society will continue to pressure companies and their boards to improve business practices in an attempt to disseminate new norms of corporate behavior. Increasingly, they will be joined by investors, proxy advisors, and other financial actors for whom ESG and financial materiality are inextricably linked. It is in the space where profitability and ESG overlap that social movements will succeed, as has been demonstrated in the case of climate change. Where social movements are unable to emphasize the financially material impacts of poor corporate behavior, it remains unlikely that business can be pressured to respond to societal concerns.

Notes

Introduction

1. This figure is much higher for neighboring countries, with people living in the Pacific one hundred times more likely to be displaced by climate-induced crises than those living in Europe.

2. This figure is difficult to calculate. The IMF estimates the cost to be US$29 billion (Caody et al. 2019), however this number includes the environmental and social price of greenhouse gas emissions. The Productivity Commission figure above only includes direct, financial subsidies.

Chapter 1

1. Dorothy Lund and Adriana Robertson (2023) rightfully note that this label and characterization are somewhat of a misnomer. Fidelity's assets under management are greater than State Street's, making it a significant player in this industry. Furthermore, while passive investing has grown in significance since the financial crisis, all funds also hold significant amounts of active investments.

2. The issues driving activists have not disappeared with the transition to majority rule. South Africa remains the world's most unequal country, beset by ongoing social and economic implications of Apartheid rule.

Chapter 2

1. In a survey of the private authority scholarship, Janina Grabs et al. (2021) demonstrate that the conclusions reached by scholars on effectiveness and applicability often depend on the ontological assumptions of researchers. This is particularly the case because scholars of private governance come from a variety of disciplines, bring with them varied assumptions, and seek to answer different questions.

2. The companies included in this research are: Origin Energy, Rio Tinto, Santos, ANZ Banking Group, BHP, Woodside Petroleum, AGL, and National Australia Bank Group.

3. This project utilized qualitative research methods to analyze a database of ESG shareholder resolutions, which included 104 substantive claims on Australian companies. The construction of the database utilized the rich open data collected, collated, and shared by the Australasian Centre for Corporate Responsibility. This data was then augmented by filling in gaps, where required, updating to the end of 2022, including the activists' claim-making, corporate responses (as appear in the Notice of AGM), and voting outcomes.

The focus of the research was then narrowed down to the eight companies where the greatest number of ESG resolutions were filed, ensuring that at least two companies from each key economic sector were included. This resulted in a total of seventy-one resolutions filed at the AGMs of Origin Energy, Rio Tinto, Santos, ANZ Banking Group, BHP, Woodside Petroleum, AGL, and National Australia Group between 2017 and 2022. The researcher attended the AGMs of the eight firms in 2021 and 2022, which were all webcast, to undertake participant observation of the meetings.

Thematic content analysis was conducted on the activist claim-making, corporate responses, and the associated interviews conducted during 2021 and 2022. Activist claim-making and corporate responses for each of the seventy-one ESG resolutions were analyzed and triangulated through interviews with key actors in this space. Codes for the analysis were derived from two read-throughs of the documents by the researcher. From this, two coding tables were established, one for activist claim-making and one for corporate responses. The seventy-one documents, and interviews, were uploaded to NVivo 12, and the program was used to extract paragraphs where these codes occurred.

The interviewees for this project were located through utilizing existing research and professional connections, approaching via email, and through use of the snowball technique whereby interviewees would suggest others for the researcher to contact. They were connected to a range of private organizations including businesses, financial services, and civil society. Job ranks varied, although most were employed at senior levels within their various organizations given their authorization to speak to a researcher. The interviews took place between September 2021 and March 2022, and via Zoom given the Covid-induced lockdowns in Australia.

The research in this book was approved by the University of Sydney's Human Research Ethics Committee on May 3, 2021.

Chapter 3

1. There are currently twenty-four coal-fired power stations in operation in Australia, of which Eraring is the largest (Australian Energy Market Operator 2021).

Chapter 4

1. In 2015, HESTA (the health and community services pension fund) responded to activist pressure by divesting from Transfield Holdings, the company responsible for managing Australia's offshore detention centers in Manus Island Papua New Guinea and Nauru. While this campaign drew the company's attention to the risks of poor social engagement, it did so through the holdings of institutional investors (O'Brien et al. 2022).

2. A break in this policy occurred between 2008 and 2012, after which the government reintroduced offshore detention on the basis that more boat arrivals had led to more deaths at sea.

3. The Closing the Gap targets are nineteen socioeconomic measures that impact the lives of Aboriginal and Torres Strait Islander people. The goal of the National Agreement on Closing the Gap is to overcome the inequality experienced by Aboriginal and Torres Strait Islander people to achieve equal lives for all Australians.

4. Successful referendums in Australia are rare; they require a majority at the national level and then of a majority of states and territories. In 2023, only the Australian Capital Territory recorded a majority "yes" vote. All other states and one remaining territory (Northern Territory) recorded a majority "no" vote.

Bibliography

ACCR. 2017. *Investor Briefing Note: ACCR Shareholder Resolution to Oil Search.* https://d3n8a8pro7vhmx.cloudfront.net/accr/pages/450/attachments/original/1494488108/ACCR_-_Oil_Search_investor_briefing_note.pdf?1494488108%3E.

ACCR. 2020a. "Rio Board Review: Financial Penalties Completely off the Mark of Damage Caused; CEO Must Go." https://www.accr.org.au/news/rio-board-review-financial-penalties-completely-off-the-mark-of-damage-caused-ceo-must-go/.

ACCR. 2020b. "Rio Tinto Takes the First Step to Recovery." https://www.accr.org.au/news/rio-tinto-takes-the-first-step-to-recovery/.

ACCR. 2022a. *Annual Report 21/22.* https://www.accr.org.au/2021-2022/.

ACCR. 2022b. "Beetaloo Divestment Will Not Reduce Emissions." https://www.accr.org.au/news/beetaloo-divestment-will-not-reduce-emissions/.

ACCR. 2023. "Brynn O'Brien." https://www.accr.org.au/about/people/brynn-obrien/.

ACCR. 2024a. "ACCR Company Engagement J-Power." https://www.accr.org.au/companies/j-power/.

ACCR. 2024b. "Highlights of 2024." https://hub.accr.org.au/impact/highlights-of-2024/.

ACCR. 2025. Australian ESG Shareholder Resolutions.

Acharya, Abhijith G., David Gras, and Ryan Krause. 2022. "Socially Oriented Shareholder Activism Targets: Explaining Activists' Corporate Target Selection Using Corporate Opportunity Structures." *Journal of Business Ethics* 178 (2): 307–23. https://doi.org/10.1007/s10551-021-04785-5. https://doi.org/10.1007/s10551-021-04785-5.

AGL. 2021. *2021 Annual General Meeting - Results of Meeting.* https://www.agl.com.au/content/dam/digital/agl/documents/about-agl/media-centre/2021/210922-agl-2021-agm-results-of-meeting.pdf.

Allam, L. 2020. "Rio Tinto Condemned by Shareholders for Seeking Legal Advice Before Blowing Up Juukan Gorge." *The Guardian (UK).* https://www.theguardian.com/business/2020/sep/07/rio-tinto-condemned-by-shareholders-for-seeking-legal-advice-before-blowing-up-juukan-gorge.

Allen, Rupert, Hugues Letourneau, and Tessa Hebb. 2012. "Shareholder Engagement in the Extractive Sector." *Journal of Sustainable Finance & Investment* 2 (1): 3–25.

Allianz Global Investors. 2024. "AllianzGI to Vote Against Woodside Energy's Climate Transition Action Plan and the Election of the Chair of the Board." https://www.allianzgi.com/en/press-centre/media/press-releases/20240410-allianzgi-to-vote-against-woodside-energys-climate-transition-action-plan.

Amenta, Edwin, Neal Caren, Elizabeth Chiarello, and Yang Su. 2010. "The Political Consequences of Social Movements." *Annual Review of Sociology* 36 (1): 287–307. https://doi.org/10.1146/annurev-soc-070308-120029. https://www.annualreviews.org/doi/abs/10.1146/annurev-soc-070308-120029.

American Securities Association. 2023. "ASA Outlines Principles for Proxy Process Reform to House Financial Services Committee." https://www.americansecurities.org/post/asa-outlines-principles-for-proxy-process-reform-to-house-financial-services-committee.

Amnesty International. 2024. "Unsafe Offshore Detention Facilities mean Asylum Seekers must be Processed in Australia." https://www.amnesty.org.au/unsafe-offshore-detention-facilities-mean-asylum-seekers-must-be-processed-in-australia/.

Ancelovici, Marcos. 2021. "Bourdieu in Movement: Toward a Field Theory of Contentious Politics." *Social Movement Studies* 20 (2): 155–73.

Anderson, Kirsten, and Ian Ramsay. 2006. "From the Picket Line to the Boardroom: Union Shareholder Activism." *University of Melbourne Legal Studies Research Paper* (255).

Anderson, Kirsten, Ian Ramsay, Shelley Marshall, and Richard Mitchell. 2007. "Union Shareholder Activism in the Context of Declining Labour Law

Protection: Four Australian Case Studies." *Corporate Governance: An International Review* 15 (1): 45–56.

Andrei, Alina G., J. Van Oosterhout, and Steve Sauerwald. 2023. "Symbolic Shareholder Democracy: Toward a Behavioral Understanding of the Role of Shareholder Voting in CEO Dismissals." *Organization Science* 34 (5): 1736–58.

Andrews, Kenneth T. 2001. "Social Movements and Policy Implementation: The Mississippi Civil Rights Movement and the War on Poverty, 1965 to 1971." *American Sociological Review*: 71–95.

ASIC. 2021. "ASIC Guidelines for Investor Meetings Using Virtual Technology."

ASIC. 2024. "ASIC's Vanguard Greenwashing Action Results in Record $12.9 Million Penalty." https://asic.gov.au/about-asic/news-centre/find-a-media-release/2024-releases/24-213mr-asic-s-vanguard-greenwashing-action-results-in-record-12-9-million-penalty/#:~:text=ASIC%20Deputy%20Chair%20Sarah%20Court,an%20enforcement%20priority%20for%20ASIC.

Australasian Centre for Corporate Responsibility. 2020a. "BHP Resolution Withdrawn: First Nations Alliance Reaches Outcome with BHP." https://www.accr.org.au/news/bhp-resolution-withdrawn-first-nations-alliance-reaches-outcome-with-bhp/.

Australasian Centre for Corporate Responsibility. 2020b. *Submission: Parliamentary Inquiry into the Destruction of 46,000 Year Old Caves at the Juukan Gorge.* https://www.accr.org.au/research/submission-parliamentary-inquiry-into-the-destruction-of-46-000-year-old-caves-at-the-juukan-gorge/.

Australian Council of Superannuation Investors. 2021. *Climate Change Policy.* https://acsi.org.au/policies/climate-change/.

Australian Energy Market Operator. 2021. *Draft 2022 Integrated System Plan.* https://aemo.com.au/-/media/files/major-publications/isp/2022/draft-2022-integrated-system-plan.pdf?la=en.

Australian Energy Market Operator. 2022. *2022 Integrated System Plan for the National Electricity Market.* https://aemo.com.au/en/energy-systems/major-publications/integrated-system-plan-isp/2022-integrated-system-plan-isp.

Australian Institute for Disaster Resiliance. 2020. "Australian Disaster Resiliance Knowledge Hub: Bushfires - Black Summer." Australian National Emergency Management Agency. https://knowledge.aidr.org.au/resources/black-summer-bushfires-nsw-2019-20/#:~:text=Six%20firefighters%20also%20died%2C%20including,during%20water%2Dbombing%20operations%20on.

Australian Institute of Company Directors. 2023. "The Lone Ranger." https://www.aicd.com.au/corporate-governance-sectors/Indigenous/business/the-lone-ranger.html.

Australian Productivity Commission. 2020. *Trade and Assistance Review 2018–19* (Canberra). https://www.pc.gov.au/ongoing/trade-assistance/2018-19/.

Australian Senate, Senate Environment and Communications Committee. 2021. *Oil and Gas Exploration and Production in the Beetaloo Basin.* https://www.aph.gov.au/Parliamentary_Business/Committees/Senate/Environment_and_Communications/BeetalooBasin/Interim_Report/section?id=committees%2Freportsen%2F024744%2F77655.

Avant, Deborah D., Martha Finnemore, and Susan K. Sell. 2010. *Who Governs the Globe?* Vol. 114. Cambridge University Press.

Backus, Matthew, Christopher Conlon, and Michael Sinkinson. 2021. "Common Ownership in America: 1980–2017." *American Economic Journal: Microeconomics* 13 (3): 273–308.

Bailey, Ian, Iain MacGill, Rob Passey, and Hugh Compston. 2012. "The Fall (and Rise) of Carbon Pricing in Australia: A Political Strategy Analysis of the Carbon Pollution Reduction Scheme." *Environmental Politics* 21 (5): 691–711.

Baines, Joseph, and Sandy Brian Hager. 2021. "Commodity Traders in a Storm: Financialization, Corporate Power and Ecological Crisis." *Review of International Political Economy*: 1–54. https://doi.org/10.1080/09692290.2021.1872039.

Bañon Gomis, Alexis J., Manuel Guillén Parra, W. Michael Hoffman, and Robert E. McNulty. 2011. "Rethinking the Concept of Sustainability." *Business and Society Review* 116 (2): 171–91.

Bansal, Pratima, and Mark R. DesJardine. 2014. "Business Sustainability: It Is About Time." *Strategic organization* 12 (1): 70–78.

Barko, Tamas, Martijn Cremers, and Luc Renneboog. 2022. "Shareholder Engagement on Environmental, Social, and Governance Performance." *Journal of Business Ethics* 180 (2): 777–812. https://doi.org/10.1007/s10551-021-04850-z.

Barnard, Jayne W. 1990. "Institutional Investors and the New Corporate Governance." *NCL Rev.* 69: 1135.

Barnes, Jamal. 2022. "Suffering to Save Lives: Torture, Cruelty, and Moral Disengagement in Australia's Offshore Detention Centres." *Journal of Refugee Studies* 35 (4): 1508–29. https://doi.org/10.1093/jrs/feac041.

Baron, David P. 2003. "Private Politics." *Journal of Economics & Management Strategy* 12 (1): 31–66.

Bartley, Tim. 2007. "Institutional Emergence in an Era of Globalization: The Rise of Transnational Private Regulation of Labor and Environmental Conditions." *American Journal of Sociology* 113 (2): 297–351.

Baumgartner, Frank R., and Bryan D. Jones. 2010. *Agendas and Instability in American Politics.* University of Chicago Press.

Bebchuk, Lucian Arye. 2004. "The Case for Increasing Shareholder Power." *Harv. L. Rev.* 118: 833.

Bebchuk, Lucian Ayre, Alon Brav, and Wei Jiang. 2015. *The Long-Term Effects of Hedge Fund Activism.* National Bureau of Economic Research.

Becht, Marco, Julian Franks, Colin Mayer, and Stefano Rossi. 2009. "Returns to Shareholder Activism: Evidence from a Clinical Study of the Hermes UK Focus Fund." *The Review of Financial Studies* 22 (8): 3093–129.

Beck, Ulrich. 2000. *What Is Globalization?* Polity.

Berenschot, Ward, Ahmad Dhiaulhaq, Afrizal, Otto Hospes, Rebekha Adriana, and Erysa Poetry. 2022. "Anti-Corporate Activism and Collusion: The Contentious Politics of Palm Oil Expansion in Indonesia." *Geoforum* 131: 39–49. https://doi.org/https://doi.org/10.1016/j.geoforum.2022.03.002.

Bernstein, Steven, and Benjamin Cashore. 2007. "Can Non-State Global Governance Be Legitimate? An Analytical Framework." *Regulation & Governance* 1 (4): 347–71. https://doi.org/10.1111/j.1748-5991.2007.00021.x.

BHP. 2019. "Industry Association Review." https://www.bhp.com/-/media/documents/ourapproach/operatingwithintegrity/industryassociations/191212_bhpindustryassociationreview2019.pdf?la=en.

BHP. 2020a. "BHP Annual General Meetings." https://www.bhp.com/-/media/documents/investors/shareholder-information/2020/200928_bhpchairmanshareholderletter2020.pdf?la=en.

BHP. 2020b. "First Nations Alliance and BHP Strengthen Heritage Protection in Australia." https://www.bhp.com/news/media-centre/releases/2020/10/first-nations-alliance-and-bhp-strengthen-heritage-protection-in-australia.

BHP. 2022. "Notice of Annual General Meeting: Bringing People and Resources Together to Build a Better World." https://www.bhp.com/-/media/documents/investors/shareholder-information/2022/221003_bhp2022noticeofmeeting.pdf.

Bice, Sara, Martin Brueckner, and Christof Pforr. 2017. "Putting Social License to Operate on the Map: A Social, Actuarial and Political Risk and Licensing Model (SAP Model)." *Resources Policy* 53: 46–55.

BlackRock. 2020. "Sustainable Investing." http://www.blackrock.com/us/individual/investment-ideas/sustainable-investing/sustainable-solutions.

Bloomberg Intelligence. 2024. "ESG AUM Set to Top $40 Trillion by 2030, Anchor Capital Markets." https://www.bloomberg.com/professional/insights/sustainable-finance/esg-aum-set-to-top-40-trillion-by-2030-anchor-capital-markets/#:~:text=ESG%20assets%20have%20proven%20resilient,3.5%25%20as%20the%20market%20matures.

Bodley, John H. 2014. *Victims of Progress.* Rowman & Littlefield.

Böhm, Steffen, and Annika Skoglund. 2022. *Climate Activism: How Communities Take Renewable Energy Actions Across Business and Society. Business, Value Creation, and Society.* Cambridge University Press.

Boone, Audra L, Stuart Gillan, and Mitch Towner. 2020. "The Role of Proxy Advisors and Large Passive Funds in Shareholder Voting: Lions or Lambs?" 2nd Annual Financial Institutions, Regulation and Corporate Governance Conference.

Bosi, Lorenzo, Marco Giugni, and Katrin Uba. 2016. *The Consequences of Social Movements.* Cambridge University Press.

Bottomley, Stephen. 2019. "Rethinking the Law on Shareholder-Initiated Resolutions at Company General Meetings." *Melbourne University Law Review* 43 (1): 93–132.

Boudet, Hilary. 2011. "From NIMBY to NIABY: Regional Mobilization Against Liquefied Natural Gas in the United States." *Environmental Politics* 20 (6): 786–806.

Bowley, Tim, and Jennifer G. Hill. 2024a. "The Global ESG Stewardship Ecosystem." *European Business Organization Law Review*: 1–40.

Bowley, Tim, and Jennifer G. Hill. 2024b. "Stewardship Codes, ESG Activism and Transnational Ordering." In *Research Handbook on Environmental, Social and Corporate Governance*, edited by Thilo Kuntz, 117–37. Edward Elgar.

Braun, Sarah. 2025. "It's Not Just DEI—Corporate ESG Initiatives Are Under Threat in the Trump Era and 80% of Companies Say They're Adjusting Their Policies." *Fortune.* https://fortune.com/2025/05/29/esg-under-threat-trump-era-majority-companies-changing-policies/.

Brav, Alon, Wei Jiang, Frank Partnoy, and Randall Thomas. 2008. "Hedge Fund Activism, Corporate Governance, and Firm Performance." *The Journal of Finance* 63 (4): 1729–75.

Briscoe, Forrest, M. K. Chin, and Donald C. Hambrick. 2014. "CEO Ideology as an Element of the Corporate Opportunity Structure for Social Activists." *Academy of Management Journal* 57 (6): 1786–809.

Briscoe, Forrest, and Sean Safford. 2008. "The Nixon-in-China Effect: Activism, Imitation, and the Institutionalization of Contentious Practices." *Administrative Science Quarterly* 53 (3): 460–91. https://doi.org/10.2189/asqu.53.3.460.

Brundtland, Gro Harlem. 1987. "Our Common Future—Call for Action." *Environmental Conservation* 14 (4): 291–94.

Bulkeley, Harriet, Liliana B. Andonova, Michele M. Betsill, Daniel Compagnon, Thomas Hale, Matthew J. Hoffman, Peter Newell, Matthew Paterson, Charles Roger, and Stacy D. Vandeveer. 2014. *Transnational Climate Change Governance.* Cambridge University Press.

Burton, David. 2024. "Financial Regulatory Agencies." In *2025 Mandate for Leadership: The Conservative Promise*, edited by Heritage Foundation.

Bush, Sarah Sunn, and Jennifer Hadden. 2025. *Crowded Out: The Competitive Landscape of Contemporary International NGOs*. Cambridge University Press.

Business Roundtable. 1997. "Statement on Corporate Governance." https://cdn.theconversation.com/static_files/files/693/Statement_on_Corporate_Governance_Business-Roundtable-1997%281%29.pdf?1566830902.

Business Roundtable. 2019. "Business Roundtable Redefined the Purpose of a Corporation to Promote 'An Economy That Serves All Americans.'" https://www.businessroundtable.org/business-roundtable-redefines-the-purpose-of-a-corporation-to-promote-an-economy-that-serves-all-americans.

Büthe, Tim, and Walter Mattli. 2011. *The New Global Rulers: The Privatization of Regulation in the World Economy*. Princeton University Press.

Butler, Ben. 2020. "'Test for the Board': UK Pension Fund Heaps Pressure on Rio Tinto Boss over Juukan Gorge Blasts." *The Guardian (UK)*. https://www.theguardian.com/business/2020/sep/09/test-for-the-board-uk-pension-fund-heaps-pressure-on-rio-tinto-boss-over-juukan-gorge-blasts.

Butler, Ben. 2021. "Rio Tinto Defends Not Stripping Bonuses from Executives Who Left Amid Juukan Gorge Outcry." *The Guardian*. https://www.theguardian.com/business/2021/may/06/rio-tinto-defends-not-stripping-bonuses-from-executives-who-left-amid-juukan-gorge-outcry#:~:text=Rio%20Tinto%20has%20defended%20its,Juukan%20Gorge%20in%20the%20Pilbara.

Butler, Dan. 2023. "These Traditional Owners Fear for Their Songlines, Saying the Northern Land Council Is Not Defending Them." *NITV*. https://www.sbs.com.au/nitv/article/these-traditional-owners-are-terrified-of-fracking-and-they/ency7tu86.

Cai, Jay, Jacqueline L. Garner, and Ralph A. Walkling. 2013. "A Paper Tiger? An Empirical Analysis of Majority Voting." *Journal of Corporate Finance* 21: 119–35.

Callaghan, Helen. 2018. *Contestants, Profiteers, and the Political Dynamics of Marketization: How Shareholders Gained Control Rights in Britain, Germany, and France*. 1st ed. Oxford University Press.

Campbell, Rod, Liz Morison, Piers Verstegen, Morgan Harrington, Alexia Adhikari, Kristen Scicluna, Evie Simpson, and Lilia Anderson. 2023. *Fossil Fuel Subsidies in Australia 2023 Federal and State Government Assistance to Fossil Fuel Producers and Major Users in 2022–23*. The Australia Institute. https://australiainstitute.org.au/wp-content/uploads/2023/05/P1378-Fossil-fuel-subsidies-2023-Web.pdf.

Caody, David, Ian Parry, Nghia-Piotr Le, and Baoping Shang. 2019. *Global Fossil Fuel Subsidies Remain Large: An Update Based on Country-Level Estimates.*

International Monetary Fund. https://www.imf.org/en/Publications/WP/Issues/2019/05/02/Global-Fossil-Fuel-Subsidies-Remain-Large-An-Update-Based-on-Country-Level-Estimates-46509.

Caradonna, Jeremy L. 2022. *Sustainability: A History.* Oxford University Press.

Carrington, Damian. 2015. "Shell Urges Shareholders to Accept Climate Resolution." *The Guardian.* https://www.theguardian.com/environment/2015/jan/29/shell-urges-shareholders-to-accept-climate-change-resolution.

Cashore, Benjamin William. 2002. "Legitimacy and the Privatization of Environmental Governance: How Non–State Market–Driven (NSMD) Governance Systems Gain Rule–Making Authority." *Governance* 15 (4): 503–29. https://doi.org/10.1111/1468-0491.00199.

Caulkin, S. 1997. "Amnesty and WWF Take a Crack at Shell." *The Observer.*

CERES. 2002. *Value at Risk: Climate Change and the Future of Governance.*

Cerrato, Davide, and Tomaso Ferrando. 2020. "The Financialization of Civil Society Activism: Sustainable Finance, Non-Financial Disclosure and the Shrinking Space for Engagement." *Accounting, Economics, and Law: A Convivium* 10 (2): 20190006.

CGI Glass Lewis. 2023a. "2023 Policy Guidelines." https://www.glasslewis.com/wp-content/uploads/2022/11/US-Voting-Guidelines-2023-GL.pdf.

CGI Glass Lewis. 2023b. "Company Overview." https://www.glasslewis.com/company-overview/.

Chau, David, and Michael Janda. 2020. "Rio Tinto Boss Jean-Sebastien Jacques Quits over Juukan Gorge Blast." *ABC News.* https://www.abc.net.au/news/2020-09-11/rio-tinto-boss-jean-sebastien-jacques-quits-over-juukan-blast/12653950#.

Cheffins, Brian R. 2010. "The Stewardship Code's Achilles' Heel." *The Modern Law Review* 73 (6): 1004–25.

Chiu, I. H., and D. Katelouzou. 2017. "From Shareholder Stewardship to Shareholder Duties: Is the Time Ripe?" In *Shareholder Duties*, edited by H. S. Mirkmose, 131. Luwer Law International.

Chiu, Iris H.-Y. 2013. "Reviving Shareholder Stewardship: Critically Examining the Impact of Corporate Transparency Reforms in the UK." *Del. J. Corp. L.* 38: 983.

Christoff, Peter. 2005. "Policy Autism or Double-Edged Dismissiveness? Australia's Climate Policy under the Howard Government." *Global Change, Peace & Security* 17 (1): 29–44. https://doi.org/10.1080/0951274052000319346.

Chuah, Kevin, Mark R. DesJardine, Maria Goranova, and Witold J. Henisz. 2024. "Shareholder Activism Research: A System-Level View." *Academy of*

Management Annals 18 (1): 82–120. https://doi.org/10.5465/annals.2022.0069.

Clapp, Jennifer. 2002. "The Distancing of Waste: Overconsumption in a Global Economy." *Confronting Consumption*: 155–76.

Clapp, Jennifer. 2014. "Financialization, Distance and Global Food Politics." *The Journal of Peasant Studies* 41 (5): 797–814.

Clark, Gordon, James Salo, and Tessa Hebb. 2008. "Social and Environmental Shareholder Activism in the Public Spotlight: US Corporate Annual Meetings, Campaign Strategies, and Environmental Performance, 2001–04." *Environment and Planning A* 40 (6): 1370–90.

Climate Action 100+. 2024. "Methodologies." https://www.climateaction100.org/net-zero-company-benchmark/methodology/.

Coffee Jr., John C. 2021. "The Coming Shift in Shareholder Activism: From 'Firm-Specific' to 'Systematic Risk' Proxy Campaigns (and How to Enable Them)." *Brook. J. Corp. Fin. & Com. L.* 16: 45.

Collins, Luke, Ross A. Bradstock, Hamish Clarke, Michael F. Clarke, Rachael H. Nolan, and Trent D. Penman. 2021. "The 2019/2020 Mega-Fires Exposed Australian Ecosystems to an Unprecedented Extent of High-Severity Fire." *Environmental Research Letters* 16 (4): 044029.

Commonwealth of Australia. 2023. *Intergenerational Report 2023: Australia's Future to 2063*. https://treasury.gov.au/sites/default/files/2023-08/p2023-435150.pdf.

Condon, Madison. 2020. "Externalities and the Common Owner." *Wash. L. Rev.* 95: 1.

Conservation Council of WA. 2024. "Choking the Energy Transition: Woodside Continues to Increase Emissions Amidst Climate Crisis." https://www.ccwa.org.au/choking_the_energy_transition.

Copland, James, David F. Larcker, and Brian Tayan. 2018. "The Big Thumb on the Scale: An Overview of the Proxy Advisory Industry." *Rock Center for Corporate Governance at Stanford University Closer Look Series: Topics, Issues and Controversies in Corporate Governance No. CGRP-72, Stanford University Graduate School of Business Research Paper* (18–27).

Corporate and Markets Advisory Committee. 2012. *The AGM and Shareholder Engagement Discussion Paper*. https://www.camac.gov.au/camac/camac.nsf/byheadline/pdfdiscussion+papers/$file/agm.pdf.

Corporations Act (2001) Cth.

Cox, Lisa. 2023. "'We Need Help': Traditional Owners Accuse Land Council of 'Facilitating Fracking.'" *The Guardian*. https://www.theguardian.com/australia-news/2023/jun/20/beetaloo-basin-traditional-owners-land-council-gas-fracking-northern-territory.

Cox, Lisa. 2025. "How an Obscure Consultancy Firm Is Helping Fracking Companies Influence Traditional Owners." *The Guardian*. https://www.theguardian.com/australia-news/2025/jun/24/consulting-firm-good-advice-empire-energy-private-deals-signatures-northern-territory-gas-sales-leaked-documents-ntwnfb.

Cox, Robert Henry, and Daniel Béland. 2013. "Valence, Policy Ideas, and the Rise of Sustainability." *Governance* 26 (2): 307–28.

Cutler, A. Claire, Virginia Haufler, and Tony Porter, eds. 1999. *Private Authority and International Affairs*. State University of New York Press.

Dashwood, Hevina S. 2012. *The Rise of Global Corporate Social Responsibility: Mining and the Spread of Global Norms*. Cambridge University Press.

Dauvergne, Peter, and Genevieve LeBaron. 2014. *Protest Inc.: The Corporatization of Activism*. Polity.

Davies, Anne. 2017. "BHP Expected to Reject Activists' Push to Give Shareholders a Greater Voice." *The Guardian Australia*. https://www.theguardian.com/business/2017/oct/19/bhp-expected-to-reject-activists-push-to-give-shareholders-a-greater-voice.

Davis, Gerald F. 2008. "A New Finance Capitalism? Mutual Funds and Ownership Re-Concentration in the United States." *European Management Review* 5 (1): 11–21.

Davis, Gerald F. 2009. *Managed by the Markets: How Finance Re-Shaped America*. OUP Oxford.

Davis, Gerald F., and Tracy A. Thompson. 1994. "A Social Movement Perspective on Corporate Control." *Administrative Science Quarterly*: 141–73.

Del Guercio, Diane, Laura Seery, and Tracie Woidtke. 2008. "Do Boards Pay Attention When Institutional Investor Activists 'Just Vote No'?" *Journal of Financial Economics* 90 (1): 84–103. https://doi.org/https://doi.org/10.1016/j.jfineco.2008.01.002.

Della Porta, Donatella. 2020. "Protests as Critical Junctures: Some Reflections Towards a Momentous Approach to Social Movements." *Social Movement Studies* 19 (5–6): 556–75.

Della Porta, Donatella, and Elias Steinhilper. 2021. *Contentious Migrant Solidarity: Shrinking Spaces and Civil Society Contestation*. Routledge.

Della Porta, Donatella, and Hanspeter Kriesi. 1999. "Social Movements in a Globalizing World: An Introduction." In *Social Movements in a Globalizing World*, 3–22. Springer.

Della Porta, Donatella, and Maria Fabbri. 2016. "Producing Space in Action: The Protest Campaign Against the Construction of the Dal Molin Military Base." *Social Movement Studies* 15 (2): 180–96.

Department of Climate Change, Energy, the Environment and Water. 2024. "Australian Energy Statistics: Renewables." https://www.energy.gov.au/energy-data/australian-energy-statistics/renewables.

Di Stefano, Mark, and Samantha Hutchinson. 2023. "Australia's Pokies Addiction Explained in Four Charts." *Australian Financial Review*. https://www.afr.com/companies/games-and-wagering/what-will-happen-if-pokies-go-cashless-20221212-p5c5os.

Dick, Samantha. 2022. "Origin Energy Quitting Beetaloo Fracking Project an 'Indicator' of Gas Industry's Future, Analyst Says." *ABC*. https://www.abc.net.au/news/2022-09-20/nt-origin-quitting-beetaloo-project-may-signal-gas-decline/101454668.

Dinshaw, Freya, Justine Nolan, Christina Hill, Amy Sinclair, Shelley Marshall, Fiona McGaughey, Martijn Boersma, Vikram Bhakoo, Jasper Goss, and Peter Keegan. 2022. *Broken Promises: Two Years of Corporate Reporting Under Austrlia's Modern Slavery Act*. https://static1.squarespace.com/static/580025f66b8f5b2dabbe4291/t/6375ce29c0dad25a4841722f/1668664881220/HRLC_Broken_Promises_2022_11_17.pdf.

Diversity Council of Australia. 2024. *Joint Diversity Council Australia, University of Sydney Business School, University of Technology Sydney Business School/Jumbunna Institute for Indigenous Education and Research Submission on the 5th Edition of the ASX Corporate Governance Council Principles and Recommendations Consultation.*

Doidge, Craig, Alexander Dyck, Hamed Mahmudi, and Aazam Virani. 2015. "Can Institutional Investors Improve Corporate Governance through Collective Action?" *Rotman School of Management Working Paper* 21.

Drucker, Peter. 1996. *The Pension Fund Revolution*. Transaction Publishers.

Eilstrup-Sangiovanni, Mette, and Laura Breen. 2024. "Issue-Adoption and Campaign Structure in Transnational Advocacy Campaigns: A Longitudinal Network Analysis." *European Journal of International Relations* 30 (2): 486–516.

Elbra, Ainsley. 2014. "Interests Need Not Be Pursued if They Can Be Created: Private Governance in African Gold Mining." *Business and Politics* 16 (2): 247–66. https://doi.org/10.1515/bap-2013-0021.

Elbra, Ainsley. 2017. *Governing African Gold Mining: Private Governance and the Resource Curse*. Palgrave Macmillan.

Elbra, Ainsley. 2020. "Fool's Gold: Business Power and the Evolution of the Conflict-Free Gold Standard." *Global Policy* 11 (3).

Elbra, Ainsley. 2023. "The AGM as a Site of Contestation: Evaluating the Tactics of Environmental Shareholder Activists." *New Political Economy*: 1–15. https://doi.org/10.1080/13563467.2023.2264211.

Elbra, Ainsley, Erin O'Brien, and Martijn Boersma. 2025. "The Political Influence of Proxy Advisors in Campaigns for Ethical Investment: Guiding the Invisible Hand." *Regulation & Governance.*

Enari, Dion, and Lisa Viliamu Jameson. 2021. "Climate Justice: A Pacific Island Perspective." *Australian Journal of Human Rights* 27 (1): 149–60.

Engine No. 1. 2021. "Reenergize ExxonMobil: Investor Presentation." https://reenergizexom.com/mater ials/engine-no-1-releases-white-paper-detailing-changing-energy-landscape-in-response-to-exxon mobil-investor-day-presentation-2.

English II, Philip C., Thomas I. Smythe, and Chris R. McNeil. 2004. "The 'CalPERS Effect' Revisited." *Journal of Corporate Finance* 10 (1): 157–74.

Environmental Defenders Office. 2020. *Submission to the Inquiry into the Destruction of 46,000 Year Old Caves at the Juukan Gorge in the Pilbara Region of Western Australia.* https://www.edo.org.au/wp-content/uploads/2020/08/200814-EDO-Submission-Inquiry-into-Juukan-Gorge-destruction.pdf.

Ertimur, Yonca, Fabrizio Ferri, and David Oesch. 2018. "Understanding Uncontested Director Elections." *Management Science* 64 (7): 3400–20.

Etchart, Linda. 2022. "Sustainable Funds and 'Cuddly Capitalism': Indigenous Land Defenders and the Greenwashing of Investment Management." In *Global Governance of the Environment, Indigenous Peoples and the Rights of Nature: Extractive Industries in the Ecuadorian Amazon*, edited by Linda Etchart, 185–222. Springer International Publishing.

Fairfax, Lisa M. 2019. "From Apathy to Activism: The Emergence, Impact, and Future of Shareholder Activism as the New Corporate Governance Norm." *BUL Rev.* 99: 1301.

Falcon Oil & Gas. 2023. "Beetaloo Sub-Basin, Australia." https://web.archive.org/web/20230401133725/https://falconoilandgas.com/beetaloo-australia/.

Falkner, Robert. 2003. "Private Environmental Governance and International Relations: Exploring the Links." *Global Environmental Politics* 3 (2): 72–87. https://doi.org/10.1162/152638003322068227.

FAO. 2024. "Our Pillars: FPIC." https://www.fao.org/Indigenous-peoples/our-pillars/fpic/en/.

Fichtner, Jan, and Eelke M. Heemskerk. 2020. "The New Permanent Universal Owners: Index Funds, Patient Capital, and the Distinction Between Feeble and Forceful Stewardship." *Economy and Society* 49 (4): 493–515. https://doi.org/10.1080/03085147.2020.1781417.

Fichtner, Jan, Eelke M. Heemskerk, and Javier Garcia-Bernardo. 2017. "Hidden Power of the Big Three? Passive Index Funds, Re-Concentration of Corporate Ownership, and New Financial Risk." *Business and Politics* 19 (2): 298–326.

Filatotchev, Igor, and Oksana Dotsenko. 2015. "Shareholder Activism in the UK: Types of Activists, Forms of Activism, and Their Impact on a Target's Performance." *Journal of Management & Governance* 19 (1): 5–24.

Fink, Larry. 2018. *Larry Fink's Annual Letter to CEOs: A Sense of Purpose.* https://aips.online/wp-content/uploads/2018/04/Larry-Fink-letter-to-CEOs-2018-BlackRock.pdf.

First Nations Clean Energy Network. 2024. "More Than Half of Australia's Critical Minerals Mines Lie on Indigenous Land: Mongabay." https://www.firstnationscleanenergy.org.au/more_than_half_of_australia_s_critical_minerals_mines_lie_on_indigenous_land_mongabay#:~:text=In%20a%20new%20study%2C%20researchers,yet%20been%20determined%20are%20included.

Fiss, Peer C., and Edward J. Zajac. 2004. "The Diffusion of Ideas over Contested Terrain: The (Non) Adoption of a Shareholder Value Orientation among German Firms." *Administrative Science Quarterly* 49 (4): 501–34.

Fitzgerald, Roxanne. 2024. "Tamboran Resources, NT Government Face Another Beetaloo Basin Fracking Challenge under Novel 'Third Party' Laws." *ABC.* https://www.abc.net.au/news/2024-09-28/beetaloo-fracking-legal-challenge-ecnt-nt-government/104404794#.

Fitzgerald, Roxanne, and Sarah Spina-Matthews. 2023. "NT Government Announces Fracking in the Beetaloo Basin Can Go Ahead." *ABC.* https://www.abc.net.au/news/2023-05-03/nt-government-fracking-decision-beetaloo-basin-gas/102295762.

Fligstein, Neil. 2001. *The Architecture of Markets: An Economic Sociology of Twenty-First-Century Capitalist Societies.* Princeton University Press.

Follow This. 2025. "Follow This Pauses Climate Resolutions for Big Oil in 2025 Amid Investor Hesitation." https://www.follow-this.org/follow-this-pauses-climate-resolutions-for-big-oil-in-2025-amid-investor-hesitation/.

Fransen, Luc. 2011. *Corporate Social Responsibility and Global Labor Standards: Firms and Activists in the Making of Private Regulation.* Routledge.

Freeburn, Lloyd, and Ian Ramsay. 2021a. "An Analysis of ESG Shareholder Resolutions in Australia." *University of New South Wales Law Journal* 44 (3): 1142–79.

Freeburn, Lloyd, and Ian Ramsay. 2021b. "Virtual Shareholder Meetings in Australia." *International Company and Commercial Law Review* 32 (2): 67–93.

Frydenberg, Josh. 2019. "Government Response to the Digital Economy Consultation." https://joshfrydenberg.com.au/latest-news/government-response-to-digital-economy-consultation/.

Galanter, Marc. 1974. "Why the 'Haves' Come Out Ahead: Speculations on the Limits of Legal Change." *Law & society review* 9 (1): 95–160.

Gallagher, D., and Erika Weinthal. 2012. "Business-State Relations and the Environment: The Evolving Role of Corporate Social Responsibility." In *Comparative Environmental Politics: Theory Practice and Prospects*, edited by Paul F. Steinberg and Stacy D. Vandeveer, 143–70. MIT Press.

Gamson, William A. 1975. *The Strategy of Social Protest.* Dorsey Press.

Gamson, William A., and David S. Meyer. 1996. "Framing Political Opportunity." In *Comparative Perspectives on Social Movements: Political Opportunities, Mobilizing Structures, and Cultural Framings*, edited by Doug McAdam, John D. McCarthy, and Mayer Zald. Cambridge University Press.

Garrett, Daniel, and Ivan Ivanov. 2022. "Gas, Guns, and Governments: Financial Costs of Anti-ESG Policies." *Jacobs Levy Equity Management Center for Quantitative Financial Research Paper.* https://papers.ssrn.com/sol3/papers.cfm?abstract_id=4123366.

Geoscience Australia. 2024. *Australia's Energy Commodity Resources 2024 Gas.* https://www.ga.gov.au/aecr2024/gas#:~:text=Trade,period%20(DISR%2C%202024).

Gibson, Connor, and Frances Sawyer. 2023. *2023 Statehouse Report: Right-Wing Attacks on the Freedom to Invest Responsibly Falter in Legislatures.* Pleiades Strategy. https://www.pleiadesstrategy.com/state-house-report-bill-tracker-republican-anti-esg-attacks-on-freedom-to-invest-responsibly-earns-business-labor-and-environmental-opposition.

Gillan, Stuart, and Laura Starks. 2000. "Corporate Governance Proposals and Shareholder Activism: The Role of Institutional Investors." *Journal of Financial Economics* 57 (2): 275–305.

Gillan, Stuart, and Laura T. Starks. 2007. "The Evolution of Shareholder Activism in the United States." *Journal of Applied Corporate Finance* 19 (1): 55–73.

Gills, Barry, and Jamie Morgan. 2022. "Global Climate Emergency: After COP24, Climate Science, Urgency, and the Threat to Humanity." In *Economics and Climate Emergency*, 253–70. Routledge.

Gilson, Ronald J., and Jeffrey N. Gordon. 2013. "The Agency Costs of Agency Capitalism: Activist Investors and the Revaluation of Governance Rights." *Colum. L. Rev.* 113: 863.

Giugni, Marco, Doug McAdam, and Charles Tilly. 1999. *How Social Movements Matter.* Vol. 10. University of Minnesota Press.

Goldfarb, Bruce. 2020. "Are Virtual Annual Meetings Good for Shareholder Democracy?" *Forbes.* https://www.forbes.com/sites/brucegoldfarb/2020/05/05/are-virtual-annual-meetings-good-for-shareholder-democracy/?sh=6b9fe40927f3.

Gómez-Baggethun, Erik, and José Manuel Naredo. 2015. "In Search of Lost Time: The Rise and Fall of Limits to Growth in International Sustainability Policy." *Sustainability Science* 10: 385–95.

Gourevitch, Peter Alexis, and James Shinn. 2005. *Political Power and Corporate Control: The New Global Politics of Corporate Governance*. Princeton University Press.

Governance Institute of Australia. 2024. *Board Diversity Index*. https://www.watermarksearch.com.au/rails/active_storage/blobs/eyJfcmFpbHMiOnsibWVzc2FnZSI6IkJBaHBBeDhQSXc9PSIsImV4cCI6bnVsbCwicHVyIjoiYmxvYl9pZCJ9fQ==--d0c909b0ef43cd4a57829a789dacc9d53dddaac4/2024%20Board%20Diversity%20Index.pdf?source=boarddirection.com.au.

Grabs, Janina, Graeme Auld, and Benjamin Cashore. 2021. "Private Regulation, Public Policy, and the Perils of Adverse Ontological Selection." *Regulation & Governance* 15 (4): 1183–208. https://doi.org/10.1111/rego.12354.

Graves, Samuel B., Sandra Waddock, and Kathleen Rehbein. 2001. "Fad and Fashion in Shareholder Activism: The Landscape of Shareholder Resolutions, 1988–1998." *Business and Society Review* 106 (4): 293–314.

Greaves, Wilfrid. 2018. "Damaging Environments: Land, Settler Colonialism, and Security for Indigenous Peoples." *Environment and Society* 9 (1): 107–24.

Green, Antony. 2025. "FED2025—Four Graphs on Labor's Landslide Victory." *Antony Green's Election Blog* (blog). https://antonygreen.com.au/category/electoral-history/.

Green, Janice, and Bradley Moggridge. 2021. "Inland Water." In *Australia State of the Environment 2021*, edited by Ian Cresswell, Terri Janke, and Emma Johnston. Department of Climate Change Energy the Environment & Water.

Green, Jessica F. 2013. *Rethinking Private Authority: Agents and Entrepreneurs in Global Environmental Governance*. Princeton University Press.

Green, Jessica F., and Jennifer Hadden. 2021. "How Did Environmental Governance Become Complex? Understanding Mutualism Between Environmental NGOs and International Organizations." *International Studies Review* 23 (4): 1792–812. https://doi.org/10.1093/isr/viab046.

Greenfield, Kent. 2019. *The Failure of Corporate Law: Fundamental Flaws and Progressive Possibilities*. University of Chicago Press.

Greenwood, Robin, and Michael Schor. 2009. "Investor Activism and Takeovers." *Journal of Financial Economics* 92 (3): 362–75.

Grewal, Jyothika, George Serafeim, and Aaron Yoon. 2016. "Shareholder Activism on Sustainability Issues." *Harvard Business School Working Paper* No. 17–003. http://nrs.harvard.edu/urn-3:HUL.InstRepos:dash.current.terms-of-use#OAP.

Griffin, Caleb N. 2019. "We Three Kings: Disintermediating Voting at the Index Fund Giants." *Md. L. Rev.* 79: 954.

Grundfest, Joseph A. 1993. "Just Vote No: A Minimalist Strategy for Dealing with Barbarians Inside the Gates." *Stanford Law Review* 45 (4): 857–937. https://doi.org/10.2307/1229199.

Guay, Terrence, Jonathan P. Doh, and Graham Sinclair. 2004. "Non-Governmental Organizations, Shareholder Activism, and Socially Responsible Investments: Ethical, Strategic, and Governance Implications." *Journal of Business Ethics* 52: 125–39.

Hadden, Jennifer, and Aseem Prakash. 2024. "Introduction: What Scholars Know (and Need to Know) about the Politics of Climate Change." *PS: Political Science & Politics* 57 (1): 17–20. https://doi.org/10.1017/S1049096523000562.

Hall, Nina, and Nina Reiners. 2025. "Challenges and Opportunities for Transnational Advocacy." *International Studies Review* 27 (3). https://doi.org/10.1093/isr/viaf015.

Hall, Rodney Bruce, and Thomas J. Biersteker. 2002. *The Emergence of Private Authority in Global Governance.* Vol. 85. *Cambridge Studies in International Relations.* Cambridge University Press.

Hannam, Peter. 2021. "Australia's Coal-Fired Power Plants Likely to Shut Almost Three Times Faster Than Expected, Report Suggests." *The Guardian.* https://www.theguardian.com/australia-news/2021/dec/10/australias-coal-fired-power-plants-likely-to-shut-almost-three-times-faster-than-expected-report-suggests.

Hannam, Peter. 2022. "Mike Cannon-Brookes Succeeds in Shaking Up AGL Board." *The Guardian.* https://www.theguardian.com/business/2022/nov/15/agl-energy-board-directors-mike-cannon-brookes#:~:text=McKenzie%20said%20that%20based%20on,veteran%2C%20ahead%20of%20the%20vote.

Haufler, Virginia. 2001. *A Public Role for the Private Sector: Industry Self-Regulation in a Global Economy.* Carnegie Endowment.

Haufler, Virginia. 2006. "Global Governance and the Private Sector." In *Global Corporate Power*, edited by C. May, 85–103. Lynne Reinner Publishers.

Hawser, Anita. 2023. "Citi, JPMorgan, Wells Fargo to Face AGM Challenges over Indigenous Rights Impact." *The Banker.* https://www.thebanker.com/Citi-JPMorgan-Wells-Fargo-to-face-AGM-challenges-over-indigenous-rights-impact-1714118559.

Herbst-Bayliss, S. 2021. "BlackRock Backs 3 Dissidents to Shake Up Exxon Board." *Reuters.*

HESTA. 2024. "Statement on HESTA's Voting Positions at Woodside AGM." https://www.hesta.com.au/about-us/media-centre/statement-on-hestas-voting-positions-at-the-woodside-agm.

Hey, Michael. 2015. "ACCR v CBA [2015] FCA 785: Nonbinding Shareholder Resolutions and Implications for Shareholder Activism." *University of Western Australia Law Review* 40 (1): 399–411.

Hillman, Alex. 2022. *Facts over Fiction: Debunking Gas Industry Spin.* ACCR.

Hirsch, Peter Buell. 2021. "There's a Change in the Weather: Corporate Reputation and Climate Change." *Journal of Business Strategy.*

Ho, Evana. 2022. *Destruction of Juukan Gorge Highlights Flaws in Native Title.* Australian National University. https://reporter.anu.edu.au/all-stories/destruction-of-juukan-gorge-highlights-flaws-in-native-title.

Ho, Virginia Harper. 2015. "Risk-Related Activism: The Business Case for Monitoring Nonfinancial Risk." *J. Corp. L.* 41: 647.

Hoffmann, Matthew J. 2011. *Climate Governance at the Crossroads: Experimenting with a Global Response after Kyoto.* Oxford University Press.

Hsueh, Lily. 2017. "Transnational Climate Governance and the Global 500: Examining Private Actor Participation by Firm-Level Factors and Dynamics." *International Interactions* 43 (1): 48–75. https://doi.org/10.1080/03050629.2016.1223929.

Hsueh, Lily. 2019. "Corporations at a Crossroads: How Multilevel Governance Interactions Shape Participation and Effort in Private Governance Regimes." *Governance* 32 (4): 715–60. https://doi.org/https://doi.org/10.1111/gove.12406.

Interfaith Center on Corporate Responsibility. 2023a. "About Us." https://www.iccr.org/about-iccr.

Interfaith Center on Corporate Responsibility. 2023b. "History of ICCR." https://www.iccr.org/about-iccr/history-iccr.

Interfaith Center on Corporate Responsibility. 2023c. "Respect for Rights of Indigenous Peoples." https://www.iccr.org/resolutions/respect-for-rights-of-indigenous-peoples/.

International Energy Agency. 2022. *A 10-Point Plan to Cut Oil Use.* https://iea.blob.core.windows.net/assets/c5043064-58b7-4066-b1e9-68d7d9203fe9/A10-PointPlantoCutOilUse.pdf.

Ivanova, Mila. 2016. "Shareholder Activism and the Ethical Harnessing of Institutional Investors: The Unique Case of ShareAction." *Critical Perspectives on International Business.*

Jefferies, Michael. 2019. "The Third Wave of Shareholder Influence and the Emergence of Informational Activism in Australia." *Australian Journal of Corporate Law* 34 (3): 305–40.

Jerolmack, Colin. 2021. *Up to Heaven and Down to Hell.* Princeton University Press.

Joergens, Catrin. 2006. "Ethical Fashion: Myth or Future Trend?" *Journal of Fashion Marketing and Management: An International Journal* 10 (3): 360–71.

Kanbur, Ravi. 2019. "Inequality in a Global Perspective." *Oxford Review of Economic Policy* 35 (3): 431–44. https://doi.org/10.1093/oxrep/grz010.

Karpf, David. 2012. *The MoveOn Effect: The Unexpected Transformation of American Political Advocacy.* Oxford University Press.

Kastiel, Kobi, and Yaron Nili. 2016. "In Search of the Absent Shareholders: A New Solution to Retail Investors' Apathy." *Del. J. Corp. L.* 41: 55.

Katelouzou, D., and Alice Klettner. 2022. "Sustainable Finance and Stewardship: Unlocking Stewardship's Sustainability." In *Global Shareholder Stewardship*, edited by D. Katelouzou and D. W. Puchniak. Cambridge University Press.

Katz, David A., Laura McIntosh, and Wachtell Lipton. 2021. "Corporate Governance Update: 'Materiality' in America and Abroad." *Harvard Law School Forum on Corporate Governance* (blog). https://corpgov.law.harvard.edu/2021/05/01/corporate-governance-update-materiality-in-america-and-abroad/.

Katz, Michael. 2023. "Indiana Amends ESG Bill to Exclude Private Markets." *Chief Investment Officer.* https://www.ai-cio.com/news/indiana-amends-esg-bill-to-exclude-private-markets/.

Keay, Andrew. 2014. "Comply or Explain in Corporate Governance Codes: In Need of Greater Regulatory Oversight?" *Legal Studies* 34 (2): 279–304.

Keck, Margaret E., and Kathryn Sikkink. 1998. *Activists Beyond Borders: Advocacy Networks in International Politics.* Cornell University Press.

Kelly, Loretta, and L. Y. Behrendt. 2007. "Creating Conflict: Case Studies in the Tension Between Native Title Claims and Land Rights Claims." *Journal of Indigenous Policy.*

Kemp, Deanna, and John Owen. 2017. "Corporate Readiness and the Human Rights Risks of Applying FPIC in the Global Mining Industry." *Business and Human Rights Journal* 2 (1): 163–69.

Keohane, Robert O. 2009. "The Old IPE and the New." *Review of International Political Economy* 16 (1): 34–46.

Ker, P. 2020. "AusSuper: Rio's Juukan Penalty Too Low." *Australian Financial Review.*

King, Brayden. 2008a. "A Political Mediation Model of Corporate Response to Social Movement Activism." *Administrative Science Quarterly* 53 (3): 395–421.

King, Brayden. 2008b. "A Social Movement Perspective of Stakeholder Collective Action and Influence." *Business & Society* 47 (1): 21–49.

King, Brayden, and Mary-Hunter McDonnell. 2012. "Good Firms, Good Targets: The Relationship Between Corporate Social Responsibility, Reputation, and Activist Targeting." In *Corporate Social Responsibility in a Globalizing World: Toward Effective Global CSR Frameworks*, edited by Kiyoteru Tsutsui and Alwyn Lim. Cambridge University Press.

King, Brayden, and Nicholas A. Pearce. 2010. "The Contentiousness of Markets: Politics, Social Movements, and Institutional Change in Markets." *Annual Review of Sociology* 36: 249–67.

King, Brayden, and Sarah A. Soule. 2007. "Social Movements as Extra-Institutional Entrepreneurs: The Effect of Protests on Stock Price Returns." *Administrative Science Quarterly* 52 (3): 413–42.

King, Leslie, and Elisabeth Gish. 2015. "Marketizing Social Change: Social Shareholder Activism and Responsible Investing." *Sociological Perspectives* 58 (4): 711–30.

Klettner, Alice. 2016. *Corporate Governance Regulation: The Changing Roles and Responsibilities of Boards of Directors.* Routledge.

Klettner, Alice. 2021. "Stewardship Codes and the Role of Institutional Investors in Corporate Governance: An International Comparison and Typology." *British Journal of Management* 32 (4): 988–1006.

Klingemann, Hans-Dieter, and Dieter Fuchs. 1995. *Citizens and the State.* Oxford University Press.

Knight, Elizabeth. 2020. "Rio Failed, Now Comes Test for Shareholders." *Sydney Morning Herald.* https://www.smh.com.au/business/companies/rio-failed-now-comes-a-big-test-for-shareholders-20200619-p554dl.html.

Knight, Elizabeth. 2024. "Qantas Baggage Haunts Under-Pressure Goyder at Woodside." *Sydney Morning Herald.* https://www.smh.com.au/business/companies/qantas-baggage-haunts-under-pressure-goyder-at-woodside-20240411-p5fj27.html.

Kramarz, Teresa, Susan Park, and Craig Johnson. 2021. "Governing the Dark Side of Renewable Energy: A Typology of Global Displacements." *Energy Research & Social Science* 74: 101902.

Kriesi, Hanspeter. 1995. "The Political Opportunity Structure of New Social Movements: Its Impact on Their Mobilization." *The Politics of Social Protest: Comparative Perspectives on States and Social Movements* 3: 167–98.

Larcker, David F., Allan L. McCall, and Gaizka Ormazabal. 2015. "Outsourcing Shareholder Voting to Proxy Advisory Firms." *The Journal of Law and Economics* 58 (1): 173–204.

Lee, Min-Dong Paul, and Michael Lounsbury. 2011. "Domesticating Radical Rant and Rage: An Exploration of the Consequences of Environmental Shareholder Resolutions on Corporate Environmental Performance." *Business & Society* 50 (1): 155–88.

Lewis, S. 2023. "Shareholder Rights: Assessing the Threat Environment." *Harv L Sch Forum on Corp Gov.* https://corpgov.law.harvard.edu/2023/08/21/shareholder-rights-assessing-the-threat-environment/.

Lewis, W. 1997. "Shell to Face Shareholder Vote on Ethics." *Financial Times.*

Ley, Aaron J., and Edward P. Weber. 2015. "The Adaptive Venue Shopping Framework: How Emergent Groups Choose Environmental Policymaking Venues." *Environmental Politics* 24 (5): 703–22.

Lightfoot, Sheryl R. 2021. "Decolonizing Self-Determination: Haudenosaunee Passports and Negotiated Sovereignty." *European Journal of International Relations* 27 (4): 971–94.

Lipsky, Michael. 1968. "Protest as a Political Resource." *American Political Science Review* 62 (4): 1144–58.

Litfin, Karen. 1994. *Ozone Discourses: Science and Politics in Global Environmental Cooperation.* Columbia University Press.

Logsdon, Jeanne M., and Harry J. Van Buren. 2008. "Justice and Large Corporations: What Do Activist Shareholders Want?" *Business & Society* 47 (4): 523–48. https://doi.org/10.1177/0007650308316524.

Logsdon, Jeanne M., and Harry J. Van Buren. 2009. "Beyond the Proxy Vote: Dialogues Between Shareholder Activists and Corporations." *Journal of Business Ethics* 87 (Suppl 1): 353–65. https://doi.org/10.1007/s10551-008-9807-z.

Lubell, Mark. 2013. "Governing Institutional Complexity: The Ecology of Games Framework." *Policy Studies Journal* 41 (3): 537–59.

Lubell, Mark, Adam Douglas Henry, and Mike McCoy. 2010. "Collaborative Institutions in an Ecology of Games." *American Journal of Political Science* 54 (2): 287–300.

Luders, Joseph. 2006. "The Economics of Movement Success: Business Responses to Civil Rights Mobilization." *American Journal of Sociology* 111 (4): 963–98.

Lund, Dorothy S., and Adriana Robertson. 2023. "Giant Asset Managers, the Big Three, and Index Investing." USC CLASS Research Paper No. 23–13. https://ssrn.com/abstract=4406204 or http://dx.doi.org/10.2139/ssrn.4406204.

Lydenberg, Steven. 2007. "Universal Investors and Socially Responsible Investors: A Tale of Emerging Affinities." *Corporate Governance: An International Review* 15 (3): 467–77.

Macdonald-Smith, Angela. 2024. "Influential Proxy Adviser Urges Vote Against Woodside Chairman." *Australian Financial Review.* https://www.afr.com/companies/energy/influential-proxy-advisor-urges-vote-against-woodside-chairman-goyder-20240404-p5fhjo#:~:text=Woodside%20Energy%20shareholders%20should%20vote,told%20its%20heavyweight%20investment%20clients.

Macey, Jonathan R. 2022. "ESG Investing: Why Here? Why Now?" *Berkeley Business Law Journal* 19 (2): 258–91. https://heinonline.org/HOL/P?h=hein.journals/berkbusj19&i=264.

Macintosh, Andrew, Don Butler, Pablo Larraondo, Megan C. Evans, Dean Ansell, Marie Waschka, Rod Fensham, David Eldridge, David Lindenmayer, Philip Gibbons, and Paul Summerfield. 2024. "Australian Human-Induced Native Forest Regeneration Carbon Offset Projects Have Limited Impact on Changes in Woody Vegetation Cover and Carbon Removals." *Communications Earth & Environment* 5 (1): 149. https://doi.org/10.1038/s43247-024-01313-x. https://doi.org/10.1038/s43247-024-01313-x.

MacLeod, Michael. 2009. "Emerging Investor Networks and the Construction of Corporate Social Responsibility." *Journal of Corporate Citizenship* (34): 69–98.

MacLeod, Michael. 2010. "Private Governance and Climate Change: Institutional Investors and Emerging Investor-Driven Governance Mechanisms." *St Antony's International Review* 5 (2): 46–65.

MacLeod, Michael, and Jacob Park. 2011. "Financial Activism and Global Climate Change: The Rise of Investor-Driven Governance Networks." *Global Environmental Politics* 11 (2): 54–74.

MacNeil, Iain, and Irene-Marié Esser. 2022. "From a Financial to an Entity Model of ESG." *European Business Organization Law Review* 23 (1): 9–45.

MacNeil, Robert. 2021. "Swimming against the Current: Australian Climate Institutions and the Politics of Polarisation." *Environmental Politics*: 1–22.

Malenko, Andrey, and Nadya Malenko. 2019. "Proxy Advisory Firms: The Economics of Selling Information to Voters." *The Journal of Finance* 74 (5): 2441–90.

Malone, Leah, Emily Holland, and Carolyn Houston. 2023. "ESG Battlegrounds: How the States Are Shaping the Regulatory Landscape in the U.S." *Harvard Law School Forum on Corporate Governance*. https://corpgov.law.harvard.edu/2023/03/11/esg-battlegrounds-how-the-states-are-shaping-the-regulatory-landscape-in-the-u-s/#19b.

Maloney, Rosanne. 2024. "UN Committee Says WA Government's Botched Handling of Aboriginal Heritage Could Be Racial Discrimination Convention Breach." *ABC News*. https://www.abc.net.au/news/2024-05-27/australian-government-breaches-racial-discrimination-convention/103886464#.

March, James G., and Johan P. Olsen. 1998. "The Institutional Dynamics of International Political Orders." *International Organization* 52 (04): 943–69.

Marens, Richard. 2002. "Inventing Corporate Governance: The Emergence of Shareholder Activism in the Nineteen-Forties." Academy of Management Proceedings.

Marinetto, Michael. 1998. "The Shareholders Strike Back: Issues in the Research of Shareholder Activism." *Environmental politics* 7 (3): 125–33. https://doi.org/10.1080/09644019808414412.

Market Forces. 2021. "99% of Rio Tinto Shareholders Vote for Paris-Aligned Emission Targets." https://www.marketforces.org.au/rio-tinto-dodges-climate-fight-for-now/.

Market Forces. 2024. "Shareholders File First Ever Climate Resolution on Australian Gas Pipeline Company." https://www.marketforces.org.au/shareholders-file-first-ever-climate-resolution-on-australian-gas-pipeline-company/.

Marks, K. 2010. "Exclamation Politics: GetUp!" *The Monthly*. http://www.themonthly.com.au/monthly-essays-kathy-marks-exclamation-politics-getup-2788.

Marquardt, Carol, and Christine Wiedman. 2016. "Can Shareholder Activism Improve Gender Diversity on Corporate Boards?" *Corporate Governance: An International Review* 24 (4): 443–61. https://doi.org/10.1111/corg.12170.

Mascher, Sharon. 2022. *Indigenous Land Rights in Australia: Lessons for a Canadian Northern Corridor*. University of Calgary. http://dx.doi.org/DOI-10.11575/sppp.v15i1.75215.

May, Christopher. 2006. "Global Corporate Power and the UN Global Compact." In *Global Corporate Power*, edited by Christopher May. Lynne Rienner Publishers.

McAdam, Doug. 2017. "Social Movement Theory and the Prospects for Climate Change Activism in the United States." *Annual Review of Political Science* 20: 189–208.

McAdam, Doug, Sidney Tarrow, and Charles Tilly. 2001. *Dynamics of Contention: Cambridge Studies in Contentious Politics*. Cambridge University Press.

McAdam, Doug, Sidney Tarrow, and Charles Tilly. 2003. "Dynamics of Contention." *Social Movement Studies* 2 (1): 99–102.

McAllister, Scott. 2024. "Shareholder Activism Is Rising Globally: How Can Boards Set Up for Long-Term Success?" *Diligent* (blog). https://www.diligent.com/resources/blog/shareholder-activism.

McAteer, Emily, and Simone Pulver. 2009. "The Corporate Boomerang: Shareholder Transnational Advocacy Networks Targeting Oil Companies in the Ecuadorian Amazon." *Global Environmental Politics* 9 (1): 1–30.

McDonald, Matt. 2021. "After the Fires? Climate Change and Security in Australia." *Australian Journal of Political Science* 56 (1): 1–18.

McDonnell, Mary-Hunter, and Brayden King. 2013. "Keeping Up Appearances: Reputational Threat and Impression Management After Social Movement Boycotts." *Administrative Science Quarterly* 58 (3): 387–419.

McDonnell, Mary-Hunter, Brayden King, and Sarah A. Soule. 2015. "A Dynamic Process Model of Private Politics: Activist Targeting and Corporate Receptivity to Social Challenges." *American Sociological Review* 80 (3): 654–78.

McGuirk, Rod. 2022. "Mine Company's Blasting of Rock Shelters Likened to Taliban." *Associated Press.* https://apnews.com/article/afghanistan-business-australia-cultures-taliban-a01018cec1f4a240e3fc19e8f975c84a.

Medecins Sans Frointieres. 2020. "Seven Years of Offshore Processing. Enough Is Enough." https://msf.org.au/article/project-news/seven-years-offshore-processing-enough-enough.

Meznar, Martin B., Douglas Nigh, and Chuck C. Y. Kwok. 1994. "Effect of Announcements of Withdrawal from South Africa on Stockholder Wealth." *Academy of Management Journal* 37 (6): 1633–48.

Michelon, Giovanna, Michelle Rodrigue, and Elisabetta Trevisan. 2020. "The Marketization of a Social Movement: Activists, Shareholders and CSR Disclosure." *Accounting, Organizations and Society* 80: 101074. https://doi.org/https://doi.org/10.1016/j.aos.2019.101074. https://www.sciencedirect.com/science/article/pii/S0361368219300674.

Mikler, John. 2018. *The Political Power of Global Corporations.* John Wiley & Sons.

Mikler, John, and Imogen Ryan. 2024. "Gaslighting Australia: The Instrumental Power of Australia's Mining and Energy Industries." *Australian Journal of Politics & History.*

Minerals Council of Australia. 2024. "Indigenous Partnerships." https://minerals.org.au/policies/sustainability/indigenous-partnerships/.

Missouri Senate. 2023. "SB 436 Modifies Provisions Relating to Fiduciary Duties for Investments of Public Employee Retirement Systems." In *1663S.03I.*

Moffat, Kieren, and Airong Zhang. 2014. "The Paths to Social Licence to Operate: An Integrative Model Explaining Community Acceptance of Mining." *Resources Policy* 39: 61–70.

Morgan, Thomas. 2024. "Tamboran and NT Government's Secretive Beetaloo Basin Gas Deal Criticised by Industry, Experts." *ABC.* https://www.abc.net.au/news/2024-04-26/concerns-over-nt-government-and-tamboran-beetaloo-gas-deal/103769966.

Morrison, Scott. 2020a. Address to the National Press Club.

Morrison, Scott. 2020b. "Gas-Fired Recovery." https://pmtranscripts.pmc.gov.au/release/transcript-43017.

Morton, Adam, and Katharine Murphy. 2020. "Australia's Chief Scientist Rejects Experts' Letter Warning Him Not to Back Gas." *The Guardian.* https://www.theguardian.com/australia-news/2020/aug/26/australias-chief-scientist-rejects-experts-letter-warning-him-not-to-back-gas.

Moss, Jeremy, and Persephone Fraser. 2019. "Australia's Carbon Majors Report." *Practical Justice Initiative, UNSW* 2 (2): 21. climatejustice. co/wp-content/uploads/2019/10/Australias-Carbon-Majors-Report-2019-1. pdf.

Mufson, S. 2021. "Representatives of Discontented ExxonMobil Shareholders Win a Third Seat on Oil Giant's Board of Directors." *The Washington Post.*

Muroi, Millie. 2023. "Size Matters, Even if Australian Banks Are No Longer at Peak Profitability." *The Sydney Morning Herald.* https://www.smh.com.au/business/banking-and-finance/size-matters-even-if-australian-banks-are-no-longer-at-peak-profitability-20230901-p5e1e6.html.

National Institute of Health and Welfare. 2024. "Socioeconomic Indexes." https://www.indigenoushpf.gov.au/measures/2-09-socioeconomic-indexes.

Native Title Act.

Nature. 2020. "Australia: Show the World What Climate Action Looks Like." *Nature* 577.

Nelson, James M. 2006. "The 'CalPERS Effect' Revisited Again." *Journal of Corporate Finance* 12 (2): 187–213.

Neville, Kate J. 2021. *Fueling Resistance: The Contentious Political Economy of Biofuels and Fracking.* Oxford University Press.

Neville, Kate J., Jackie Cook, Jennifer Baka, Karen Bakker, and Erika S Weinthal. 2019. "Can Shareholder Advocacy Shape Energy Governance? The Case of the US Antifracking Movement." *Review of International Political Economy* 26 (1): 104–33.

Newell, Peter J. 2001. "Managing Multinationals: The Governance of Investment for the Environment." *Journal of International Development* 13 (7): 907–19. https://doi.org/10.1002/jid.832.

Nikolakis, William, Harry W. Nelson, and David H. Cohen. 2014. "Who Pays Attention to Indigenous Peoples in Sustainable Development and Why? Evidence from Socially Responsible Investment Mutual Funds in North America." *Organization & Environment* 27 (4): 368–82.

Nilsson, Jonas. 2008. "Investment with a Conscience: Examining the Impact of Pro-Social Attitudes and Perceived Financial Performance on Socially Responsible Investment Behavior." *Journal of Business Ethics* 83: 307–25.

North, Gill. 2020. "Corporate Management and Communication of Environmental and Social Risks in Australia: Pressures Are Mounting." *Australian Journal of Corporate Law* 2018 (33).

Northern Territory Government. 2024. "Our Territory Gas Plan: Beetaloo Sub-Basin." https://territorygas.nt.gov.au/projects/beetaloo-sub-basin.

O'Brien, Erin, Ainsley Elbra, Martijn Boersma, and Justine Coneybeer. 2023. "Political Investorism in Australia: Unnatural Insiders and The Insider/Outsider Dynamics of Market Lobbying." *Australian Journal of Political Science.* https://doi.org/10.1080/10361146.2023.2166813.

O'Brien, Erin, Hope Johnson, and Yu-An Murray. 2023. "Banning Indirect Boycotts: Contentious Interactions and the Role of the State in Marketplace Activism." *Business and Politics* 25 (4): 393–408.

O'Brien, Erin, Justine Coneybeer, Martijn Boersma, and Alice Payne. 2022. "Political Investorism: Conceptualising the Political Participation of Shareholders and Investors." *International Political Science Review* 44 (5): 01925121221098863.

O'Faircheallaigh, Ciaran. 2023. *Indigenous Peoples and Mining: A Global Perspective.* Oxford University Press.

O'Faircheallaigh, Ciaran. 2021. "Explaining Outcomes from Negotiated Agreements in Australia and Canada." *Resources Policy* 70: 101922. https://doi.org/https://doi.org/10.1016/j.resourpol.2020.101922.

O'Rourke, Anastasia. 2003. "A New Politics of Engagement: Shareholder Activism for Corporate Social Responsibility." *Business Strategy and the Environment* 12 (4): 227–39.

Office of the Chief Economist. 2023. Resources and Energy Quarterly (September). https://www.industry.gov.au/publications/resources-and-energy-quarterly-september-2023.

Origin Energy. 2018. *Notice of Meeting 2018.* https://www.originenergy.com.au/wp-content/uploads/Origin_2018_Notice_of_Meeting.pdf.

Origin Energy. 2019. *Notice of Meeting 2019.* https://www.originenergy.com.au/wp-content/uploads/Origin-NOM-FINAL.pdf.

Origin Energy. 2021. *Notice of Annual General Meeting 2021.*

Origin Energy. 2022. *Notice of Annual General Meeting 2022.* https://www.originenergy.com.au/wp-content/uploads/Notice_of_Annual_General_Meeting_2022_ASX-Release_20220916.pdf.

Owen, John R., Deanna Kemp, Alex M. Lechner, Jill Harris, Ruilian Zhang, and Éléonore Lèbre. 2023. "Energy Transition Minerals and Their Intersection with Land-Connected Peoples." *Nature Sustainability* 6 (2): 203–11.

Owen, John R., Deanna Kemp, Jill Harris, Alex M. Lechner, and Éléonore Lèbre. 2022. "Fast Track to Failure? Energy Transition Minerals and the Future of Consultation and Consent." *Energy Research & Social Science* 89: 102665. https://doi.org/https://doi.org/10.1016/j.erss.2022.102665.

Packham, Colin. 2022. "AGL Bows to Shareholders and Hastens Coal Exit." *The Australian Financial Review.* https://www.afr.com/companies/energy/agl-accelerates-exit-from-coal-20220929-p5bluw.

Parfitt, Claire. 2024. "False Profits of Ethical Capital: Finance, Labour and the Politics of Risk."

Pargendler, Mariana. 2020. "The Rise of International Corporate Law." *Wash. UL Rev.* 98: 1765.

Parker, A. Rani. 2003. "Prospects for NGO Collaboration with Multinational Corporations." In *Globalization and NGOs: Transforming Business, Government, and Society*, edited by Jonathan P. Doh and Hildy Teegen. Praeger.

Parliament of Australia. 2020. *Inquiry into the Destruction of 46,000 Year Old Caves at the Juukan Gorge in the Pilbara Region of Western Australia.*

Parliament of Australia. 2023. "2023 Referendum Results." https://www.aph.gov.au/About_Parliament/Parliamentary_departments/Parliamentary_Library/pubs/Dashboards/2023Referendum.

Pattberg, Philipp. 2007. *Private Institutions and Global Governance. The New Politics of Environmental Sustainability.* Edward Elgar.

Peach, Joshua. 2025. "Macquarie, IFM-Backed Net Zero Group Suspends Itself as Trump Looms." *Australian Financial Review.* https://www.afr.com/markets/equity-markets/macquarie-ifm-backed-net-zero-group-suspends-itself-as-trump-looms-20250114-p5l42c.

Peetz, David, and Georgina Murray. 2013. "Financialization of Corporate Ownership and Implications for the Potential for Climate Action." In *Institutional Investors' Power to Change Corporate Behavior: International Perspectives.* Emerald Group Publishing Limited.

Pelosi, Nick, and Rebecca Adamson. 2016. "Managing the 'S' in ESG: The Case of Indigenous Peoples and Extractive Industries." *Journal of Applied Corporate Finance* 28 (2): 87–95.

Pender, Howard. 2011. "Carbon Price Assumptions."

Pender, Howard, and ACCR. 2014. *Financed Emission,"Unburnable Carbon" Risk and the Major Australian Banks.* ACCR. https://accr.org.au/wp-content/uploads/BankReportWeb.pdf.

Pepper, Mia, Michael Hughes, and Yvonne Haigh. 2021. "Loophole or Lifeline? The Policy Challenges of Mines in Care and Maintenance." *The Extractive Industries and Society.*

Pepper, Rachel. 2018. *Final Report of The Scientific Inquiry into Hydraulic Fracturing in the Northern Territory.*

Perkins, Reed M., and Stefan Michael Krause. 2018. "Adapting to Climate Change Impacts in Yap State, Federated States of Micronesia: The Importance of Environmental Conditions and Intangible Cultural Heritage." *Island Studies Journal* 13 (1).

Pickrell, John. 2020. "Smoke from Australia's Bushfires Killed Far More People Than the Fires Did, Study Says." *The Guardian.* https://www.theguardian.com/australia-news/2020/mar/21/smoke-from-australias-bushfires-killed-far-more-people-than-the-fires-did-study-says.

Piven, Frances Fox, and Richard A. Cloward. 1977. *Poor People's Movements: Why They Succeed, How They Fail.* Pantheon.

Polletta, Francesca, and James M. Jasper. 2001. "Collective Identity and Social Movements." *Annual Review of Sociology* 27 (1): 283–305. https://doi.org/10.1146/annurev.soc.27.1.283.

Pollman, E. 2021. "Corporate Social Responsibility, ESG, and Compliance." In *Cambridge Handbook of Compliance*, edited by B. van Rooij and D. D. Sokol. Cambridge University Press.

Porter, Terry, and Robbin Derry. 2012. "Sustainability and Business in a Complex World." *Business and Society Review* 117 (1): 33–53.

Pralle, Sarah B. 2006. *Branching Out, Digging In: Environmental Advocacy and Agenda Setting*. Georgetown University Press.

Pralle, Sarah B. 2010. "Shopping Around: Environmental Organizations and the Search for Policy Venues." In *Advocacy Organizations and Collective Action*, edited by Aseem Prakash and Mary Kay Gugerty, 177–202. Cambridge University Press.

PwC. 2023. *Global Investor Survey*. https://www.pwc.com/gx/en/issues/c-suite-insights/global-investor-survey.html.

Pye, Oliver, and Jayati Bhattacharya. 2013. *The Palm Oil Controversy in Southeast Asia: A Transnational Perspective*. Institute of Southeast Asian Studies.

Qantas. 2018. *Notice of Meeting 2018*. https://investor.qantas.com/FormBuilder/_Resource/_module/doLLG5ufYkCyEPjF1tpgyw/file/agm/QAN-2018-AGM-Notice-of-meeting.pdf.

Qantas. 2019. *Notice of Meeting 2019*. https://investor.qantas.com/FormBuilder/_Resource/_module/doLLG5ufYkCyEPjF1tpgyw/file/agm/notice-of-meeting-2019.pdf.

Radzyminski, G. 2022. "Proxy Advice Shake-Up's Real Target Is Shareholder Social Activism." *Australian Financial Review*.

Raeburn, Nicole Christine. 2004. *Changing Corporate America from Inside Out: Lesbian and Gay Workplace Rights*. Vol. 20. University of Minnesota Press.

Rawling, Michael. 2006. "Australian Trade Unions as Shareholder Activists: The Rocky Path Towards Corporate Democracy." *Sydney Law Review* 28 (2): 227–58.

Read, Michael. 2023. "Australia's Floods Were Fourth Most Costly Global Disaster in 2022." *Australian Financial Review*. https://www.afr.com/policy/economy/australia-s-floods-were-fourth-most-costly-global-disaster-in-2022-20230110-p5cbhx.

Read, Paul, and Richard Denniss. 2020. "With Costs Approaching $100 Billion, The Fires Are Australia's Costliest Natural Disaster." *The Conversation*. https://theconversation.com/with-costs-approaching-100-billion-the-fires-are-australias-costliest-natural-disaster-129433.

Rehbein, Kathleen, Jeanne M. Logsdon, and Harry J. Van Buren. 2013. "Corporate Responses to Shareholder Activists: Considering the Dialogue Alternative." *Journal of Business Ethics* 112 (1): 137–54.

Reid, Erin M., and Michael W. Toffel. 2009. "Responding to Public and Private Politics: Corporate Disclosure of Climate Change Strategies." *Strategic management journal* 30 (11): 1157–78.

Reisberg, Arad. 2015. "The UK Stewardship Code: On the Road to Nowhere?" *Journal of Corporate Law Studies* 15 (2): 217–53.

Reuters. 2024. "J-Power May Close up to Five Coal Power Plants by Fiscal 2030." *The Japan Times*. https://www.japantimes.co.jp/business/2024/05/10/companies/j-power-coal-plants/.

Riddell, Garth. 2016. "Environmental Shareholder Activism in Australia after ACCR v CBA." *Australian Resources and Energy Law Journal* 35 (2): 172–77.

Ringe, Wolf-Georg. 2022. "Investor-Led Sustainability in Corporate Governance." *Annals of Corporate Governance* 7 (2): 93–151.

Rio Tinto. 2021. *Rio Tinto 2021 AGM Results*. https://cdn-rio.dataweavers.io/-/media/content/documents/invest/shareholder-information/agms/2021/rt-plc-agm-2021-voting-results.pdf?rev=110179f72d6a46c88f5db43382ceaba2.

Rock, Edward B. 2020. "For Whom Is the Corporation Managed in 2020? The Debate Over Corporate Purpose." *Bus. Law.* 76: 363.

Rodman, Kenneth A. 1998. "'Think Globally, Punish Locally:' Non-State Actors." *Multinational Corporations, and Human Rights Sanctions* 12.

Rudd, Kevin. 2013. "If You Come by Boat You Will Never Permanently Live in Australia." https://youtu.be/kIapYIBRZIs.

Ruggie, John. 2004. "Reconstituting the Global Public Domain—Issues, Actors, and Practices." *European Journal of International Relations* 10 (4): 499–531.

Ruggie, John. 2007. "Global Markets and Global Governance: The Prospects for Convergence." *Global Liberalism and Political Order: Toward a New Grand Compromise*: 23–50.

Ruggie, John. 2011. "Business and Human Rights: Interview with John Ruggie." Edited by Michael Connor. *Business Ethics*.

Rumpff, Libby, Sarah Legge, Stephen van Leeuwen, Brendan A. Wintle, and John C. Z. Woinarski, eds. 2023. *Australia's Megafires: Biodiversity Impacts and Lessons from 2019–2020*. CSIRO Publishing.

S&P Dow Jones Indices. 2022. "S&P/ASX 200." https://www.spglobal.com/spdji/en/indices/equity/sp-asx-200/#overview.

Sadler, David. 2004. "Anti-Corporate Campaigning and Corporate "Social" Responsibility: Towards Alternative Spaces of Citizenship?" *Antipode* 36 (5): 851–70.

Sauerwald, Steve, J. Van Oosterhout, Marc Van Essen, and Mike W. Peng. 2018. "Proxy Advisors and Shareholder Dissent: A Cross-Country Comparative Study." *Journal of Management* 44 (8): 3364–94.

Say on Climate. 2024. "Who We Are and What We Do." https://www.sayonclimate.org/say-on-climate-who-we-are-and-what-we-do/#:~:text=The%20Say%20on%20Climate%20initiative,held%20accountable%20for%20delivering%20them.

Schanzenbach, Max M., and Robert H. Sitkoff. 2020. "Reconciling Fiduciary Duty and Social Conscience: The Law and Economics of ESG Investing by a Trustee." *Stan. L. Rev.* 72: 381.

Scherer, Andreas Georg, Dorothée Baumann-Pauly, and Anselm Schneider. 2013a. "Democratizing Corporate Governance: Compensating for the Democratic Deficit of Corporate Political Activity and Corporate Citizenship." *Business & Society* 52 (3): 473–514.

Scherer, Andreas Georg, Dorothée Baumann-Pauly, and Anselm Schneider. 2013b. "Democratizing Corporate Governance:Compensating for the Democratic Deficit of Corporate Political Activity and Corporate Citizenship." *Business & Society* 52 (3): 473–514. https://doi.org/10.1177/0007650312446931. https://journals.sagepub.com/doi/abs/10.1177/0007650312446931.

Schmalz, Martin C. 2018. "Common-Ownership Concentration and Corporate Conduct." *Annual Review of Financial Economics* 10 (1): 413–48.

Scholtens, Bert. 2006. "Finance as a Driver of Corporate Social Responsibility." *Journal of business ethics* 68 (1): 19–33.

Schueth, Steve. 2003. "Socially Responsible Investing in the United States." *Journal of Business Ethics* 43 (3): 189–94. https://doi.org/10.1023/A:1022981828869.

Schurman, Rachel. 2004. "Fighting 'Frankenfoods:' Industry Opportunity Structures and the Efficacy of the Anti-Biotech Movement in Western Europe." *Social Problems* 51 (2): 243–68.

Seabrooke, Leonard, and Duncan Wigan. 2018. "Tax Justice Activists in Global Wealth Chains." In *Business, Civil Society and the "New" Politics of Corporate Tax Justice*, edited by Richard Eccleston and Ainsley Elbra. Edward Elgar Publishing.

Seabrooke, Leonard, and Duncan Wigan. 2024. "Getting Action for Global Economic Justice: The Micro-Foundations of Transnational Activism." *Socio-Economic Review* 22 (3): 1313–334.

Seabrooke, Leonard, and Lasse Folke Henriksen. 2017. *Professional Networks in Transnational Governance*. Cambridge University Press.

Semenova, Natalia, and Lars G. Hassel. 2019. "Private Engagement by Nordic Institutional Investors on Environmental, Social, and Governance Risks in

Global Companies." *Corporate Governance: An International Review* 27 (2): 144–61. https://doi.org/10.1111/corg.12267.

Sethi, S. Prakash, and Oliver F. Williams. 2000. *Economic Imperatives and Ethical Values in Global Business: The South African Experience and International Codes Today.* Springer Science & Business Media.

ShareAction. 2017. "Shareholders' Capital at Risk as BP and Shell Drag Feet on Binding Shareholder Resolutions." https://shareaction.org/shareholders-capital-at-risk-as-bp-and-shell-drag-feet-on-binding-shareholder-resolutions/.

Sharfman, Bernard S. 2020. "The Risks and Rewards of Shareholder Voting." *SMU L. Rev.* 73: 849.

Shariati, Ahmad Ali. 2024. "The Purpose of Corporations in the Context of ESG Concerns: Continuing Shareholder Primacy or Countenancing Radical Reform?" *European Business Law Review* 35 (5).

Sharma, Vigya, and Julia Loginova. 2024. "Just Transition out of Coal-Fired Power: Policy Lessons from Australia's Automotive Sector Closure." *Environmental Innovation and Societal Transitions* 51: 100835. https://doi.org/10.1016/j.eist.2024.100835.

Shawki, Noha. 2010. "Political Opportunity Structures and the Outcomes of Transnational Campaigns: A Comparison of Two Transnational Advocacy Networks." *Peace & Change* 35 (3): 381–411.

Sheehy, Benedict. 2017. "Conceptual and Institutional Interfaces Between CSR, Corporate Law and the Problem of Social Costs." *Va. L. & Bus. Rev.* 12: 93.

Sheehy, Benedict. 2022. "Sustainability, Justice and Corporate Law: Redistributing Corporate Rights and Duties to Meet the Challenge of Sustainability." *European Business Organization Law Review* 23 (1): 273–312.

Sheehy, Benedict, Howard Pender, and Ben Jacobson. 2021. "Corporate Social Responsibility/ESG Shareholder Activism in Australia: A Case Study of the Australasian Centre for Corporate Responsibility." *Australian Journal of Corporate Law* 36 (2): 156–77.

Sheehy, Benedict, Howard Pender, and Juan Diaz-Granados. 2023. "Restraint of Shareholder Voice in Australia: Corporate Governance, Corporate Law and Politics." *Australian Journal of Corporate Law.*

Shu, Chong. 2022. "The Proxy Advisory Industry: Influencing and Being Influenced." *USC Marshall School of Business Research Paper.*

Shu, Ei, and Arie Y. Lewin. 2024. "Caught in the Crossfire: Anti-Corporate Activism and Non-Market Strategies of Corporate Targets in the Creation of Emissions Controls." *Organization Studies*: 01708406241286302.

Simmonds, Kate, and Kate Donnelly. 2022. *Changing Pathways for Australian Gas: A 1.5C Scenario Analysis of New Australian Gas Projects.* Investor Group on Climate Change. https://igcc.org.au/wp-content/uploads/2022/04/IGCC-Changing-pathways-for-Australian-gas-FINAL.pdf.

Sjåfjell, Beate, and Christopher M. Bruner. 2019. "Corporations and Sustainability." In *Cambridge Handbook of Corporate Law, Corporate Governance and Sustainability*, edited by Beate Sjåfjell and Christopher M. Bruner, 1–12. Cambridge University Press.

Sjåfjell, Beate, and Mark B. Taylor. 2019. "Clash of Norms: Shareholder Primacy vs. Sustainable Corporate Purpose." *International and Comparative Corporate Law Journal* 13 (3): 40–66.

Sjöström, Emma. 2008. "Shareholder Activism for Corporate Social Responsibility: What Do We Know?" *Sustainable Development* 16 (3): 141–54.

Smith, Michael P. 1996. "Shareholder Activism by Institutional Investors: Evidence from CalPERS." *The journal of finance* 51 (1): 227–52.

Smith, Timothy. 2024. "ExxonMobil's Lawsuit Against Its Shareholders: A Cautionary Tale." *Harvard Law School Forum on Corporate Governance* (blog). https://corpgov.law.harvard.edu/2024/06/12/exxonmobils-lawsuit-against-its-shareholders-a-cautionary-tale/.

Snow, David, and Sarah A. Soule. 2010. *A Primer on Social Movements.* W. W. Norton.

Snow, David, Sarah A. Soule, and Hanspeter Kriesi. 2004. *The Blackwell Companion to Social Movements.* 1st ed. *Blackwell Companions to Sociology.* Blackwell Pub.

Sorkin, Andrew. 2018. "BlackRock's Message: Contribute to Society, or Risk Losing Our Support." *New York Times.*

Soule, Sarah A. 1997. "The Student Divestment Movement in the United States and Tactical Diffusion: The Shantytown Protest." *Social Forces* 75 (3): 855–82.

Soule, Sarah A. 1999. "The Diffusion of an Unsuccessful Innovation." *The Annals of the American Academy of Political and Social Science* 566 (1): 120–31.

Soule, Sarah A. 2009. *Contention and Corporate Social Responsibility.* Cambridge University Press.

Soule, Sarah A., Anand Swaminathan, and Laszlo Tihanyi. 2014. "The Diffusion of Foreign Divestment from Burma." *Strategic Management Journal* 35 (7): 1032–52. https://doi.org/https://doi.org/10.1002/smj.2147.

Soule, Sarah A., Brayden King, Donatella Della Porta, and Mario Diani. 2015. "Markets, Business, and Social Movements." In *The Oxford Handbook of Social Movements*, edited by Donatella Della Porta and Mario Diani, 1–15. Oxford University Press.

Southalan, John, and Joe Fardin. 2019. "Free, Prior and Informed Consent: How and from Whom? An Australian Analogue." *Journal of Energy & Natural Resources Law* 37 (4): 365–88.

Spatt, Chester S. 2021. "Proxy Advisory Firms, Governance, Market Failure, and Regulation." *The Review of Corporate Finance Studies* 10 (1): 136–57.

Steffen, Will, and Simon Bradshaw. 2021. *Hitting Home: The Compounding Costs of Climate Inaction.* Climate Council of Australia. https://www.climatecouncil.org.au/wp-content/uploads/2021/01/hitting-home-report-V7-210122.pdf.

Stringer, Tara, Gary Mortimer, and Alice Ruth Payne. 2020. "Do Ethical Concerns and Personal Values Influence the Purchase Intention of Fast-Fashion Clothing?" *Journal of Fashion Marketing and Management: An International Journal* 24 (1): 99–120.

Super Members Council. 2025. "Australians' Super Savings on Track to Become Second Largest Globally by the Early 2030s." https://smcaustralia.com/news/australians-super-savings-on-track-to-become-second-largest-globally-by-the-early-2030s/.

Tarrow, Sidney. 1994. *Power in Movement: Collective Action, Social Movements and Politics.* Cambridge University Press.

Tarrow, Sidney. 2005. *The New Transnational Activism: Cambridge Studies in Contentious Politics.* Cambridge University Press.

Tarrow, Sidney. 2013. *The Language of Contention: Revolutions in Words, 1688–2012.* Cambridge University Press.

Tarrow, Sidney, and Donatella Della Porta. 2005. *Transnational Protest and Global Activism.* Rowman and Littlefield.

Taylor, Maria. 2014. *Global Warming and Climate Change: What Australia Knew and Buried . . . Then Framed a New Reality for the Public.* ANU Press.

The Church of England. 2019. "Church of England Pensions Board Tables Shareholder Resolution at BHP Group." https://www.churchofengland.org/media/finance-news/church-england-pensions-board-tables-shareholder-resolution-bhp-group.

The Goldman Environmental Prize. 2023. "Julien Vincent - Goldman Environmental Prize." https://www.goldmanprize.org/recipient/julien-vincent/.

The White House. 2025. "Putting America First in International Environmental Agreements." https://www.whitehouse.gov/presidential-actions/2025/01/putting-america-first-in-international-environmental-agreements/.

Thompson, Brad. 2023. "WA to Backflip on Controversial Aboriginal Heritage Laws." *Australian Financial Review.*

Thomson, Jo-Anne R., and Joe Dortch. 2022. "A Missed Opportunity for a Paradigm Shift: The Rescinded 'Western Australian Aboriginal Cultural Heritage Act 2021.'" *Historic Environment* 34 (1/2/3): 20–34.

Thrall, Calvin. 2021. "Public-Private Governance Initiatives and Corporate Responses to Stakeholder Complaints." *International Organization* 75 (3): 803–36. https://doi.org/10.1017/S0020818321000199.

Tillotson, Pete, Raphael Slade, Iain Staffell, and Krista Halttunen. 2023. "Deactivating Climate Activism? The Seven Strategies Oil and Gas Majors Use to Counter Rising Shareholder Action." *Energy Research & Social Science* 103: 103190. https://doi.org/https://doi.org/10.1016/j.erss.2023.103190.

Tilly, Charles. 1977. *From Mobilization to Revolution*. McGraw-Hill.

Tilly, Charles, and Sidney Tarrow. 2015. *Contentious Politics*. Oxford University Press.

Toscano, Nick. 2020. "Rio Tinto's Board Under Pressure to Review Cave Blast Sanctions." *The Sydney Morning Herald*. https://www.smh.com.au/business/companies/rio-tinto-s-board-under-pressure-to-review-cave-blast-sanctions-20200908-p55tg7.html.

Toscano, Nick. 2021a. "Coal's Struggles 'Threaten Value' in AGL's Plan to Split." *Sydney Morning Herald*. https://www.smh.com.au/business/companies/coal-s-struggles-threaten-value-in-agl-s-plan-to-split-20210331-p57fi5.html.

Toscano, Nick. 2021b. "Rio Tinto Swings Behind Activist Shareholder Demands on Climate." *Sydney Morning Herald*. https://www.smh.com.au/business/companies/rio-tinto-swings-behind-activist-shareholder-demands-on-climate-20210318-p57c3y.html.

Toscano, Nick, and Elizabeth Knight. 2020. "Colonial Rabble Rousers: How a Group of Australian Funds Toppled Rio's Chief." *Sydney Morning Herald*. https://www.smh.com.au/business/companies/colonial-rabble-rousers-how-a-group-of-australian-funds-toppled-rio-s-chief-20200918-p55wxl.html.

Towie, Narelle. 2023. "Divisive, Confusing and Stressful: Western Australia's Aboriginal Cultural Heritage Laws in a Mess." *The Guardian*. https://www.theguardian.com/australia-news/2023/aug/13/divisive-confusing-and-stressful-western-australias-aboriginal-cultural-heritage-laws-in-a-mess.

UK Financial Conduct Authority. 2023. *Sustainability Disclosure Requirements (SDR) and Investment Labels*. https://www.skadden.com/-/media/files/publications/2024/01/fca-finalises-uk-sustainable-investment-rules/policy-statement.pdf?rev=fc919dcfdc4f4052973e9e6768325069&hash=B06D45273109777C54A1FDD5BB089453.

UN Environment Programme Finance Initiative. 2005. *A Legal Framework for the Integration of Environmental, Social and Governance Issues into Institutional Investment*. https://www.unepfi.org/fileadmin/documents/freshfields_legal_resp_20051123.pdf.

UN Global Compact, UN Environment Programme Finance Initiative, and PRI. 2015. *Inquiry: Design of a Sustainable Financial System*. Fiduciary Duty in the 21st Century.

United Kingdom Home Office. 2024. "Failed Asylum Seekers Detained for Removal to Rwanda." https://www.gov.uk/government/news/failed-asylum-seekers-detained-for-removal-to-rwanda.

United Nations Global Compact. 2005. *Who Cares Wins: Connecting Financial Markets to a Changing World.* https://documents1.worldbank.org/curated/en/280911488968799581/pdf/113237-WP-WhoCaresWins-2004.pdf.

United Nations Global Compact. 2024. "UN Global Compact." https://unglobalcompact.org.

United Nations Permanent Forum on Indigenous Issues. n.d. *Indigenous People Indigenous Voices Fact Sheet: Indigenous Peoples and Industrial Corporations.* https://www.un.org/esa/socdev/unpfii/documents/PFII8_FS3.pdf.

United Nations Principles for Responsible Investment. 2023. About Us.

United Nations Special Rapporteur on the Rights of Indigenous Peoples. 2017. *Report of the Special Rapporteur on the Rights of Indigenous Peoples on Her Visit to Australia.* United Nations General Assembly Human Rights Council. https://un.arizona.edu/sites/default/files/2021-11/UNSR_VTC_Country_Report_Australia_2017_English.pdf.

UNPRI. 2022. *The Investor Case for Responsible Political Engagement.* https://www.unpri.org/governance-issues/the-investor-case-for-responsible-political-engagement/9366.article.

US Supreme Court. 1976. *TSC Industries v. Northway Inc.*

van den Broek, Onna M., and Robyn Klingler-Vidra. 2022. "The UN Sustainable Development Goals as a North Star: How an Intermediary Network Makes, Takes, and Retrofits the Meaning of the Sustainable Development Goals." *Regulation & Governance* 16 (4): 1306–24.

Villalonga, Belén, Raphael Amit, María-Andrea Trujillo, and Alexander Guzmán. 2015. "Governance of Family Firms." *Annual Review of Financial Economics* 7 (1): 635–54.

Vogel, David. 1978. *Lobbying the Corporation: Citizen Challenges to Business Authority.* Basic Books.

Vogel, David. 2006. *The Market for Virtue: The Potential and Limits of Corporate Social Responsibility.* Brookings Institute Press.

Vromen, Ariadne. 2015. "Campaign Entrepreneurs in Online Collective Action: GetUp! in Australia." *Social Movement Studies* 14 (2): 195–213.

Vromen, Ariadne. 2017. "Hybrid Online Campaigning Organisations." In *Digital Citizenship and Political Engagement: The Challenge from Online Campaigning and Advocacy Organisations*, 77–126. Palgrave Macmillan UK.

Wahlquist, Calla. 2020. "Rio Tinto Blasts 46,000-Year-Old Aboriginal Site to Expand Iron Ore Mine." *The Guardian.* https://www.theguardian.com/australia-news/2020/may/26/rio-tinto-blasts-46000-year-old-aboriginal-site-to-expand-iron-ore-mine.

Weible, Christopher M. 2007. "An Advocacy Coalition Framework Approach to Stakeholder Analysis: Understanding the Political Context of California

Marine Protected Area Policy." *Journal of Public Administration Research and Theory* 17 (1): 95–117.

Weible, Christopher M., and Paul A. Sabatier. 2007. "A Guide to the Advocacy Coalition Framework." *Handbook of Public Policy Analysis: Theory, Politics, and Methods*, 123.

West, Michael. 2012. "Ethics Brawl at Ethical Investment." *Sydney Morning Herald*. https://www.smh.com.au/business/ethics-brawl-at-ethical-investment-20120328-1vy2x.html.

Westphal, James D., and Edward J. Zajac. 2013. "A Behavioral Theory of Corporate Governance: Explicating the Mechanisms of Socially Situated and Socially Constituted Agency." *Academy of Management Annals* 7 (1): 607–61.

Wilburn, Kathleen M., and Ralph Wilburn. 2011. "Achieving Social License to Operate Using Stakeholder Theory." *Journal of International Business Ethics* 4 (2).

Wilderness Australia. 2023. "Give a Dam." https://www.wildernessaustralia.org.au/give_a_dam.

Woodside Energy Group Limited. 2024. "2024 Annual General Meeting Voting Results." https://www.woodside.com/docs/default-source/asx-announcements/2024/2024-annual-general-meeting-voting-results.pdf?sfvrsn=5922395f_6.

Yadin, Sharon. 2023. *Fighting Climate Change through Shaming*. Cambridge University Press. https://www.cambridge.org/core/elements/fighting-climate-change-through-shaming/FE9DA69D7DE60C8FDA2FBD2521FD540A.

Young, Emma, and Nick Toscano. 2020. "'Incomprehensible': How Rio Tinto Reduced 46,000 Years of History to Rubble." *Sydney Morning Herald*. https://www.smh.com.au/business/companies/incomprehensible-how-rio-tinto-reduced-46-000-years-of-history-to-rubble-20200605-p54zx7.html.

Zald, Mayer N., and Michael A. Berger. 1978. "Social Movements in Organizations: Coup d'etat, Insurgency, and Mass Movements." *American Journal of Sociology* 83 (4): 823–61.

Zald, Mayer N., Calvin Morrill, and Hayagreeva Rao. 2005. "The Impact of Social Movements on Organizations." *Social Movements and Organization Theory*: 253–79.

Index

Note: Page numbers in *italics* refer to figures and tables.

FSC
www.fsc.org
MIX
Papier | Fördert gute Waldnutzung
FSC® C083411

Kolibri 360 GmbH
Ferdinand-Jühlke-Straße 7
99095 Erfurt, Deutschland
produktsicherheit@kolibri360.de